Mastering
MOUNTAIN
BIKE Skills

BRIAN LOPES
LEE McCORMACK

Human Kinetics

Library of Congress Cataloging-in-Publication Data

Lopes, Brian.
  Mastering mountain bike skills / Brian Lopes, Lee McCormack. -- 2nd ed.
    p. cm.
  Includes index.
  ISBN-13: 978-0-7360-8371-3 (soft cover)
  ISBN-10: 0-7360-8371-5 (soft cover)
  1. Mountain biking--Training. I. McCormack, Lee. II. Title.
  GV1056.L66 2010
  796.6'3--dc22

                              2010012431

ISBN-10: 0-7360-8371-5 (print)
ISBN-13: 978-0-7360-8371-3 (print)

The Web addresses cited in this text were current as of January 2010, unless otherwise noted.

Acquisitions Editor: Justin Klug; **Developmental Editor:** Anne Hall; **Assistant Editor:** Cory Weber; **Copyeditor:** Patsy Fortney; **Indexer:** Dan Connolly; **Permission Manager:** Martha Gullo; **Graphic Designer:** Bob Reuther; **Graphic Artist:** Tara Welsch; **Cover Designer:** Keith Blomberg; **Photographer (cover):** Manfred Stromberg; **Photography (interior):** all photos appear courtesy of Lee McCormack—see page 245 for individual credits; **Photo Asset Manager:** Laura Fitch; **Visual Production Assistant:** Joyce Brumfield; **Photo Production Manager:** Jason Allen; **Art Manager:** Kelly Hendren; **Associate Art Manager:** Alan L. Wilborn; **Illustrator:** Lee McCormack, unless otherwise noted; **Printer:** Premier Print Group

Human Kinetics books are available at special discounts for bulk purchase. Special editions or book excerpts can also be created to specification. For details, contact the Special Sales Manager at Human Kinetics.

Printed in the United States of America   10 9 8 7 6 5 4 3 2

Human Kinetics
Web site: www.HumanKinetics.com

United States: Human Kinetics
P.O. Box 5076
Champaign, IL 61825-5076
800-747-4457
e-mail: humank@hkusa.com

Canada: Human Kinetics
475 Devonshire Road Unit 100
Windsor, ON N8Y 2L5
800-465-7301 (in Canada only)
e-mail: info@hkcanada.com

Europe: Human Kinetics
107 Bradford Road
Stanningley
Leeds LS28 6AT, United Kingdom
+44 (0) 113 255 5665
e-mail: hk@hkeurope.com

Australia: Human Kinetics
57A Price Avenue
Lower Mitcham, South Australia 5062
08 8372 0999
e-mail: info@hkaustralia.com

New Zealand: Human Kinetics
P.O. Box 80
Torrens Park, South Australia 5062
0800 222 062
e-mail: info@hknewzealand.com

E4849

Mastering
MOUNTAIN
BIKE Skills

CONTENTS

1 Choose Your Weapon 7

2 Become One With Your Bike 43

3 Make Great Power 61

4 Brake Better to Go Faster 73

Carve Any Corner 81

Wheelie and Hop Over Anything 103

Pump Terrain for Free Speed 119

Drop Like a Feather 131

Jump With the Greatest of Ease 139

Flow on Any Trail 163

Handle Crazy Conditions 177

Avoid Injuries 189

Race Like a Champ 205

INTRODUCTION

Would you rather repeat old failures or create new successes? If you're satisfied with your riding, keep doing what you're doing. If you want to ride better/safer/faster, you must consciously practice the skills that will get you there.

One thing at a time.   Whenever you're out riding, concentrate on one skill or component of a skill. Look ahead in the corners, stay low over the jumps, weight your outside pedal, or whatever. Think about executing the move perfectly. Soon you'll be doing it without thought, and then you can move on to the next thing.

Don't let bad habits take over.   It's OK to make some mistakes while you're learning. But when you keep making the same mistake, it becomes a bad habit.

Research by Wendy Wood, a psychologist at Texas A&M University, provides some tips for overcoming bad habits. Wood no doubt had habits like smoking and Xbox in mind, but these tips apply to bad bike habits as well. Let's say that as you do a big double jump, you stare into the gap and abort the mission.

- Make it difficult to continue the bad habit. You could attach a blinder to the mouthpiece of your full-face helmet, so you can't look down. If you tend to grab the brakes for no reason, wrap your fingers around the grips until there's a reason to brake.

- Change your environment. After you stop on the lip a few times, you probably will not go for it. Come back later or try a similar jump elsewhere. When your mind gets caught in a rut, a new situation can shake it free.

- Enjoy the short-term rewards. When you finally get that double, or at least take off without staring into the gap, give yourself a Lemon Zest Luna Bar. Yummy.

For additional info, refer to www.duke.edu/~wwood/Ouellette.Wood.1998.pdf.

Practice your attack position. See page 46.

Think about what you want to do rather than what you're trying to avoid. If you think "don't stare into the hole," where do you think you'll stare? Many coaches recommend repeating a positive mantra: "I will fly over there. I will fly over there."

Precision now, speed later. Don't make yourself a human missile and hope you learn something before you explode. When you're working on a new skill, do it slowly on easy terrain. We want to train effective habits here. Going too fast will introduce errors and greatly increase the danger. Stick this to your refrigerator: *Smoothness first. Speed later.*

CONSIDER GETTING SOME COACHING

You will learn a lot from this book, but there's no substitute for a qualified skills instructor. By having a coach, you will be able to:

- ◎ Learn in your own style. A good instructor reaches you using words, demonstrations, and on-bike doing.

- ◎ Get immediate feedback. It might feel perfect the first time, but it rarely is. A good coach zeroes in on what you're doing well, and what you can do better.

- ◎ Improve much faster. Avoid wasting time on bad habits. Build perfect new skills, and the confidence that goes with them.

Time and money spent on skills gets you higher performance—and more fun—than any equipment upgrade. We encourage you to learn at least the basics from a qualified instructor. For information on Lee's coaching programs, check out www.leelikesbikes.com.

Lee demonstrates the fine points of braking at a clinic in Nathrop, Colorado.

Step Up to a Higher Level

When you become a mountain biker, you begin a never-ending journey of self-improvement and good times. You have the most fun when your skills match the current challenge. When you step up your skills, you step up the challenge, and vice versa. Beginners and experts enjoy the same stoke. When you nail your first little double jump, you'll be just as stoked as Brian was when he won his fourth world championship.

As your skills evolve, so does your relationship with terrain. You get more confident and you learn to work a trail the way a surfer works a wave. Although your kung fu changes with the situation (you might be a confident trail rider but a sissy jumper), you probably spend most of your time at one of the following three levels.

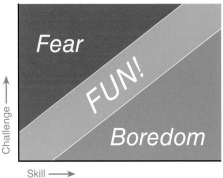

Fun happens where challenge meets skill

Level 1: The Trail Works You

Your bike feels new and strange, and you have little faith in your ability to survive a trail. You keep all of your muscles tense, all of the time. You drag your brakes whenever your bike points downhill. You creep slowly over obstacles and frequently stop dead or flop over your handlebars. You don't lean enough in turns, and your constant braking keeps your bike from cornering smoothly.

Riding at level 1 is herky-jerky and, to be honest, not all that fun. You hear experienced riders talk about flow and groove and flying over stuff, but you have no idea what they're talking about. Heck, you might even think they're crazy.

Unfortunately, most people who own mountain bikes never get out of this stage. They either wallow in beginnerdom forever, or they just plain give up and stick to the road. If you're at level 1, don't give up. This isn't what mountain biking is about. The real fun is still to come.

LEAP FROM LEVEL 1 TO LEVEL 2

1. Relax. This is so important, we'll keep beating you over the head with it. If you find yourself tensing up, stop what you're doing and return with a fresh mind. If the tension remains, go work on something that doesn't scare you. Fear and tension make riding unproductive and unfun.

2. Lay off the brakes unless there's a specific reason to slow down. "I'm going really fast right now" is not a valid reason to brake. When it's time to brake, do it like you mean it.

3. Try carrying more speed into rough sections. Get light on your bike to get through more smoothly.

4. Have faith in your bike's ability to roll. That's what bikes do. They roll.

5. Dial in your attack position. This is key!

Level 2: You Survive the Trail

Now mountain biking becomes fun. You've learned to relax a bit. You coast between corners. You roll, clatter, and fly straight over obstacles. In corners you lay off the brakes, lean, and carve like a butcher.

You've become a competent rider. On a smooth, curvy trail you enjoy the sensations of speed and flow. When things get gnarly, you tend to tense up. You bog down in rough terrain, and you get bucked out of control when you hit obstacles at speed. You have trouble making corners when traction is iffy.

The majority of satisfied mountain bikers ride happily somewhere in level 2, blissfully unaware of the next level. When they see pros whiz by with utmost speed and control, they just shake their heads and assume superhero powers are involved. Truth is, being born on Krypton has little to do with achieving ultimate skill (but it can't hurt).

LEAP FROM LEVEL 2 TO LEVEL 3

1. Relax. Yes, even more than ever.
2. Commit. The ups and downs of porpoiseful riding require snap.
3. Scrutinize the trail. Not just any line will do. Look for banks to turn on and downslopes to pump.
4. Don't bash into stuff. It's no longer good enough to point your wheel downhill and let it run into whatever's in the way. Instead, try to unweight, wheelie, hop, or jump over the obstacles. When you stop crashing into things, you'll immediately increase your speed and control.
5. Pump backsides. Anytime the trail turns downward, press down for some free speed. We're talking any surface here: rocks, stumps, mounds, washing machines, anything. Pumping is the key to that flowy world you've been hearing about.
6. Develop your own style. Experiment to learn what works best for your skills, body type, and equipment. For example, if you can't muscle your bike through rough sections but you rail corners, you might tend to ride around gnarly rocks, which is fine. What isn't fine is thinking you rule at rocks but actually sucking, then bashing into the business end of a boulder. Know yourself.
7. Dial in your attack position. Yes, even more. More automatic. More fluid.

YOU'RE ONLY AS GOOD AS YOUR HABITS

When you're under stress—in a race, on a new trail, with a potential mate—you'll always revert to your habits. Do you usually ride stiff and upright? If so, you'll do the same under pressure. So take the time to build good habits!

Level 3: You Work the Trail

This is the ultimate. You ride with relaxed aggression. You never let your front wheel hit a rock, and you never let a backside go by unpumped. The trail is a piece of clay, and you sculpt it to suit your fancy. Your line is as vertical as it is horizontal. You unweight or fly over obstacles, and you press hard into corners. You porpoise through rough sections, gaining speed and control the whole time.

When you reach level 3, be proud—you're in small company. But just because you can hop a boulder's face and pump its backside doesn't mean you're all that. As you get stronger and better at reading terrain, you'll learn to manipulate trails in even better ways.

FIND YOUR STYLE

Although the core riding skills shown in this book are pretty constant, the way you apply them is up to you. Definitely practice the key moves, but, as you master them, relax and rock them in your style. Are you compact like a road racer or upright like a motocrosser? Do you stay low or go for the big air? Do you turn around boulders or bash right over them? It's all good. Just find the style that works best for you.

Disclaimer

Mountain biking is dangerous. You can break your equipment, and you can hurt yourself. That's what makes it so exciting. Ride within your abilities, and always wear the proper protective gear for the type of riding you're doing. Always wear a helmet and gloves. If you're anyplace you expect to crash, consider elbow and knee pads, body armor, and a full-face helmet. We also suggest eye protection.

The best technique and gear will not prevent all crashes or injuries. If you go out and hurt yourself, it's your own fault. Ride hard and take chances, but don't be an idiot.

Welcome to the exciting, gratifying world of high-level mountain biking. Remember that becoming a great rider is a long-term process. Be patient, take it one step at a time, and have fun! But before you go out and rip, let's make sure your bike is up to the task.

Choose Your Weapon

If you're reading this book, you're serious about ripping on a mountain bike. (Right on!) Buy a quality bike that matches the type of riding you do, and set it up to match your body and your style. Your bike is an extension of your body—you wouldn't settle for off-the-shelf arms and legs, would you?

Buy the Right Bike

Aside from your house and your car, your bike is probably your biggest investment. Actually, if you're a hard-core mountain biker, you'll probably spend less on your car than on your bike. So, aside from buying a house, buying a bike is the most important purchase of your life.

Spend as much as you can afford. Higher-level frames and components work better and last longer than low-end ones. You don't need the ultra-high-end Shimano XTR group to have fun, but it will outlast and outperform XT, just as XT destroys LX, and so on down the line. If you buy a cheap department store bike, you'll get what you pay for. It will fight your attempts to ride well, and you'll end up soured on the whole experience.

Buy from your local bike shop. You can find great deals online, especially on accessories, but a local bike shop will help you select the right bike, get you fitted, and keep your rig dialed. If you find a shop with knowledgeable staff and the parts you need, establish a relationship with the staff. You might pay a bit more than you would online, but the experience and convenience will more than make up for the difference. Try bringing your mail-order bike to a shop for a night-before-the-ride repair and see how it goes.

Take it easy on the upgrades. Don't sweat the components on your bike. Just ride the thing. Here are the most important upgrades:

- ○ Saddle. It's hard to have fun sitting on a plastic anvil.
- ○ Stem and handlebars. They should fit your body and riding style.
- ○ Tires. Choose ones that match your riding conditions.

Run everything else stock until it breaks or wears out.

Hardtail or Full Suspension?

Back in the day, there was no choice because everything was rigid. When suspension forks first came out, downhillers gobbled them up, but the weight weenies stayed rigid in their ways. Now, almost every mountain bike comes with a suspension fork. In the same way, when rear suspension first became available, only downhillers went for it. As the designs got better and lighter, rear suspension appeared on all bikes from the high end on down—for hard-core downhilling and for epic cross-country.

Hardtails are still lighter and cheaper than suspension bikes with the same components, and they can perform better in two particular conditions: cross-country riding on smooth trails and **dirt jumping** and **bikercross** on smooth courses. The lighter, stiffer bikes transmit more power to the ground. That's why some racers almost always race on a hardtail.

SUSPENSION PROS AND CONS

What's Great About Suspension

Mountain bike suspension has become the norm for a simple reason: It works. But what, exactly, does it do? (Hint: It does more than let you ride poorly without being properly punished.)

- It smoothes the ride.
- It improves control.
- It improves braking.
- It allows you to absorb greater impacts.
- And, of course, it looks super cool on top of your car.

Potential Drawbacks of Suspension

On the bike, as in life, nothing comes for free. Suspension is most certainly awesome, but what does it cost?

- Weight
- Complexity
- Cost
- Lost energy
- Impaired performance (in certain situations)

It's easy to do it wrong. Ninety-nine percent of all riders' suspension systems are not set up correctly. If you don't have the wherewithal to dial in your front and rear shocks, buy some wool jerseys and stick to rigid bikes.

So . . . the best suspension designs maximize the cool factor while minimizing the poopie factor. Six popular solutions are mentioned here.

In almost all other off-road situations, **full suspension** lets you ride faster and on rougher terrain with more comfort and more control. Riding is simply more fun—despite a little extra weight and, perhaps, a skosh of lost energy. For most mountain bikers, full suspension is the way to go.

Although suspension bikes have become the norm for serious trail riding, many hard-core riders have become even more committed to riding fully rigid—with non-suspended rears *and* fronts. Fully rigid bikes are extra light and extra efficient (on smooth ground), and they promote a purity of flow you can't achieve with suspension. Everything is glorious as long as you're in phase with the terrain; if you get out of phase, beware the punishment!

Know Your Suspension Designs

Although bike designers are always innovating, bicycle suspension designs have converged on a few basic ideas, each with its benefits and potential costs.

FSR LINK

What it is: This four-bar design has a pivot at the end of the chainstay. The rear axle pivots with the seat stay. This keeps the chain length pretty constant throughout the shock stroke.

Pro: Reduces the amount of chain and brake feedback.

This says a lot: Lance Armstrong can ride any Trek bike he wants, and he raced the Colorado State Championships on a fully suspended Fuel 9.9 SSL.

Con: This neutrality can encourage the rear suspension to bob with pedaling. Damped shocks are required to maintain a bob-free ride. Specialized owns the patent in the United States, and other manufacturers must pay to use this design.

Example: Specialized

SINGLE PIVOT

What it is: This is the simplest design. A large swingarm pivots on a single point, which is typically mounted in line with the middle or large chainring.

Pro: Simplicity. Light weight. Strategic pivot placement gives the bike any characteristics the designer wants.

Con: Considerable chain and brake interference, especially when the chain is not in line with the pivot.

Examples: Orange, Mountain Cycles

FOUR-BAR SINGLE PIVOT

What it is: A frame design with multiple bars and links, but the axle is attached to the chainstay. The main pivot is usually low, near the small ring.

Pro: Can be made light and stiff. Lots of tuning possibilities and shock ratios.

Con: Despite the extra bars, it still behaves like a single-pivot bike. When the chain is not in line with the pivot, the bike may display chain and brake feedback.

Examples: Trek, Kona

VPP

What it is: This design uses multiple links to move the rear axle in an S-shaped curve. The "belly" of the S is in the natural sag position, and that's where the chain tends to pull the suspension.

Pro: Because the chain pulls the suspension to the neutral sag position and tends to hold it there, VPP bikes—even long-travel models—are very efficient pedalers.

Con: There is some brake and pedal feedback, especially if the sag isn't set correctly.

Examples: Santa Cruz, Intense

DW LINK

What it is: This "anti-squat" design keeps the suspension from compressing as the rider rocks backward with each pedal stroke.

Pro: Reduced pedal bob while maintaining plushness.

Con: Slight pedal feedback.

Examples: Ibis, Turner, Independent Fabrications

MONO LINK

What it is: The bottom bracket rides on a swing link between the front triangle and the rear triangle. The rear shock is a structural member of the rear triangle.

Pro: Efficient pedaling.

Con: Some pedal and brake feedback.

Examples: Maverick, Spot Brand

Which Is Best?

Although we all have our favorites (Lee: Specialized FSR! Brian: Ibis DW Link!), the fact is that all modern bikes work pretty well. Test-ride the bikes at your local bike shop. Pick a design that suits your terrain and riding style. Get the best model you can afford. Get your suspension tuned for you. And learn to ride it.

Choose the Right Bike for Your Riding Style

There are as many types of bikes as there are types of riding. If you can't collect bikes the way some people collect shoes or golf clubs, then you need to pick one that suits your typical riding style. Every bike manufacturer has a unique interpretation of mountain bike categories, but some universal types exist.

Hardtail bikes.   Hardtails cover the entire performance spectrum, from entry-level rides to high-end racing machines. The layout and geometry have been perfected over the years. If you're a smooth-course racerhead, a hardtail is the weapon of choice. If you ride lots of pavement with occasional smooth trails, a hardtail will work for you, too.

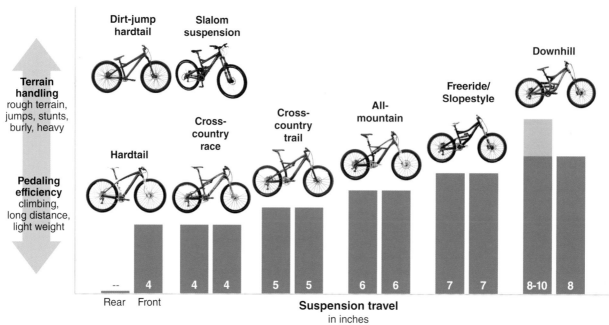

Terrain handling
rough terrain, jumps, stunts, burly, heavy

Pedaling efficiency
climbing, long distance, light weight

Dirt-jump hardtail

Slalom suspension

Hardtail

Cross-country race

Cross-country trail

All-mountain

Freeride/Slopestyle

Downhill

| -- | 4 | 4 | 4 | 5 | 5 | 6 | 6 | 7 | 7 | 8-10 | 8 |

Rear   Front

Suspension travel
in inches
(These are the emerging standards. There is still some variation among bike makers.)

Cross-country race bikes.   Do you want to cover off-road miles as fast as possible? With 3 to 4 inches (8 to 10 cm) of **travel**, steep angles, and a weight-forward riding position, cross-country race bikes track well on moderate terrain, handle quickly, and pedal like the dickens.

Cross-country trail bikes.   Cross-country trail bikes are hot tickets for all-around trail riding. They climb well and cover distance with maximum comfort and efficiency. Travel ranges from 4 to 5 inches (10 to 13 cm); 5 inches has become the standard. If you want to enjoy a wide variety of rides, this is your bike.

All-mountain bikes.   If you're willing to climb a mountain, but only if you get a rad descent, sign up here. Compared with the geometry of trail bikes, all-mountain bikes' slacker geometry and more rearward position provide greater stability in the steep and rough. Travel is usually about 6 inches. All-mountain bikes can handle light stunt work, and they truly excel on rough natural terrain. They work well for downhillers and freeriders who want to ride trails.

Freeride bikes.   More travel and greater durability qualify heavy-duty freeride bikes for mega stunts and punishing flat landings. Precise low-speed handling helps you stick to skinnies and nail narrow lines. Travel ranges start at 6 inches (15 cm) and go up from there. Many freeride bikes have dual front rings so you can pedal, rather than push, to the top.

Downhill race bikes.   Downhill race bikes want to flow down rough trails. They're perfect for riders who prefer speed rather than violence and jumping to **backside** rather than landing flat. You can certainly sprint to clear a gap, but think twice before you tackle that 10-mile (16 km) climb. Burly frames with 7 or more inches (18+ cm) of travel handle speed well and endure a decent pounding, but they won't endure stunts as long as purpose-built freeride bikes.

Dirt-jump hardtails.   Dirt-jump hardtails—the unruly cousins of XC hardtails—are burlier and slacker, and they have more front travel than XC hardtails. Their go-for-it handling traits make these the bikes of choice for dirt-jump varmints, urban cowboys, purist bikercross racers, and pump trackers. For many urban-based riders, especially those on budgets, a dirt-jump hardtail is an affordable, versatile all-around bike.

Slalom suspension bikes.   Slack geometry, 3 to 5 inches (8 to 13 cm) of travel, and low bottom brackets make **slalom** suspension bikes corner like they're on rails. You sacrifice some burliness and efficiency over hard-core dirt-jumping hardtails, but the increased traction and error margin serve racers well.

Not sure what to get?   Throw a dart at the chart on the facing page. Hopefully, you'll hit near the middle, which is perfect. A trail or all-mountain bike with a 4- to 6-inch (10 to 13 cm) travel will climb as well as it needs to, and it'll treat you right on a wide variety of terrain. These bikes are very adaptable. If you want to ride epic, run a long stem and light tires. For a more downhill feel, run a short stem and sticky meats. If you're more concerned with climbing and covering distance than ripping descents, go for a trail bike. If you climb only to earn your turns, go for an all-mountain model.

XC, trail, DJ, DH . . . all bikes are fun, but there's a lot to say for a mid-travel bike upon which you can ride up and rip down. Brian rocks one of his Ibis Mojos.

29ers

Most mountain bikes have 26-inch (66 cm) wheels. Twenty-six is not a magical number handed down from Zeus on a strip of sweet Mt. Olympus singletrack. It just happens to be the diameter of the wheels that were widely available when mountain bikes started crawling out of the primordial road bike/cruiser ooze.

Twenty-six-inch wheels have proven themselves to work fine. Rim manufacturers make them strong and light and in every style and price range to fit everyone from weekend bike-pathers to World Cup downhill racers. But can bike wheels be better?

Many say, "Yes, bike wheels can be better!" and their answer is the 29-inch (74 cm) wheel. As you might guess, a 29-inch wheel has a 3-inch greater diameter than a 26-inch wheel. Just a few years ago, **29ers** were found only on niche bikes; today every major bike maker offers at least one 29-inch model—and the 29-inch trend has solidified into a viable category all its own.

Advantages of 29-Inch Wheels

Bigger wheels roll more easily over rough terrain than smaller wheels do. To be more precise: On a rough trail, a 29-inch wheel rolls about 6 percent more easily than a 26-inch wheel.

With 29-inch wheels, you can pedal at the same speed as with 26-inch wheels with less effort, or you can pedal faster with the same effort, or you can just coast faster than with 26-inch wheels.

Bigger wheels are more stable than smaller wheels. Depending on your riding style, you might love this or hate this. Keep reading.

2009 National XC Championships: Adam Craig is leading on his 26-inch suspension bike, but Jeremy Horgan-Kobelski (right behind him) won the title on his sub-20-pound 29er.

Why 29ers feel smoother over bumps

A bigger wheel impacts a bump with a slightly lower angle of incidence than a smaller wheel. This gives the bigger wheel a smoother ride and less rolling resistance.

Approximate angles of incidence for a four-inch, square-edged bump:

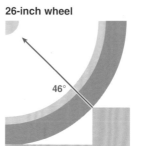

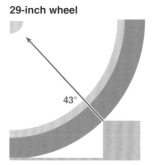

Plus: A bigger wheel stays higher over consecutive bumps, which lowers the angle of incidence even more:

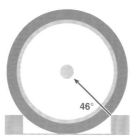

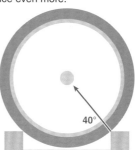

Disadvantages of 29-Inch Wheels

Bigger wheels are heavier. The increased circumference adds about 10 percent to the weight of the rim, rim strip, tube, and tire. In a world where grams are worth their weight in titanium, do you want to make your bike heavier?

Bigger wheels are harder to accelerate. All that extra weight is on the outside of the rotating body, where it has the greatest effect on rotational inertia. If you consider the extra 10 percent of mass and the fact that the mass is about 10 percent farther from the center of the hub, you can see that the result is an increased rotational inertia of almost 40 percent. That makes 29-inch wheels much less responsive in the sprint but much more stable on rough terrain.

Bigger wheels are more fragile. Because the lever arm between the rim and hub is longer, the wheel is more susceptible to lateral violence. To make a bigger wheel just as stiff as a small one requires more material, which increases the rotating weight.

Bigger wheels make bigger bikes. You need a longer fork, longer chainstays, longer top tube—pretty much longer everything. Twenty-nine-inch wheels do not work with small fame sizes (they just don't fit), and they don't work with lots of suspension (the resulting bike is just too big and unwieldy). But 29-inch wheels work great in fully rigid bikes, hardtails, and short-travel suspension bikes.

Historically, the availability of quality 29er-compatible tires, forks, and frames has been very limited, but that is changing.

OPINIONS ON 29ERS

Brian on 29ers

Wagon wheel bikes . . . circus bikes . . . Barnum & Bailey . . .

I don't see any reason to ride one. I've heard about all the benefits, but they don't accelerate as quickly. I hear they roll through stuff better, but I never have problems rolling through anything.

Johnny O'Mara (ex pro motocross racer and longtime MTB racer) has one. I was on it for two minutes. I went to hop a curb and barely made it.

It's a bike for people who are old and lazy and need something better. If you have an aggressive riding style, you're not riding a 29er."

But Brian, how do you really feel?

29ers can rip: Michael Hayes, MTB coach at the Colorado Rocky Mountain Academy in Carbondale, CO, launches his XC 29er during a clinic with Lee.

Lee on 29ers

I've coached many racers on 29ers, and I've ridden a few myself, and this is what I've observed:

- 29ers roll noticeably well through the rough, jumbly sections.
- Cornering requires a bit more input, but I adjusted quickly.
- Big wheels don't give you as much pump as smaller wheels do. This is most noticeable on smaller, steeper bumps.
- Some people flat-out rip on 29ers.

Overall, I can see rocking 29s. Maybe because I'm old and lazy and need something better?

But That's Not All

Yes, there's another wheel trend. The 650B wheel has a diameter of 27.5 inches (70 cm)—the midpoint between 26- and 29-inch wheels. The 650B wheels supposedly provide the benefits of bigger wheels without the drawbacks. The 650Bs are starting to appear on niche brands, especially on smaller-sized bikes that can't accept 29-inch wheels.

Are 650Bs the ultimate solution or just a weak compromise? We'll know in a few years. I think we know what Brian thinks!

ROCKING THE BMX

We will not suggest that you ride a BMX bike on your favorite gnarly **singletrack**, but we will suggest that a BMX bike is the ultimate way to improve your bike-riding kung fu.

Even compared with a stiff DJ hardtail, BMX bikes are unbelievable responsive, exhilarating, and—when you screw up—punishing. BMX bikes require quicker, more precise movements than mountain bikes do. Studies show that when you improve your fast movements, you also improve your slow movements, but not the other way around. No wonder every good BMX rider is a great mountain biker, but not the other way around.

Lee spent the winter on an Intense Factory Alloy 20 (fun!), and by spring mountain bikes felt like slow motion.

If you're an adult or teen coming from a mountain bike, you'll want a Pro or Pro XL- sized BMX bike. Your next choice is wheel size:

20-inch—The **20s** have 20-inch wheels, and they are considered the only "real" BMX bikes. If you can master one of these temperamental beasts, you will be a superhero on your mountain bike. And the BMX kids won't make *too* much fun of you.

24-inch cruiser—Cruisers have 24-inch wheels, and, to be honest, real BMXers consider them kind of lame because cruisers are less responsive and more forgiving than 20s—which makes them perfect for mountain bikers!

Most adult MTBers find 20s too much of a handful, at least at first. Start with a cruiser; then work your way down (up?) to a 20. A winter, or even the occasional play ride, on your BMX bike will do wonders for your riding skills.

The Upshot

The list of drawbacks of 29ers is longer than the list of advantages, but for some riders the advantages—faster rolling and increased stability—outweigh everything else. The facts are these:

○ Twenty-nine-inch wheels provide some of the advantages of suspension without the extra weight or complexity. Especially in moderately rough terrain, 29ers make great hardtails and fully rigid bikes.

○ Twenty-nine-inch wheels make your bike feel more tame and controllable. If you feel sketchy on rough terrain, the bigger wheels will help calm you down.

- If you want to cover a lot of ground with utmost efficiency, 29ers are hard to beat. For this reason, many ultra-endurance racers favor the big wheels.
- Because of the weight, fragility, and compatibility issues, very few short-distance and gravity racers use 29-inch wheels.

Women-Specific Mountain Bikes

About five years ago, the major bike companies seemed to realize, "Hey, half of humanity is female!" They saw an untapped market, and they started building women-specific bikes. Although some companies merely did the "shrink and pink" (made men's bikes smaller and painted them to appeal to women), the good companies did their research and created lines of bikes that offered real performance advantages for women. Today most major bike companies offer women-specific bikes.

Although some women ride just fine on "men's" bikes (standard bikes are designed for men), many are well served by women-specific designs. The average woman's body is smaller and lighter than the average man's body, and women have relatively shorter torsos and arms than men do. If your build fits this model, you might be well served by a women-specific design.

Here are some common women-specific features:

Frame.   Shorter top tubes to fit relatively shorter torsos. Compared with men, women tend to have proportionately longer legs and shorter torsos.

Low stand-over heights for shorter legs. Although women have relatively longer legs than men do, they tend to be shorter overall.

Lighter and thinner tubes save weight and give lighter riders a more resilient ride.

Handlebars.   Narrower to fit narrower shoulders. In his clinics, Lee often sees 5-foot (152 cm) women with 28-inch (71 cm) downhill bars that some genius sold them ("Hey, dude, these are the bars I use"). Hold the ends of a broomstick. Now imagine riding like that. Silly.

Stems.   Shorter to fit those shorter torsos. This is a good thing because having a shorter stem is an easy way to improve your bike's handling.

Cranks.   Shorter to fit shorter legs. Many extra-small mountain bikes come with the same 175-millimeter cranks found on mediums. Many women find themselves rocking their hips to get full extension with cranks that are too long. The right length—down to about 165 millimeters—gives women a much smoother, stronger pedal stroke.

Saddles.   Women's saddles tend to be a bit wider to fit their wider-set pelvic bones.

Grips.   Smaller diameters to fit smaller hands. (Tip: Many men benefit from low-profile grips; they're easier to hold on to.)

Narrower handlebars, shorter top tubes, shorter stems, and shorter cranks all give women a much more comfortable ride. (Pictured is the Specialized S-Works Safire.)

Judy loves her light, zippy women-specific 2008 Scott Contessa Scale. She worked with Nat Ross at www.probikecenter.com to get the fit just right.

Brake levers. Shorter reach, so they're easier to reach with smaller hands. So many women strain to reach standard levers; using levers with a shorter reach makes it easier for you to control your bike—and it reduces your stress.

Suspension. Women-specific forks and shocks are sprung and damped for lighter riders. Unless your suspension is dialed for your weight, you'll be getting a rougher ride than you should.

Tires. Light and fast-rolling, to make the most of your power.

Colors. Color is the last bastion of sexism. Women's bikes are almost always pink or lavender, with maybe a touch of baby blue. Insist on fit first, color second.

You love your bike, but the fit isn't quite right. If you find yourself reaching or straining, you might try the following upgrades. The most important, easiest, and least expensive are listed first.

- Well-fitted saddle
- Shorter stem
- Narrower bars
- Low-profile grips
- Short-reach brake levers
- Shorter cranks

Let air out of your tires. If you weigh 30 percent less than your male riding partners, you can ride with about 30 percent less air. This will give you a much smoother ride and better cornering traction.

Understand the Bike's Geometry

Magazine reviews and bike brochures bombard us with all sorts of numbers, but the only number most of us understand is price. When you buy a bike from a real bicycle company, the angles and dimensions will fit the intended purpose of the bike. Just hop on and ride, and everything will be fine. That said, brands differ, and many bikes these days are adjustable. So it helps to know how the key specs affect the ride of your bike.

Head angle

Head Angle

The **head angle** number has the biggest effect on the way your bike feels. The higher the number, the "steeper" the head angle; the lower the number, the "slacker" or more "raked out" the head angle.

Steep bikes feel nimble. They're easy to steer and easy to keep on track while climbing. On the downside, they feel sketchy on steep descents.

BRIAN'S QUIVER

✓ Ibis Silk

✓ Ibis Hakkalugi

✓ Ibis Tranny, small frame, for bikercross and dual slalom racing

✓ Ibis Tranny, small frame, for dirt jumping

✓ Ibis Mojo, small frame, for dual slalom racing

✓ Ibis Mojo small frame, for jumps/drops/freeriding

✓ Ibis Mojo, medium frame, for trail riding

✓ Ibis Mojo, medium frame, for all-mountain/enduro riding/racing

✓ Ibis Mojo, medium frame, for downhill

✓ KTM 530 EXC enduro motorcycle

LEE'S QUIVER

✓ Specialized Stumpjumper

✓ Specialized Enduro

✓ Specialized Demo 8

✓ Specialized P.3

✓ Specialized SX

✓ Specialized S-Works TriCross

✓ Intense BMX Pro 20

✓ Intense BMX Pro Cruiser

✓ 1992 GT Pro Cruiser (sweet!)

✓ Honda CRF450X enduro motorcycle (*braaap!*)

Slack bikes feel stable at speed and on rough terrain. On the downside, they resist turning, and once they turn, they like to flop to the side. You can feel this in a parking lot. When you veer off line on a climb, a slack bike is harder to correct than a steep bike. You have to muscle a slack bike through slow, tight corners.

Many forks these days allow you to reduce travel (and height) for climbing. A Fox Shox 32 Talas fork adjusts on the fly from 6 inches (15 cm) of travel to about 4 inches (10 cm). Dropping your front end by 2 inches (5 cm) will steepen your head angle by 1.5 to 2 degrees, which makes your bike climb significantly better but descend like a mess if you forget to dial out your travel at the top of the hill.

By the way, an experienced rider can feel a difference of just 0.25 degrees.

Our advice on head angle: If you're into steep, gnarly descending, buy a bike with a slack head angle. Dial your fork all the way out, or lower your bottom bracket to

TYPICAL HEAD ANGLES

Bike type	Measurement
Cross-country	70 to 71 degrees
All-mountain	71 degrees
Slalom, freeride, and downhill	66 to 68 degrees

slacken the head angle even more. With a slack angle, you're dialed for the downhills, and you can manhandle your bike through the tight stuff. A steep angle handles best on flat terrain and is easier to ride overall, but it feels sketchy on the descents.

Bottom-Bracket Height

Your bottom-bracket height determines the amount of ground clearance you have and how high your weight is suspended above the ground. The lower your center of gravity—and your bottom bracket—the better your bike will corner.

Ultra-low bottom brackets like to smash pedals and chainrings onto rocks, logs, and varmints. When you run a low bottom bracket, you have to watch where you pedal. But if it's that rough or bumpy, you should be pumping.

Bottom-bracket height

Long-travel bikes ride high to make clearance for suspension sag and rough terrain. Slalom and bikercross bikes, made for smooth courses, ride low for supreme corner **railing**.

Our advice on bottom-bracket height: For the best handling, select a bike with the lowest bottom bracket that suits your style and terrain. If it's adjustable, run it as low as you can without bashing your pedals all the time.

Random tip: Slow, technical riding rewards high bottom brackets. If chainring clearance is an issue, run a smaller ring or a bash guard.

TYPICAL BOTTOM-BRACKET HEIGHTS

Bike type	Measurement
Hardtails	11.5 to 12 inches (29 to 30 cm)
Slalom	12 to 13 inches (30 to 33 cm)
Cross-country suspension	13 inches (33 cm)
All-mountain	14 inches (36 cm)
Freeride and downhill	14.5 to 16 inches (37 to 41 cm)

Chainstay Length

Short stays are happy stays. They snug the rear wheel under your body for great climbing traction, and they make it easy to loft your front wheel.

You might be asking yourself, "If short stays rock so hard, why don't all bikes come with short stays?" Well, it's difficult for bike designers to achieve long travel, lots of tire clearance, and the proper chain line with short stays. They usually end up making compromises.

Our advice on stays: Get the bike with the shortest stays that still meets your requirements for tire size and rear travel.

Caveat: A bike with longer stays puts you closer to the middle of the bike, which can aid cornering. Longer-travel bikes tend to have longer stays by necessity, but some racers and riders prefer extra-long stays for cornering and high-speed stability.

Chainstay length

Seat angle

Seat Tube Angle

A steep seat tube angle, like what you find on a cross-country bike, places you on top of your pedals for optimal pedaling. A slack seat angle moves you back a bit for downhilling. You can still make power, but not as well as you can with a steep seat angle.

Traditionally, a bike's seat angle has mirrored the head angle to suit the intended type of riding. Both were steep for cross-country; both were slack for downhill. But today's all-mountain bikes are encouraging a new kind of compromise: midtravel to work everywhere, slack head angles for descending, and steeper seat angles for pedaling.

Because your seat tube angle determines where your saddle is in relation to your top pedals, it has an enormous effect on the way you pedal your bike. You can learn to pedal well with just about any seat angle, but it can be hard to switch between bikes with vastly different angles.

How do you know whether you're sensitive? Do you feel much stronger or weaker on one bike? Do your knees hurt when you switch? If so, decide which bike is most important that you rip on; then adjust your other bikes to match. See the Saddle section.

LEE'S SEAT ANGLE

For the past several years I've ridden slack mountain bikes everywhere. When I tried to ride a road bike or steep XC bike, I felt weak, and my knees hurt. Once I realized what was going on, I adjusted all of my saddle positions to be similar fore and aft, and now I feel better.

Customize Your Bike for Your Riding Style

A few of us have a bike for every situation—XC, DH, DJ, SD, CX, and so on—but most of us have to pick one bike and make it work everywhere.

Although improving technologies have made bikes more specialized than ever—ultra light and efficient for cross-country, super burly and bottomless for downhill—the same technologies have made the "middle" bikes more versatile than ever. A modern trail or all-mountain bike climbs as well as or better than an old XC bike, and it definitely descends better than a DH bike from just 10 years ago.

If you can have only one bike, pick one that fits most of your riding; then customize it to suit your specific needs.

Here are the parts that most dramatically affect the ride of your bike; the easiest and least expensive to change are listed first.

Tires

Lighter, faster-rolling tires make your bike feel much quicker. Heavier, grippier tires make your bike feel much more capable. Tire manufacturers give you a wide continuum of tires to choose from; pick the best compromise for your riding style (or swap tires for special occasions). There is no quicker, more dramatic change than going from ultra-light XC treads to full-on DH meats.

Stem

For many riders, the stock stem on a trail bike feels great in the parking lot and on climbs, but its length makes it hard to maintain a good **attack position** and move fluidly on the bike. For many riders, a shorter stem is a quick solution. Default these days is about 90 to 110 millimeters. Switching to a 70- or even a 50-millimeter stem will make it much easier to unweight your front end and rip in general. When you go shorter, be sure to go higher as well.

This is pretty unusual, but if you want to improve your climbing and give yourself a more stretched-out roadlike position, you can switch to a longer, lower stem. Fact is, a shorter stem almost always helps your bike handle better, and you can always learn to pedal with a shorter stem.

Wheels

Lighter wheels make any bike feel quicker. If quick acceleration is your goal, lighter wheels and tires are your most cost-effective upgrade. Lighter and quicker are the holy grail of bike upgrades. For 99.99999 percent of riders, lighter, quicker wheels are all good and no bad. If you want to ride aggressively or fit big tires, you should rock wider, stiffer rims.

Bars

When you shorten your stem, it often pays to get a bar with a higher rise.

If you're a big rider, you might need wider bars. A too-narrow bar compromises your strength and control, especially in rough sections. It's like doing push-ups with a very narrow grip.

If you're a small rider, you might need narrower bars. A too-wide bar limits your range of motion, especially in tight turns and off drops. It's like doing push-ups with a very wide grip.

Seatpost

You can spend a lot of money on a seatpost that's lighter and has a tricker seat clamp, but that seems pretty silly. The only great reason to upgrade a seatpost is

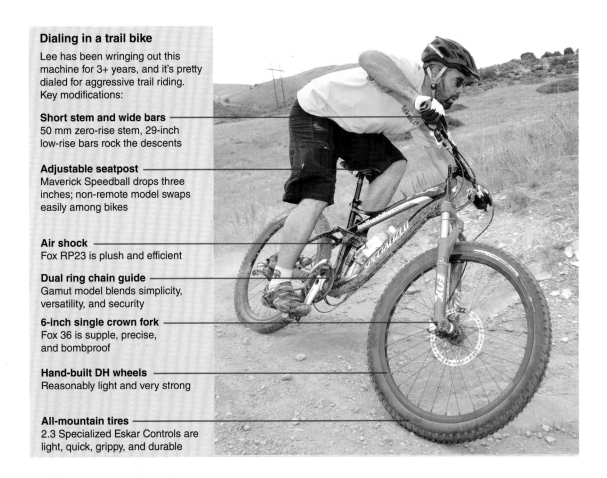

Dialing in a trail bike

Lee has been wringing out this machine for 3+ years, and it's pretty dialed for aggressive trail riding. Key modifications:

Short stem and wide bars
50 mm zero-rise stem, 29-inch low-rise bars rock the descents

Adjustable seatpost
Maverick Speedball drops three inches; non-remote model swaps easily among bikes

Air shock
Fox RP23 is plush and efficient

Dual ring chain guide
Gamut model blends simplicity, versatility, and security

6-inch single crown fork
Fox 36 is supple, precise, and bombproof

Hand-built DH wheels
Reasonably light and very strong

All-mountain tires
2.3 Specialized Eskar Controls are light, quick, grippy, and durable

to rock a remotely adjustable model, which is a great idea if your rides intersperse pedaling with cornering, pumping, hopping, dropping, and the other fun stuff. You can crank along at full seat height, then—click—rip a turn with the seat down 3 to 5 inches (8 to 13 cm).

The biggest brands are GravityDropper, CrankBrothers, and Specialized. Most make versions with levers under the seat or on the handlebar. If you decide to spend the money on one of these posts, go all the way and get the handlebar switch. You'll find yourself adjusting the post way more often than you think. If you ride trail, this is a great upgrade.

Gears

- Triple rings for general riding
- Dual rings with a guide for freeride, all-mountain, and aggressive trail riding
- Single ring with a guide for downhill, 4X, dirt jump, and slalom

Fork

Increasing travel slackens your geometry, which makes your bike more stable at speed, and gives you a plusher ride while being able to take bigger impacts. Most riders increase travel; few reduce it.

Adjustable travel lets you dial in your fork for the conditions. Dial your fork lower for more precise climbing and technical riding. Raise it all the way for more stable downhilling.

Air forks are lighter than coils. Air forks are the ticket on bikes that will be pedaled uphill.

Coil forks are plusher than air. Coil forks are the ticket on bikes that will be hoisted or shuttled uphill.

Stiffer forks (with burlier tubes and burlier axles) give you more precise handling in aggressive, high-g conditions. You'll get used to whatever you ride. You won't know you have a flexy fork until you try a stiffer one.

Shock

This is the toughest upgrade of all, because most shocks are custom made, tuned for each frame, or both.

Switching from a coil shock to an air shock will make your bike lighter and firmer for pedaling.

Switching from an air shock to a coil shock will make your bike more plush, hook up better in rough terrain, and better handle ultra-big hits.

Suspension Tuning

Getting your fork and shock custom tuned can make a huge improvement in your ride—especially if you're much smaller, bigger, slower, or faster than the "average" rider that suspension is typically designed for.

Lee rode the same Specialized Enduro for several years with stock suspension, and he loved it. After his shock was tuned by Push Industries, Lee rode it on the same rocky trails he always rode, and the bike felt far better. Specifically, PUSH revalved the rear shock to allow faster oil flow on quick, square-edged bumps. You never know how good it can be until you try it.

By changing some or all of these things, you can gently nudge your bike into a more ideal style, or you can make it a completely different machine.

Bike Setup

Because our bodies and styles are unique, we should adjust our bikes to match. Much of a bike's setup comes down to personal preference, but here are some tips to get you going.

Controls

Proper placement of your brake levers and shifters gives you maximum control with minimum effort. Most new bikes are set up wrong, so definitely take a look.

Brake Levers

Lee has worked one-on-one with hundreds of riders over the past few years, and 99 percent of them have had their brake levers set too far outboard and too high. Bikes are set up wrong at the shops, and few people know the difference. Proper brake setup has a huge impact on your control and confidence.

In and out. If you have good brakes, one finger should do the trick. Most of us use our index fingers, but some crude riders use their middles. Position your lever

BRIAN'S MOJOS

The Ibis Mojo is a 5.5-inch (14 cm) do-all mountain bike, somewhere between the trail and all-mountain categories. As a sponsored Ibis racer, Brian has lots of Mojos, with a variety of builds to suit various situations. Although few of us get a half dozen or more frames from anyone, these builds show you how a middle-of-the-road bike can be adapted for very different riding styles.

Brian races his dual slalom Mojo.

Downhill—Medium frame. 160 mm coil fork, coil shock, short stem, downhill casing tires, wider rims, single chainring with MRP chain guide, road cassette, wider handlebars.

Slopestyle—Small frame. A pretty burly build for video and photo shoots when he goes super big.

Super D—Medium frame. 160 mm Marzocchi 55 air fork, air shock with external reservoir, 2.3-inch (5.8 cm) single-ply tires, single chainring with MRP chain guide, mountain cassette, telescopic seatpost.

Cross-country—Medium frame. 140 mm air fork, air shock, 2.1-inch (5.3 cm) tires, triple chainring, mountain cassette.

Dual slalom—Small frame. 140 mm air fork, air shock, 2.1-inch (5.3 cm) tires, single chainring with MRP chain guide, road cassette.

Every mountain bike Brian rides has a 65-millimeter stem and 27-inch (69 cm) bars (except his DH bike, which has 28-inch [71 cm] bars; braaap!).

so that when you reach out, you grab the very end of the lever. This gives you max leverage. Pulling the end of the lever rather than the middle of the lever can double your braking power.

Tilt. When you reach for the brakes, your forearm, wrist, hand, and finger should be in line. In general, if you brake moderately on flat terrain (as on a cross-country bike), point your levers downward. If you brake violently on steep terrain (downhill), point them forward. Once your brake levers are set up, position your shifters wherever you can easily reach them—and wherever they fit.

Shifters

First, put your brake levers in the right place. That is crucial. Then, see where you can fit your shifters. (If you have integrated brake levers/shifters, we suppose you should run your shifters wherever they are.)

Just about all bikes come with the shifters inward of the brake levers. The problem can be that when you set your brake levers in the proper place, you can't reach the shifters. If this is the case, try running your shifters to the outside of your brake levers.

You might have to remove the little shifting window. If your knuckles accidentally hit the shifters, move the shifters back in so you have to reach for them.

When you buy shift levers and brake levers from different companies, it can be tricky to make them fit well together. If you have to compromise, make sure your brake levers are in the right place.

Saddle

Of all the touch points on your bike, the saddle is definitely the most . . . uh . . . sensitive. As with all things, the right saddle setup is all about compromise: comfort for maneuverability, power for flow.

Width

Bike seats were adapted from horse saddles more than 125 years ago, and they must reach a delicate balance: give you enough support to be comfortable while allowing your legs to move, and be narrow enough so you can move around.

Traditionally, racers chose narrow saddles and grandparents chose wide ones and that was it. Cruiser riders were comfortable, and performance riders suffered.

But there's more to saddle fit than that. Your saddle should support your sitting bones (aka ischial tuberosities), the bones at the bottom of your pelvis that you sit on. If the rear of the saddle is too narrow, you press down between your sitting bones, into the soft tissue (not fun!). If your saddle is too wide, it's just in the way.

So, the key is finding a saddle that fits your anatomy. Over the past few years, some companies (Specialized and Bontrager) have introduced devices to measure your sitting bones and a range of saddle widths to suit your anatomy perfectly. You basically sit on a gel pad, the bike shop tech measures the space between your sitting bones, and then he sells you a saddle with the proper width. With this kind of precision, saddles have padding right where you need it, so the saddles are smaller, lighter, easier to move around on—and more comfortable.

When it comes to finding your ideal saddle, we encourage you to experiment. Don't use the narrowest saddle because it's fashionable. Try lots of saddles to find our which feels best to you.

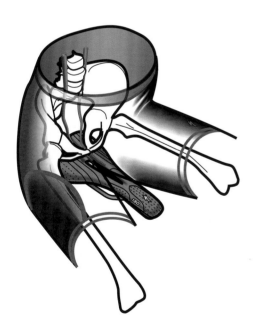

Your ideal saddle supports your sitting bones so your weight doesn't press on soft tissue—which can be a painful and/or numbing experience. Specialized makes saddles in multiple widths to fit individual sit bones.

Padding

When it comes to bike seats, padding is a double-edged sword. (Ouch, that doesn't sound so good.)

Although many types of padding might feel good in the parking lot, over time your sitting bones can push down toward the hard base, and your soft parts start to press into the padding. Not only is this uncomfortable, but the increased contact and friction can slow you down.

With very little padding, all of your weight rests on your sitting bones. This leaves very little contact with your soft parts, which is a good thing, but it too can be uncomfortable—especially for occasional riders.

We suggest that you go for a soft saddle if your rides are short and infrequent. If your rides are long and often, rock a harder one.

The sleek Specialized Phenom (left) is designed for easy movement and powerful pedaling. The wider, more padded Sonoma Gel is made for more casual riding. Both are available in multiple widths to suit individual riders.

Angle

Nose down to go up.   For lots of climbing, try pointing the nose down a bit. This concentrates your weight on the blunt rear of the saddle, especially when your bike is pointed uphill. If you plan to climb on a long-travel bike, point the nose down so it doesn't violate you when your rear end sags.

Nose up to go down.   For downhilling, jumping, and the like, try pointing the nose up. When your bike points down a steep slope or starting gate, the saddle ends up pretty level. Also, you can use the front of the saddle for control, but the rear stays out of the way when you need to move back on your bike.

Fore–Aft Position

Traditionally speaking, with your pedal at 3 o'clock, the bone right below your knee should be directly above your pedal spindle. Among experienced riders and bike fitters, this is not gospel, but it is dogma.

How far your seat is behind your bottom bracket has a huge influence on how you pedal.

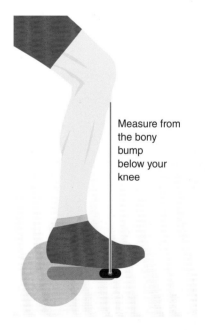

Measure from the bony bump below your knee

- ○ Seat farther forward means more quads and knees.
- ○ Seat farther back means more glutes and hips. (As Lee's knees get older, he's running his seat farther back.)

Traditional fore–aft saddle positioning places the bony bump below your knee above the pedal spindle.

WEAR BIKE SHORTS

Along with a properly fitting saddle, a good pair of cycling shorts is mandatory—unless you like chafing and saddle sores. The chamois (saddle pad) supports your sitting bones, cushions you from shock, and wicks away moisture.

Don't worry: You don't have to be a Lycra Death Sausage. If you're not willing to ride with just a thin layer of synthetic fabric between your stuff and the world, rock a pair of baggy MTB shorts with a liner, or wear any old shorts with Lycra underneath. No one has to know about your inner roadie.

This **fore–aft position** also affects the way you ride your bike.

○ Seat forward puts you in a better position for climbing.
○ Seat back puts you in a better position for descending.

No wonder XC race bikes have steep seat tube angles, whereas downhill bikes have slack ones.

Of course you have to compromise. Pedaling is A-1 Most Important. Position your seat wherever it needs to be for you to pedal powerfully and comfortably. Once that's set, you can learn to corner, pump and hop around that position.

Switching Between Bikes

Because your seat position determines your muscle recruitment and joint angles, many riders enjoy more power and less pain when they maintain the same pedaling position on all their bikes. If you have young joints of Teflon, and you have no idea what we're talking about, don't sweat it.

But if when you switch bikes your pedaling feels awkward or painful, try this:

○ Pick which bike is most important. If you are an XC or **super D** racer, definitely pick your race bike.
○ Get a friend to do a plumb bob test on you.
○ Record the distance and direction from your knee to your pedal spindle.
○ Adjust your other bikes to match.

Do this for all your "sit and spin" bikes: cross-country, all-mountain, road, **cyclocross**. It isn't so important for nonpedaling bikes such as dirt jumpers and downhillers.

Making the Adjustment

Make small adjustments by sliding your saddle back and forth on its rails. (Beware: If your saddle is too far off center, you risk damaging it or your seatpost.) If you need more than, say, 1/2 inch (1.3 cm) of adjustment, try a layback seatpost (a seatpost that is bent toward the rear). Riders with long torsos swear by layback posts.

Gearing

The original mountain bikes had three front gears (chainrings) in front and wide-ratio cogs in back. That gave them big gears for downhills, tiny gears for climbs, and everything in between. This versatility is at the heart of mountain biking's origins. These days, riding is more specialized. Riders are going faster, harder, and bigger; and we have more options to suit our needs.

The new Hammerschmidt crankset from SRAM uses an internal two-speed shifter and a dedicated chain guide to give riders the best of two worlds: dual-ring versatility and single-ring security.

Gearing tradeoffs

With a traditional chain/gears/derailleurs drivetrain, the more versatile your gearing, the less secure it is.

Less security means a greater chance of your chain falling off your chainring(s).

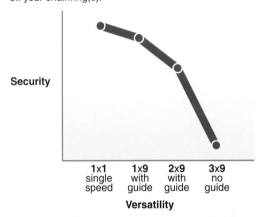

Trail—3×9

Most mountain bikes come with three gears in front (typically 22/32/44) and a wide-ratio cassette in back (typically an 11-34). This works everywhere. But if you ride hard or fast enough, your chain is likely to fall off the rings.

All-Mountain—2×9

This is the newest class of bike, and the drivetrains are achieving an awesome balance of versatility and security.

Rear: Wide-ratio mountain cassettes.

Front: Two rings, typically either a 22/34 or a 24/36, with a chain guide. "Dual" guides have a roller at the bottom. The front derailleur handles the top.

What about the big ring? Unless you're racing other people who have big rings, the 44t isn't that important. You need gears to get up hills and accelerate out of slow sections. Once you're up to speed, it's best to tuck and pump.

Gravity—1×9

Downhillers, go-big freeriders, bikercross racers, and dirt jumpers opt for the security of a single front ring encased in a chain guide. Dedicated one-ring guides have channels or rollers (or both) at the top and bottom of the ring, plus a bash guard to ward off impacts. Deraillments should be very rare (but anything can happen).

For extra ground clearance, tighter ratios, and better shifting, run a smallish front ring (36 to 40 teeth instead of 42 to 46 teeth) and a tight road cluster (11 to 25 teeth instead of a mountain bike's 11 to 34). Give yourself a gear tall enough to achieve ramming speed without spinning and low enough to blast out of the starting gate and zip out of the slowest corner. Lower and higher gears are wasted. To guarantee you don't end up in the wrong gear, use your derailleur adjuster screws to block out the ones you don't need.

Single Speed—1×1

For the ultimate in purity, simplicity, low-speed torque, and high-speed spin, one gear is all you need. No shifters, no derailleurs, no chain slap, and one fewer thing to think about.

Most single speeders run about a 2:1 gear ratio (36 in front, 18 in back).

Single speeds can be fast: Some years ago, Mark Weir set a 24-hour one-lap record on a single speed. That's partly because he's a freak, but also because, if he's turning that gear, he's going fast.

Single speeds are awesome for moderately steep, rolling terrain, and they work great for jump/park/pump bikes.

Warning: When you choose a single speed, you tread into cult territory. The chances of riding a hardtail with a rigid fork, wearing wool, drinking beer, and selling your car increase exponentially.

Tires

Back in the late '80s and early '90s, we all ran Tioga Farmer John or Specialized Ground Control tires. That's all we had, and we ran them everywhere, all the time. Nowadays, mountain biking is hyperspecialized, and there's a tire for every day of the week. Although it's strangely fun to take soil samples before each ride and change tires as if they were shoes, you'll get more out of your tires if you pick ones that suit your conditions and run them all the time. Get a feel for how much braking traction your tires have and when they're about to break loose in corners.

Soft rubber compounds improve cornering traction but increase rolling resistance. Some tires get the best of both worlds with soft side knobs and hard center knobs. Thick casings improve durability and reduce pinch flats, but you pay with extra weight. When it comes to compounds and casings, you have to roll whatever suits your situation.

For general conditions—everything from concrete to dirt to rocks to roots to mud—it's hard to beat a tire with sticky rubber and medium, widely spaced knobs. That said, certain situations call for special meat. On hard pack, nothing rolls faster than **semi-slicks**—tires with lots of tiny, closely spaced knobs. In sloppy mud, a spike tire grips like male Velcro. You wouldn't want to run these tires everywhere, but in their element they can't be beaten.

The chart on page 33 shows some general tread types. All tire makers have their own interpretations, but most of their tires fit into one of these categories.

The right tire pressure balances speed and traction, cushiness, and pinch flats. Experiment to see what works for you. Start on the high side and let out a bit of air at a time until your tires start to squirm or they pinch flat.

A whole lot goes on where rubber meets dirt. As long as you're confident and know what to expect, it's all good.

Some of you freeriders and downhillers love the 2.7-inch (7 cm) tires with thick casings for flat prevention and low pressure for traction. Most people in most situations should run smaller tires with light casings, which accelerate and roll faster. Rely on your tread and compound for traction. To avoid pinch flats, try cleaner lines and smoother riding.

Square vs. Round Profile

Now we're getting extra tricky. Look across the top of your tire. Do the knobs form a round shape or a square one?

A round tire has knobs evenly spaced from its center to its edge. This makes a consistent, predictable tire that holds well at all angles, with no surprises. Most riders, especially on harder terrain, are well served with rounder tires.

Examples: Specialized Purgatory, Maxxis Ardent, WTB Mutano Raptor

A square tire has a gap between the center knobs and the side knobs. By further exposing the side knobs, this tire gets more ultimate cornering traction, especially in loose conditions. The tradeoff: When you're on the gap, the tire can feel a bit vague and disconnected. A square tire requires more commitment in the corners: you really have to lean it onto the side knobs; otherwise, the tire feels sketchy. Mark Weir at WTB calls these "expert" tires. If your terrain is soft and your cornering is aggressive, give these a try.

Examples: Specialized Eskar, Maxxis High Roller, WTB Weir-Wolf

Round profile
Specialized Purgatory

Square Profile
Specialized Eskar   Gap

Tube vs. tubeless

Tire with inner tube
Air pressure is contained within the inner tube.

Tubeless tire
Air seal is formed between tire, rim, and valve stem.

Tire
Inner tube
Rim
Valve stem

Should You Go Tubeless?

That's a personal decision.

Dedicated tubeless tires have extra rubber on their insides to make them airtight, as well as softer beads to create air seals. Tubeless-ready rims have no spoke holes on the tire surface, and they are shaped to help the tire seal when inflated. The most common standard is UST. Many (new) UST rims and tires can be easily mounted with a floor pump.

Tubeless conversion systems, like Stan's, use a special rim strip and sealant to make almost any tire and rim tubeless. This is a slick setup but often requires an air canister or compressor.

PROS OF TUBELESS TIRES

Reduced pinch flats. There's no tube to pinch.

Self-sealing. If you run sealant inside your tires (and you should), small punctures seal themselves.

Reduced weight. Some dedicated systems might be a bit heavier than standard ones, so check the specs (and don't forget the weight of your sealant). Stan's kits are almost always lighter than standard setups.

Lower air pressure. You can run lower air, which improves traction and control for most riders. Brian, who rides aggressively, still runs lots of air.

CONS OF TUBELESS TIRES

Pain-in-the-butt factor. Installing and repairing tires is a lot more involved than with standard tires and tubes. Depending on which system you use, you need a perfect tire and tube, and you might even need an air canister or compressor. Always carry a tube, just in case.

Burping air. Hard sideways compressions can rip your bead away from the rim and let air "burp" out. When he rides tubeless, Brian finds himself riding lighter—and slower—in spots where burping can happen: sideways jumps, hard **berms**, and so on.

What We Think

Brian like tubeless tires for trail riding because of the reduced pinch flats and the reduced weight (he uses standard tires and rims with Stan's conversions). For bikercross and **dual slalom**, where there is little chance of a pinch flat and he needs to ride aggressively, he runs tubes. For downhill, he uses tires with downhill casings and tubes.

Lee has experimented with tubeless systems, and they've proved to be such a pain that he's back to tubes. At least for now.

Tread style	Advantages	Use	Examples
Semi-slick with side knobs Specialized Renegade	Very fast rolling; decent cornering traction	Very hard-packed trails or race courses	Maxxis High Roller Semi Slick, WTB Vulpine, Kenda Short Tracker, Specialized Renegade
Small; closely spaced knobs Specialized Fast Trak	Fast rolling; good cornering traction	Dry and hard-packed trails	Maxxis Larsen TT, WTB Nano Raptor, Specialized Fast Track, Kenda Small Block Eight
Medium; moderately spaced knobs Specialized Eskar	Decent rolling; great all-around traction	All-around terrain from dry to wet. Ramped knobs speed rolling. Grooves in the knobs increase traction.	Maxxis High Roller, Maxxis Minion, WTB Prowler MX, Specialized Eskar, Kenda Nevegal
Spike tire with pointy, widely spaced knobs Specialized Storm	Good penetration and mud clearance	Horrific mud and wet grass. Squirmy on any hard surface. For gravity racing only.	Maxxis Swampthing, Maxxis Wet Scream, Michelin Mud, Specialized Storm, Kenda King of Traction

BRIAN'S SIGNATURE TIRE

The Kenda "El Moco"—Spanish for "the booger"—is tweaked for Brian's riding style:

- ○ The center knobs are small and ramped, for fast rolling.
- ○ The side knobs are big and open, for aggressive cornering in loose dirt.
- ○ Brian's signature No. 55 is molded into the knobs.

Bar and Stem

Product managers spec bars and stems to match the intended use of the bike and the likely size of the rider. This is a fine starting point, but you might want to customize to suit your riding style.

If climbing is your thing, run a long, low stem—say, 90 to 120 millimeters with 0 to 10 degrees of rise. This creates a powerful pedaling position, and it weights the front end for climbing. Run a flat or 1-inch (2.5 cm) rise bar to keep you nice and stretched out.

Cockpit comparison
Race: Long and low

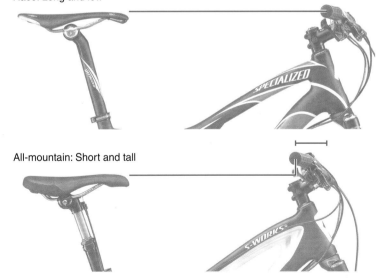

All-mountain: Short and tall

Note: Handlebar placement in general, even on race bikes, is getting higher than in the past. Bikes just tend to handle better that way.

Bikes: Specialized Epic (top) and Enduro (bottom).

If you're more concerned with descending, jumping, and other tomfoolery than ultimate climbing domination, run a 40- to 70-millimeter stem. This makes it easier to move back for steep terrain, and it gives you a bigger **cockpit** for controlling your bike. Use a stem with 10 to 15 degrees of rise, a bar with 1.5 to 2.5 inches (3.8 to 6.4 cm) of rise, or both.

When it comes to your bar and stem, long and low works, and short and high works. But long and high feels like you're reaching for help, and short and low feels like you're digging for worms. Not cool.

Riders prefer different bar widths, depending on their size and the tightness of their forests. Do what feels right, but make sure all of your bikes are the same.

To Clip In or Not to Clip In

There are two kinds of pedals these days: (1) flat BMX-style pedals you stand on with soft rubber soles and (2) clipless pedals you click into with metal cleats on stiff soles.

You young whippersnappers might be wondering why they call the pedals you clip into "clipless." Back in, like, 1492, you slipped your foot into a metal or plastic cage, called a clip, and cinched your feet to the pedals with a leather strap. These are terrible for off-roading: If you leave the straps loose, they barely help you pedal; and if you make the straps tight, you're doomed. We used to tighten our straps at the bottom of hills and loosen them at the top, which is pretty clunky—and what if you forget to uncinch for a gnarly descent?

When the mechanical pedal-and-cleat systems came out, they lacked the big ol' clips, so they were called clipless. That's like calling a car horseless. Whatever. We will now call these pedals **clip-ins**, or **clips**.

Anyway, clips give you significantly more power than flats. They also improve control, especially on rough terrain—you can float over rough stuff and you don't have to worry about your feet bouncing off the pedals. A few downhillers still insist on running flats, but they're in the minority. You quickly learn how to clip in and out, and in a crash your feet almost always release. *Almost* always.

Flat pedals definitely give you more leeway in certain situations. They're a must for learning to jump and manual, and they make it easier to jettison your bike when North Shore stunts go awry. You can tweak your legs out and lift part of your foot for more balance, and when you take your foot off for corners, you can resume pedaling sooner than with clips.

A lot of people (including the authors, back in the day) believe they can attack harder and push the limits more with flats. If you're most comfortable with flats, go ahead and run 'em, especially when you're just goofing off. For racing, we suggest you get used to pushing the limits on flats and then switch to clips for their increased power and control.

Flat pedals work best with soft, relatively flat soles. Leave the macho lugs for hiking. This pedal is made by Specialized Bicycle Components.

Clip-in pedals require shoes with holes in their soles to accommodate the metal cleats. When your sole wears out, the cleats make a cool "click, clack" sound on hard floors. This pedal is made by Shimano.

Flat pedals teach you to stay poised over the pedals and let your bike do its thing. Check out that rear suspension on this chatter bump.

Do this: Learn how to ride smoothly and confidently with flat pedals. This will force you to overcome your terrible clipped-in riding habits (yes, you have them) and will greatly improve your fluidity and flow. Ride flats during the winter; rip in clips during the summer.

Suspension

Properly dialed suspension makes your bike ride like a dream. Poorly adjusted suspension makes it ride like a nightmare. Properly dialed suspension does two things: It isolates your bike and body from violence, and it keeps your tires in contact with the ground.

Suspension setup can get very complex. Here are the basics:

Fork parts

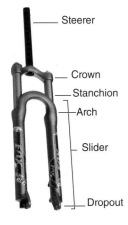

- Steerer
- Crown
- Stanchion
- Arch
- Slider
- Dropout

Shock parts

- Reservoir
- Preload collar
- Coil spring

Spring Rate and Preload

Your spring controls the amount of force it takes to compress your suspension. The higher the spring rate, the stiffer the spring. You fine-tune coil-spring shocks by turning the **preload** collar. With air shocks, you add or remove air.

You want your spring stiff enough to support your weight but soft enough to sag while you're on your bike. This sag allows your wheels to stay on the ground while you traverse little bumps and dips. The softer your suspension, the more stuck to the ground you'll feel. The stiffer your suspension, the bigger hits you can take without bottoming out. You want your suspension to be as soft as possible without bottoming out all the time. If you use the full travel range a few times per ride, that's perfect.

Most cross-country bikes should sag through about 25 percent of their travel. Longer-travel downhill and freeride bikes should sag about 33 percent. A few designs require up to 40 percent sag. Your bike's manual will tell you what's up.

Put a small zip tie on your fork stanchion and an O-ring on the shaft of your rear air shock. Get on the bike with your weight distributed as if you're riding, and see how far your high-tech indicators move in relation to the available stroke. With coil shocks, measure the distance between the shock mounting bolts. Sit on the bike and have someone measure the shock again. The difference is your sag. Of course, it helps to know the total stroke of your shock. If you've lost your manual, remove the coil spring and see how far you can compress the shock by hand.

With air shocks, increase or decrease the air pressure until you get the right sag. With coil-spring shocks, tighten or loosen the knurled metal collar on the end of the spring. This changes the preload. If you can't get enough preload with two turns, you need a stiffer spring. Too much preload makes your wheel chatter on small bumps and can damage your shock. If you loosen the collar so much that your spring is rattling around on the shock, you need a softer spring.

The placement of the o-ring (shock) and zip tie (fork) show the proper amount of sag for this 2008 Specialized Stumpjumper Pro Carbon.

Rebound Damping

The rebound circuit on your shock slows your spring's extension after you hit a bump. Without **rebound damping**, your spring would spring back full force and buck you like Buck Rogers—into the 25th century.

If you have too much rebound damping, your shock can't extend after you hit a bump, and as you hit more bumps, your shock "packs" lower and lower into its travel, giving you a harsh experience. The faster you go and the more rapid the hits, the faster your rebound must be. If you have too little rebound damping, your bike will bounce—boing, boing—after bumps and drops.

Set your rebound as fast as possible without it feeling springy or hard to control. Also, check your setting every time you change your spring. Your front and rear should rebound at the same speed.

SUSPENSION SETUP TIPS

- ○ Experiment with the extremes. Dial your rebound or compression all the way in or out and see how that feels.
- ○ Change only one thing at a time.
- ○ Make notes of your settings and how the bike feels.
- ○ Once you get your bike dialed, don't mess around with it too much. Just ride it and get used to it.

Compression Damping

Only higher-end forks and shocks have compression-damping adjustment. Factory settings usually work just fine, and besides, you can mess up your bike's ride with the wrong settings.

Although your spring determines how much force it takes to compress the suspension, your **compression damping** controls how fast your suspension can compress. Lots of compression damping reduces pedaling bob but can make your bike feel harsh. A low amount of compression damping makes your bike feel plush, but it might wallow or bottom out.

Tip: "More rebound" means more rebound *damping,* which makes your suspension rebound slower. Same with compression. "Adding compression" means adding compression *damping,* which makes your suspension compress slower.

For a plush ride, run as little compression damping as you can without blowing through your travel. For efficient pedaling, run as much compression damping as you can without feeling harsh.

Some higher-end suspensions give you two flavors of compression damping:

Low-speed compression is not for when you're riding slowly. It regulates low-frequency movements, like the ones you create when you pedal or hit the brakes. Less low-speed compression makes your bike extra plush on smaller bumps, but it can make your bike feel too bouncy and vague. More low-speed compression makes your bike stiffer for pedaling and cornering, and it reduces brake dive, but it can make your bike a bit sketchier on small bumps.

Tip: Start with very little low-speed compression damping. Add one click at a time until your bike stops bouncing when you pedal.

High-speed compression is not for when you're riding fast (although it often comes into play when you're **pinned**). It regulates high-frequency movements, like the ones you create when you bash into a rock or drop off your roof. Less high-speed compression lets your bike use its full travel more easily. More high-speed compression limits the travel and helps prevent bottoming.

Tip: Start with very little high-speed compression damping. Add one click at a time until your bike stops bottoming harshly.

BRIAN AND COMPRESSION DAMPING

I don't like any of that pedaling platform stuff. I only want the suspension stiff if I'm climbing on the road. Otherwise, I want it to be as active as possible. (Note: Brian's Ibis Mojo uses a DW link, which is known for inherently stable pedaling. Other suspension designs benefit more from pedal platforms.)

I get as close as I can with the spring. From there I fine-tune with damping if I have to. For example, if my fork is nice and supple but it's diving or bottoming too much, I might add a few clicks of compression. If I added air, it would take away the suppleness.

SUSPENSION BRACKETING

This nugget comes from Mark Fitzsimmons at Fox Racing Shox. He works with Fox's elite racers to develop new products.

Use bracketing for any adjustment: rebound, compression, or even pedaling platform (in Fox's case, it's called ProPedal). You'll be comparing two settings, picking your favorite, and gradually working your way to your final setting. Let's say you have 15 clicks of adjustment.

Pair 1: All the way in and 15 clicks out.

Pair 2: Which felt better? If 15 clicks out felt better, your next comparison will be 15 clicks out versus 7 clicks out.

Pair 3: Which felt better? If 7 clicks out felt better, your next comparison will be 7 clicks out versus 11 clicks out.

And so on, until you reach your final setting.

Suspension bracketing

Idea from Mark Fitzsimmons at Fox Racing Shox. This is for ProPedal adjustment on DHX rear shocks, but the approach applies to all suspension settings.

Start at the extremes. Compare your favorite (red) with the halfway point (blue). Compare that favorite with the next halfway point, and so on until you're dialed.

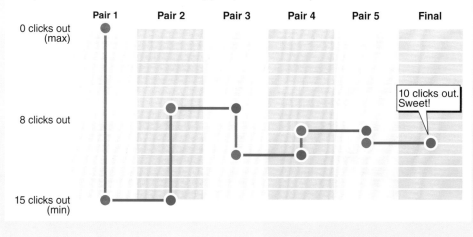

SUSPENSION TROUBLESHOOTING

Before you mess things up worse, make sure your sag (and, thus, your spring rate) is correct.

Problem: Bike bounces up and down (boing, boing) after hitting a bump or dropping off a curb.

Solution: Increase rebound damping.

Problem: Bike feels good over the first bump but gets harsher over subsequent bumps.

Solution: Your shock is "packing up." Decrease rebound damping.

Problem: Excessive bottoming (even with correct spring rate); too much bouncing while pedaling.

Solution: Increase compression damping.

Problem: Bike feels harsh on big bumps, feels harsh or chatters on small bumps, has poor traction in corners, is not using full travel.

Solution: Decrease compression damping.

Tune Your Suspension for Your Riding Style

Your suspension setup has an enormous effect on the way your bike rides. Once you pick a fork and shock, there's still a lot of tuning to do. Here are some tips:

Optimize for the average. If you're doing a two-hour loop with 1:45 of climbing, set your bike stiff for the climb. If your ride has tons of small rocks, set it up loose. If it has 100 big drops, set it up stiff.

Brian's home trails in Southern California have lots of small rocks. He sets his trail bike extra soft, so it tracks through the small and medium bumps without chatter. He lets the bike handle those; then, when he hits the occasional g-out or drop, he sucks it up with his arms and legs. His suspension is bottoming out, but he's not getting blown off the bike.

Lee's home trails in Colorado have bigger rocks with more smooth sections in between. He sets his trail bike extra stiff, so it holds up to high-g turns and bigger impacts. In the smaller bumps he deals with more sketchiness, but that's the compromise he's made.

For dirt jumping, run your bike stiff. When you're dirt jumping, you need to handle high g's and potential impacts. You're not worried how the bike tracks through chattery turns or rough sections. You're not riding that stuff—or you're just coasting though on your way to the next jump.

How strong or aggressive are you? Here's an old-school tip: Go out right now, get on your bike, and bounce up and down as hard as you can. How much travel did you use? If you bottomed out harshly, stiffen things up. If you used only a small portion of your suspension,

Setting up a trail bike for this gnarl is a tricky compromise. Supple enough to erase the chatter, but stiff enough to control the big hits. Patrick Hooper makes five inches work.

soften it. You want your bottom-out force to match the highest strain you can handle. If you're not strong or aggressive enough to use all of your suspension, why lug it around?

With short-travel bikes, you have to choose soft or stiff.   Because you don't have much space for transitions with short-travel bikes, you either get a supple bike that bottoms easily or a bottom-resistant bike that chatters through the rough sections.

With long-travel bikes, you can have the best of both worlds.   Because long-travel bikes give you more room to work with, you can achieve both a supple beginning and a smooth transition to a bottomless bottom. This is one of the real benefits of longer travel. Brian: "The more travel you have, the easier it is to adjust for everything. If you have only 3 inches (8 cm), it's hard to make it super supple and then ramp up. There isn't enough room in there. But if you have 8 inches (20 cm), there's plenty of room to start supple and then ramp up."

It's OK to bottom out.   You have 5, 6, or 8 inches (13, 15, or 20 cm) of travel. You paid for it, and you're dragging it up the hills. Use it. At some point on your average ride, you should bottom out. Not violently, but you should use all the travel. Brian says this is like choosing his gear back in his BMX days. At the end of the first straight, entering the first turn, he wanted to be completely spun out. Why have that extra tooth if you're not using it?

For steep trails, try softening your rear suspension.   Softening the rear suspension drops the rear end, raises the front end, and slackens your geometry.

Respect your frame.   Every bike design has a unique leverage ratio, presumably designed to complement the bike's intended use. Hopefully the frame maker and shock maker worked together, so you don't have to worry about what's inside your shock.

Don't be stupid with your fork.   Although each frame is made for a specific shock, you can theoretically slap on any fork you want. Don't go too tall, or you'll whack out your geometry and void your warranty. Don't go too low, either. Few people install shorter-travel forks, but many drop their forks for climbing.

Beware the adjustable fork.   Adjustable forks can be a great way to help your bike both climb and descend better, but a lot of people forget to raise (or unlock) their forks for the downhill. What a waste of perfectly good potential energy. Also (and this is rarely spoken about), some rear suspension designs actually pedal worse if the front end is too low. Brian says he and Richie Schley experienced this on their GT and Rocky Mountain bikes.

When you land hard on flat ground, you should bottom your suspension. That's what it's for.

Stop messing with it. If you race or travel, you might have reasons to dial in your suspension for a specific course or trail. But if you, like most of us, ride the same local trails all the time, find a setting that works—and rock it. Stop tinkering and blaming your bike for bad days. Find a setting, learn it, and leave it alone.

A freshly dialed bike is truly a thing to be proud of—the sweet frame, the dialed suspension, the perfectly adjusted controls. But a new bike is merely a thing. It takes a few great rides—a brush with death, a glimpse of greatness, a moment of exultant flow—to bring your steed to life. A perfectly functioning bike becomes more than an assembly of expensive parts. It becomes an individual, a friend, a part of you.

READ THE MANUAL!

There are so many suspension designs and a variety of knobs—compression, rebound, low-speed compression, high-speed compression, lower your fork, lock your fork, plus, minus, a bunny and a turtle—and there are no standards.

And then there's the whole issue of positive and negative air chambers, not to mention the adjustable air volume *and* adjustable air pressure.

No matter how experienced you think you are, read your manual and follow the manufacturer's recommendations.

CHAPTER 2

Become One With Your Bike

Lee teaches riders of all types and levels, and, based on that experience, he'll respectfully tell you these things:

1. You probably suck.
2. You suck more than you realize.
3. You suck because you're too stiff and passive on the bike.

If you want to suck less, you must loosen up and learn to use your entire cockpit in a fluid and balanced way. Everything you do on your bike starts here, in this chapter. These fundamentals are the core of Lee's curriculum, and they are the key to not sucking (or at least sucking less).

YOU MIGHT NOTICE . . .

. . . that this section repeats a few key themes over and over again. Heavy feet, light hands! Attack position!

1. They are crucial to great riding.
2. The more we say 'em, the more likely you'll learn 'em!

Hey, we're just trying to help.

Learn How to Touch Your Bike

Nothing gives you as much pleasure (or pain) as your bike. The least you can do is learn how it likes to be touched. You contact your bike in three places, each with its own purpose.

Ride from the waist down. This rider drives all of his weight, and the force of hitting the rock, straight into his pedals. The rest of his body is relaxed. Perfect.

Pedals

These little spinning platforms form the basis of your relationship. When you stand on your pedals, your weight runs through your bottom bracket and spreads about 45/55 to the front and rear wheels. This is where your weight belongs. Here's why:

○ Front–rear balance. Your weight stays safely between your wheels, and your front stays just a bit lighter than the rear.

○ Low center of gravity. With your weight focused 12 or so inches (30 cm) off the ground, your bike whips easier than a strap of leather.

○ Your biggest muscles bear your immense weight . . . ha!

○ Your hands stay light on the bars. This is the A-1 key to effective riding. Keep reading.

Handlebars

Believe it or not, your handlebars are *not* for holding your upper body up. You have a lot to do with your bars—steering, pulling yourself forward, pushing yourself back, pressing down to weight, and pulling up to unweight—so the less you lean on them for basic support, the better. Here's why:

○ More comfort. You place less stress on hand nerves and shoulder muscles.

○ Better handling. Your bike steers more easily, and a light grip allows your front wheel to flop around as it whips into corners and bashes into things.

○ Ready for action. When you lean on the bar, you half-commit in the downward, lazy direction. When you hover over your bar, you're poised to push, pull, steer, lean, or leap over tall buildings.

And, most important:

○ Perfect balance. Leaning forward onto the bars makes the front wheel too heavy. Leaning back away from the bars makes the front wheel too light. Unless you're intentionally pulling an expert move, your hands should be neutral on the bars. This lets your weight drive through the bottom bracket and into both wheels, which is perfect.

Saddle

We should all feel close to our saddles, but we shouldn't sit too often or too heavily. Your bike saddle is not a seat—at least not the kind you want to sit on—but it does serve three purposes:

○ A place to rest. When you pedal very hard, all of your weight pushes down on the pedals. This is a good thing, for as long as you can keep it up. Your saddle lets you rest while you pedal softly. The lighter you pedal, the heavier you sit. Here's a vicious cycle: The more uncomfortable you are, the softer you pedal. The softer you pedal, the heavier you sit. The heavier you sit, the more uncomfortable you are. If you feel yourself crumpling lazily onto your saddle, buck up and pedal harder. You'll feel better, and you'll reach the top faster.

Tea Party Fingers. Lisa Myklak is pinning a downhill run, yet her hands are daintily neutral.

Disengaging from the seat gives Judy Freeman the freedom to take this smart line into a blown out corner.

○ A platform for efficient pedaling. Even if you aren't sitting with your full weight, your saddle helps smooth your pedal stroke and saves energy you'd otherwise spend holding your body upright. Also, when you push across the top of the stroke, you brace against the rear of the saddle.

○ A point of control. Back in the day, there was a BMX bike with no saddle for maximum lightness, and it was really hard to ride. Even if you don't sit on the seat, you use it to control your bike's side-to-side movement. Sitting back on the seat increases rear traction for climbing and cornering.

When you plant yourself on the saddle, you limit yourself to smooth terrain, mellow cornering, and soft braking. When you cross rough terrain, corner hard, or brake with authority, get up and off that saddle. Even a slight unweight is better than a full sit. In summary: Stand on your pedals. Use your handlebars for control. Use your saddle sparingly, for rest and control.

Get Into Attack Position

Read this carefully, because it's the A-1 key to ripping.

Although mountain biking is (and should be) dynamic, you should have a neutral base position—a position you can start with and return to. We call it the attack position, because it positions you to attack the trail, rather than survive it.

When you're in your attack position, you can quickly and seamlessly push, pull, lean, twist, and basically rock. The more centered you are, the more range you have in every direction, and the more ready you are to attack the trail.

Keys to a Good Attack Position

Weight Driving Into Your Pedals

How: In almost every situation, a red dotted line should drive your weight from your belly button to your bottom bracket. As you ride, subtly shift your hips forward or backward to keep your feet heavy and your hands light.

Why: This is the best way to ensure perfect fore–aft balance. It's not about how your hips are related to your seat, or how your shoulders are related to your bars. The only thing that truly matters is, are your feet heavy and your hands light?

Knees Bent

How: Lower your hips and upper body until you're halfway between standing fully straight and hitting your seat. The lower your seat, the lower that is.

You should never ride with completely straight knees because (1) you become stiff and unyielding, and (2) if you hit something super hard, you're risking a hyperextension injury. Bending your knees might seem simple, and it is, but you must also flex at your hips. Keep reading.

Why: Bent knees give you built-in suspension. Lowering your body to the midpoint between standing and hitting the seat places you in a position in which you can quickly move up or down to deal with terrain. Also, a lower center of gravity is a happier center of gravity.

Attack position checklist
With the seat all the way up, this Specialized Stumpjumper Pro Carbon has a very neutral trail-riding position. Whenever you ride, check on these key points. They will make you smoother, faster and—in general—readier.

☐ Hips back

☐ Torso level

☐ Head and eyes up

☐ Shoulders back

☐ Elbows out

☐ Knees bent

☐ Weight driving into pedals

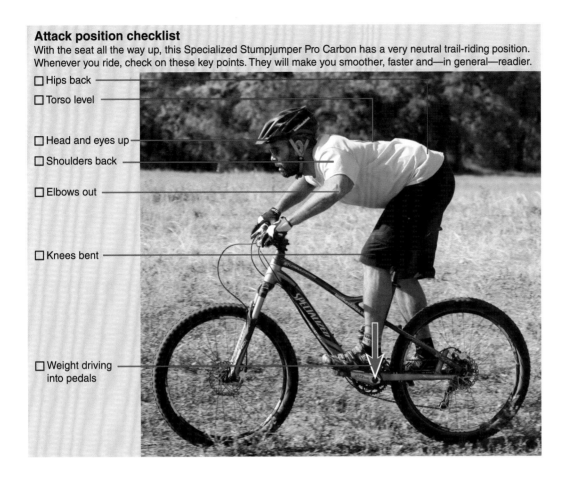

Hips Back, Torso Level

How: This is tricky for most riders. *Do not* try to accomplish this by lowering your shoulders toward the bars. This will shift your weight forward in a bad way. Instead, push your hips back. Keep your spine and tailbone in line, and let your torso fold forward. Your hips will push back. Your shoulders will swing forward. They will balance each other, and your belly button will be right over your bottom bracket.

Why: A couple of reasons: (1) Pushing your hips back lets you recruit some of the most powerful muscles in your body—your glutes. You ride with more power and less fatigue. (2) This helps you maintain proper balance over your bottom bracket. Most people tuck their hips forward under them. Bad news.

Shoulders Down

How: When you push your hips back and bring your torso level, your shoulders will come down automatically. It's all part of the same motion, but low shoulders deserve special attention.

Why: The lower your shoulders are, the more arm range you have for cornering, pumping, manualing, jumping, and all the fun stuff. When you obey your natural instinct to protect your skull by raising your head away from danger, you are limiting your

LOWER THAT SEAT!

Unless you're racing cross-country, you should try lowering your seat for downhills. Heck, if you're racing cross-country, you might still try a remotely adjustable post. The lower your seat, the more you can rip.

arm range and pretty much guaranteeing that you'll ride poorly. You need that arm range. The gnarlier it gets, the lower your shoulders should be.

Getting your shoulders (and head) close to the bars (and trail) runs counter to a whole lot of evolution, but trust us—it really helps. Look at any photo or video of Brian racing. His shoulders are always low. Now you know why.

Side note: Shoulder blades down and back, not hunched forward. You shouldn't hunch forward at your computer, and you definitely shouldn't hunch on your bike.

Elbows Out

How: Hold your elbows out until they're in line with your shoulders. Try for a 90-degree angle between your forearm and upper arm, and a 90-degree angle between your upper arm and your torso.

Why: Get down and do 100 push-ups. OK, 10 will do. Try them with your elbows close to your body; then rock 'em with your elbows out. It's easier with your elbows out, isn't it? When you ride with your elbows out, you are stronger, and you have more range of motion for pushing, pulling, and leaning.

Head Up and Eyes Out

How: Lift your head. Imagine leading with your chin. Look as far ahead as you can. This is probably the simplest thing to say, but it's the most important, and it's the first thing you'll forget to do.

Why: (1) Balance. Dropping your head to stare at that big rock shifts your weight forward—never a good thing, especially as you encounter a big rock. (2) Confidence. You're not apologizing—you're charging! (3) Anticipation. The farther ahead you look, the more time you have to react to terrain. This is one of the keys to avoiding crashes.

Perfect Practice!

This position will feel strange at first, and you'll learn that your shoulders, back, hips, hamstrings, and calves aren't as strong and flexible as you thought. Stick with it. Focus on one element at a time. Eventually, the attack position will become instinctual, and you will rip like never before.

While you're out there, be aware of these common mistakes:

Riding too high. You think you're low, but you're not. Get lower!

Too stiff and static. This is just your base position. As you ride along a trail, you'll pass through your attack position on your way to other positions. Stay neutral, but stay loose and flexible.

Too far forward or back. You're pressing down or pulling up with your hands, aren't you? We knew it. Whatever happens, make sure your hands are perfectly neutral on the bars.

Butt near the seat. It seems like there's a glass well about 1 inch (2.5 cm) behind everyone's saddles. Push your hips back! In your attack position with your torso level and perfectly balanced, the back of your butt will be a bit behind your saddle. That's perfect.

A good, neutral-attack position is the A-1 key to riding well. If you're having a bad day, go back to your attack position checklist:

- Hips back
- Torso level
- Head up and eyes forward
- Shoulders down
- Elbows out
- Knees bent
- Heavy feet, light hands

Bonus: No matter what you're doing or how slow you're going, a good attack position makes you look fast. Elbows out!

THE FOUNDATION OF EVERY SKILL

When Lee teaches his skills clinics, he always starts with the attack position. Whether you're a beginner or a pro, young or old, male or female, endurance or gravity, your attack position helps you execute every move with more grace and power.

Optimize Your Sense of Balance

You're zipping down a wooded singletrack, and a log appears across the trail. Your inner ears sense downward acceleration. Your skin senses pressure and cold. Your muscles and joints tell you you're crouched on your bike, with your weight planted nicely on your pedals and your bar dancing in your loose grip. Your memory reminds you that if you clip that log at an angle, your tires will slide out and you will crash.

All this information (and more) collides in your brain stem, which sorts it out and fires off the instructions to slow down, approach the log at a right angle, and then hop like a yoked bunny—all in a fraction of a second, without conscious thought.

You perform impressive acts of balance every day—for example, kicking a door open with your arms full of groceries or in-line skating with your dog on a leash. Heck, you're great at staying upright. If you just relax and trust your innate ability to keep your ass below your teakettle, you'd be amazed at the situations you can ride through. That said, here are some things to keep in mind:

Relax.   Tension is the enemy of balance. On and off the bike.

Keep moving.   Balance is not a static action. Anyone who's bounced on a pogo stick or done a **track stand** knows this. The more actively you use your cockpit, pump, and basically move and groove, the more fluid—and more balanced—you'll be.

Stay out of it.   Your calculations are way too rapid and complex for conscious thought. If you butt in and try to help, you'll screw everything up. The instant you start thinking, "I'd better stay upright," it's all over. This is especially difficult anytime you're cracking through your skill or fear ceiling. You might track stand without a care in front of Starbucks, but balancing on a skinny bridge will get your inner mother screaming.

Look where you want to go.   When you look somewhere, you tell your brain and body that's where you want to go. Next time you stare at a scary rock, notice how your head drops and you smash directly into that rock. As they say in every driving and motorcycle-riding program, "Look where you want to go; go where you look."

Practice.   Not only riding, but also balancing. Work on track stands. Practice slow riding. Stand on one foot while you wash your hair. Anything that improves your balance improves your bike riding.

Carry a really long pole everywhere you go.   Especially on tightropes.

Stay Between Your Wheels

Imagine yourself running along a trail. You cross ferny flats, climb rooted rises, drop into rutted ravines, and leap spongy stumps. You lean forward when you go up, lean backward when you go down, and lean sideways when you turn. As long as your weight stays between your feet, you stay balanced, and everything is fine.

Staying balanced on your bike is pretty much the same, except your feet are wheels. The better you get at keeping your center of gravity between your wheels, the more time you'll spend smiling on your bike, rather than cartwheeling beside it.

No matter what you're doing, try to keep your feet heavy and your hands light. As long as you do that, you'll stay balanced between your wheels.

Side note: Side-to-side balance has everything to do with cornering forces. For more about cornering, check out chapter 5.

Flat Ground

On flat ground there's plenty of leeway for you to move forward or back. As long as you focus your weight on the pedals or saddle, you're unlikely to go flying off the front or back of your bike. That said, your bike will brake and corner best if you keep your weight centered on the pedals. Heavy feet, light hands!

On flat ground you should be in your sweet attack position, with your belly button right over your bottom bracket.

○ If you're too far forward, you'll feel pressure on your bars. Your front wheel will catch on obstacles, and your cornering might feel herky-jerky.

○ If you're too far back, you'll feel pulling on your bars. Your front wheel will be too light to track correctly, and your rear wheel will hit obstacles extra hard, which can actually lead to the dreaded forward buck.

Uphill

As your front wheel comes up, you have to move forward. It's all about keeping your weight centered on the pedals.

Sitting: Bend your arms and pull your torso forward to keep your weight centered over the bike. The less weight you put onto your saddle, and the more you drive into your pedals, the better. On really steep climbs, you might be on the very tip of the

While climbing a steep incline in the saddle, pull your torso down and forward to bring your center of mass closer to your bottom bracket. (On a decently steep incline, the front of the bike will still be light).

When riding up an incline, shift your weight forward to keep your weight over your bottom bracket.

saddle. Some saddle brands, such as WTB, slope the nose downward so you can perch at the end and not feel too violated. Long stems help position you for climbing.

- ○ If you're too far forward, you might feel pressure on your hands. Your rear tire will spin.
- ○ If you're too far back, you'll feel a strong pull on your hands. Your front end will wander.

Standing: Pull yourself forward until you're balanced on your pedals.

- ○ If you're too far forward, you'll feel your hands pushing on the bar. Your rear wheel slides out. Or you spontaneously do a front flip. Whammo!
- ○ If you're too far back, you'll feel your hands pulling on the bar. Your front end comes up, and your wheel wanders from side to side.

Downhill

The steeper it gets, the farther back you need to be. But don't overdo it: Volumes of magazine articles have convinced people to get behind their saddles whenever they descend. This not only is unnecessary, but also makes your bike handle poorly. Your front wheel gets too light, and it dances randomly instead of tracking precisely.

When riding down a decline, shift your weight backward to keep your weight over your bottom bracket. (If your hands are weightless, as Lee's are here, you are golden.)

When you coast down a trail, you should be balanced—guess where—on your pedals. If the grade is 10 percent, you only need to lean back about 10 degrees. Any farther than that and your front wheel is too light for effective braking and cornering.

On steep descents, shift your hips back until—you guessed it—all your weight is on the pedals.

○ If you're too far forward, you'll feel pressure on your hands. Your front wheel will catch, your rear wheel will bounce, and an over-the-bars experience is just a matter of when.

○ If you're too far back, you'll feel pulling on your hands. Your front wheel will wash, your rear wheel will buck, and you'll feel like you're getting pulled down into every drop.

To get a feel for balancing on your pedals, coast down a slight grade and stand on your bike with some weight on your hands. Move your body backward until your hands hover lightly on the bars. This is perfect.

If you lean so far back that you have to pull with your hands, you went too far. This light-handed place makes a good base of operations. For cornering, you want more handlebar pressure; for rough terrain, you want less handlebar pressure.

Although there are situations in which you want to push and pull on the bars—manuals, hops, pumping, jumping, advanced cornering, and so on—your default setting should be (you guessed it) . . . heavy feet, light hands.

On the Brakes

When you slow down, momentum carries your weight forward. The harder you brake, the farther you must lean back. If you're not back far enough, your rear wheel skids (this could be a case of too much rear brake) or comes off the ground (this is definitely because you're too far forward).

If you have dual suspension, your rear end will jack up and your front end will dive. This steepens your head angle and makes your bike very sketchy, just when you need it to be the least sketchy. If you're too far back, your unweighted front wheel skips around like a stone on water. If it locks and suddenly catches traction, *you'll* skip like a stone on water.

When you brake, shift your weight back and drive your weight into your pedals, *not* your bars. See chapter 4 on braking.

Don't try this on your home trail. If your hands are this neutral, you know all your weight is in your feet—right where it belongs.

WHEN IT GETS REALLY STEEP...
STAY ON YOUR FEET!

No matter how steep the trail gets, remember to balance on your feet and keep your hands neutral (have you noticed a common theme?).

In the case of a very steep drop, your arms will be very straight, and you'll feel like you're way back on the bike. But your center of mass should be—you know where—right over your pedals. Like always.

Heavy feet. Light hands!

On a very steep decline, it'll feel like you're shifting waaaay back . . . but you should still be right over your feet.

Accelerating

No doubt you have a hard time controlling your power. You're forever roosting your friends and tearing up cobbles. Not only that, but your front wheel tends to come up while you accelerate.

Wheelying down a bikercross start ramp won't kill you, but you have to control that power out on the trail. Lean forward while you're on the gas, especially if you're climbing something steep. See the Sprinting section in chapter 3.

While you're on the gas, you have to shift your weight to account for the grade plus your acceleration. It's all about driving your weight into your pedals.

Forward, to the side and twisted 45 degrees: Real fun demands full access to your cockpit—and the ability to let your body and bike act independently.

Using Your Entire Cockpit

Enjoying a trail—railing turns, hopping logs, and pumping humps—is all about shifting your weight fore and aft, side to side, and up and down fluidly and dynamically. To do this effectively, you must move around. Your cockpit has to give you space to work, and you must be loose and energetic enough to use the space.

Explore the limits of your bike's cockpit:

◦ Pull forward until your tender bits hit your stem.

◦ Push back until your arms straighten or your bum gets the knobby treatment.

◦ Lean all the way to the side until your saddle hits your thigh or, with a low saddle, your frame hits your shin.

◦ Stand so high you can touch the sky.

◦ Crouch down and look at the bottom of your bottom bracket.

◦ Do the Hokey Pokey and turn yourself around. That's what it's all about!

The more comfortably you can use your entire cockpit, the better. Move around a lot. Never try to maintain any one position—in turns, while climbing, or whenever. Conditions change constantly, and you have to change with them.

STRANGER IN A STRANGE LAND

When I (Lee) was in Fontana, California, coaching the InCycle downhill team, the team captain took me down the track they'd been racing. He was pinning it on a track he knew well; I was just enjoying the coarse flow and random rock features. We were ripping along—having a great time—when, all of a sudden, Jason disappeared over a huge boulder.

As I crested, the setting sun lit up my glasses, and I couldn't see anything. All I remember is thinking, "Get low!"

I got super low and kept my hands light. Good thing, too, because the track went straight down the boulder face, then dropped into a tight switchback. If I was upright and stiff, it would have been messy. But I was low and flowy, and it was sweet.

The moral of this story: Whatever is going on, and especially in unknown conditions, find your attack position. From there you'll have the range and flow to get the job done.

Loading and Unloading

Have you ever seen a really smooth rider just floating along a rough trail? He passes over rocks like water over porcelain, bounds over logs like a porpoise over a skiff, and gains speed without even pedaling. He might have a deal with the devil, but chances are he accomplishes these feats by strategically weighting and unweighting his bike.

Try this experiment:

- Stand on a spring-loaded bathroom scale. Let's say you weigh 150 pounds (68 kg).
- Suddenly crouch down (unload the scale). Depending on how fast you drop, the scale might go down to 50 pounds (23 kg) or even to 0 pounds.
- Pause at the bottom. The scale reads 150 pounds again.
- Stand up quickly (load the scale). Depending on your explosive power, the scale might tip 300 pounds (136 kg) or more.
- Rapidly crouch down; then immediately spring back up (preload the scale). By loading your moving mass against the scale, you generate even more force. With good timing, you can hit 400 pounds (181 kg) plus.
- Imagine the scale has a handle attached to it. If you pull upward as you leap upward, you can lift the scale off the ground and read a negative weight. This is a massive unload, like when you hop and jump.

Weighting and **unweighting** your bike works the same way. When you learn to control the pressure between your bike and the ground, a whole new level of riding opens to you. You can pump terrain, find traction in corners, hop across logs, hover over rocks, and soar over jumps.

Here are the keys to that new world:

Always be light or heavy.   Say you weigh 150 pounds (68 kg). When you ride over rocks, try to weigh 0 pounds. When you carve corners, try to weigh 300 pounds (136 kg).

Great practice: Lee designed this bike park in Lyons, CO to mimic the heavy-light-heavy flow of a rocky trail.

You are a sine wave. Rather than just sitting or standing on your bike, you should cultivate an oscillation—heavy, light, heavy, light. Not only does this feel playful, but it also leads to awesome rippage.

Match the terrain. You are a wave, and so is the trail. Even the roughest, most random-seeming sections have an overall up-and-down and side-to-side flow. Ignore the details. Time your wave so you're heavy in the (relatively) smooth spots and light in the rough spots.

Accelerate! When you fall or rise at a constant speed, you weigh however much you weigh. Sorry. To change the scale, you have to gain speed the whole way. Let your body fall unfettered. Drive upward with gusto.

Spread it out. The preceding tips work only as long as you can push or pull. Because you only have so much arm and leg range, you have to decide how you'll spend it. Push hard and fast to hop a big rock; push slow and easy to create traction in a sweeping turn.

Be decisive. Most riders are way too static on their bikes. Change direction rapidly. Moves like jumps and hops require rapid, massive loads with sudden releases and drastic unloads. Make it count. You are a Super Ball. Boing!

Time your suspension. Suspension makes preloading absolutely necessary. When you press down to make a hop, you want your power to drive into the ground, not into a spring and shock. Preload so your suspension is completely compressed when you begin your takeoff. The more travel your bike has, the longer this takes. When you first try a diving board or trampoline, you bounce up and down to get a feel for the amount of flex, and then you time your jumps so you sink all the way down and spring all the way up. It's the same on your freeride bike.

Think three-dimensionally. Once you learn to load and unload over trail features, two-dimensional riding will no longer suffice. Don't just roll along a flat ribbon. Bounce up, drive down, and throw your weight all around.

Apply it. Check out the chapters on braking (chapter 4), cornering (chapter 5), hopping (chapter 6), pumping (chapter 7), and jumping (chapter 9). The following table also shows what happens when you use different weight in different situations. When you learn to control your weight, you'll enjoy these skills at an even higher level.

DIFFERENT STATES OF WEIGHT

Weight	Amount of gravity	Situation	Application
Negative weight	Negative g's	Pulling your bike away from the ground toward your body	Clearing a rock or jump; unloading over a frontside
Weightless	0 g	Flying, freefall	Hopping, dropping, jumping
Light	0–1 g	Lightening the bike over rough terrain	Skimming over roughness, preparing to preload
Normal	1 g	Sitting or standing	Just riding along
Heavy	>1 g	Pressing the bike into the ground	Gaining traction, pumping backside, loading before a hop or jump

Getting Lighter—Unloading Your Bike

Riders who seem to float over rough terrain are often described as "sucking up" the bumps or riding "light on their bikes," which is exactly the case.

When you sit statically on your bike, the two of you behave like one heavy object. Anytime you lift your bike upward or let your body fall toward the bike, you act like two separate objects: (1) your bike, which is light but has to bash into everything, and (2) you, who are not so light and would rather not bash into anything. The faster you lift your bike, the lighter it gets. Here are some uses for temporary lightness:

A little lighter—suck up a bump. You're zooming down a fire road, and a 3-foot-tall (about 1 m) water bar appears in your path. When you hit it, relax your arms and legs and let your bike push up into you. If you and your suspension suck up 2 feet (60 cm) of the bump, your body rises only 1 foot (30 cm).

A lot lighter—absorb a shock. As you're cruising along a nice little trail, you encounter a 6-inch (15 cm) root. When your front wheel hits the front of the root, bend your arms to let the bars come up toward you and then let the wheel roll down the back of the root. When your rear wheel hits the root, relax your legs to let the bike roll over; then straighten on the backside. Your lightened bike will buck up and over the root, but your body will carry smoothly down the trail.

Ultimate lightness—pick up over an obstacle. You're **hauling the mail** down a race course, and an 18-inch (45 cm) rock squats in your path. Preload your bike into the ground, and then, as you reach the rock, hop your bike sharply upward. This will unweight the bike so much, it'll come off the ground.

Jagged slabs of sandstone are a great time to get very light on your bike.

Getting Heavier—Loading Your Bike

Although most of the people in the United States are too heavy and want to be lighter, mountain bikers, who tend to be light, should try to make themselves heavier—at least sometimes. The harder you press into the ground, the heavier you get. This is an awkward time to bash into a rock, but there are some wonderful uses for this temporary heaviness. Here are some of them:

Press down—pump terrain. You've unloaded up the face of a water bar, and you crest with your bike sucked up into your body. When you reach the backside, press your bike down into the ground until you're standing straight. The downslope will convert some of this downforce into forward speed. Cool, eh?

Drop and stop—brake harder. You're zooming down a hill, and you need to brake really hard to make a corner. Just before it's time to brake, stand up. Drop your body toward your bike, and at the instant you reach bottom, hit the brakes. The extra downforce yields extra traction love.

Drop, stop, and press—generate traction. You're tooling along a dirt road, and a tight corner seems too slick for your speed. As you approach the corner, drop your weight toward your bike. All at once, as you begin your turn, stop your fall and push yourself back up. This loads your tires into the ground and gives you megatraction.

Preload your bike—catch some air. To hop over a huge log, you need more up force than you can muster from a static crouch. Approach the log standing up. Drop your body toward your bike. This creates downward momentum. As soon as you reach bottom, explosively push yourself back up. Your downward momentum combines with your downward push, and you get a huge upward surge. The faster you drop and the more suddenly you push back up, the bigger your hop.

Before you can un-load over that stone, first you gotta pre-load. The suspension is about to be bottomed out from the downforce.

Mounting and Dismounting

Getting on and off your bike might seem like the most basic of skills, which they are, but the faster you can get to your feet, get past an obstacle, and get back onto the pedals, the better. Nobody carries their bikes faster than cyclocross racers. Practice these moves, and soon you'll cross the unrideable (and recover from crashes) with your speed (and pride) intact.

ROLLING DISMOUNT

1. Unclip your right foot and swing it behind your bike. Always dismount to the left, to avoid those nasty rookie marks from your chain.

2. Swing your right foot forward between your left foot and the bike.

3. As you set your right foot onto the ground, unclip your left foot and hit the ground running, right foot first.

Practice doing this at higher and higher speeds. You'll be amazed at how fast you can do this. Soon you'll bound over inflatable alligators with no loss of speed.

RUNNING MOUNT

1. Run alongside your bike and thrust yourself upward with your left leg. While you're in the air, swing your right leg over the saddle.

2. Land on your right inner thigh. We don't have to tell you to be careful, do we?

3. Find your right pedal and push down. Catch your left pedal as it crosses the top of your stroke; then get out of there!

Try to land on your saddle with your feet already on the pedals. When you master the cyclocross mount, the tough thing will be resisting the urge to wear knickers and a wool jersey.

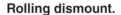 

Rolling dismount.   **Running mount.**

SHOOT YOUR TROUBLES

Problem: Your arms are getting tired, and your eyes are rattling in your head. Every time you hit a bump it gets worse.

Solution: You're too far forward. Shift your hips back until your palms stop pressing on the bars and your hands are weightless. That'll keep you centered.

Problem: When you hit water bars and other obstacles at speed, especially on downhills, you feel the back end kick up. You might even get bucked over the bars. Not good.

Solution: Believe it or not, you're too far back. Shift your hips forward until your fingers stop pulling on the bars and your hands are weightless. That'll keep you centered.

Problem: Your shoulders or triceps get tired when you climb.

Solutions: You're slumping and putting too much weight on your bars. Sit up straighter and put more pressure into the pedals. Also, your bike size and stem length could be wrong. Visit a quality shop for a fit.

Problem: On steep, seated climbs, your front tire wanders around like a balloon on a windy day.

Solution: Your weight is too far back. Crouch low and pull yourself forward until the front tire starts to track.

Problem: You struggle for balance. Maybe you find yourself swinging your bars back and forth and waving your knees all over the place as you try to make a turn or get over an outcropping.

Solutions: Relax and look as far ahead as possible. If low-speed sections give you trouble, speed up! Kidding. Sort of.

If you want to ride better, safer, or faster (or all of these), you have to loosen up, explore your cockpit, dial in your attack position, and learn to stay on your feet. This will improve everything you do on the bike—and it's the key to sucking less.

Make Great Power

Bikes are cool because you propel them with your own power. You fly through nature, running on pasta and listening to your breathing. Bikes suck because you propel them with your own power. You labor up hills, gasping for dear life and trying not to puke.

When it comes to making power, most people and publications emphasize fitness. Basically, riding faster and longer enables you to ride even faster and even longer. But no matter how hard you work, you eventually crash into your genetic and motivational ceilings. So, assuming you're already as strong as you can be (or deserve to be), it makes sense to become more efficient. You'll use less energy for the same power, the same energy for more power, or, as your fitness improves, more energy for even more power.

BRIAN KNOWS PEDALING

Don't think for a second that because Brian is best known for biker-cross, which requires explosive starts and downhill sprints, he can't blast flats and hammer climbs with the best of them. One of the strongest pedalers in the world, Brian has won on all kinds of trails, tracks, roads, and courses.

Build a Perfect Pedal Stroke

A basic pedal stroke can be simple. You push down and your bike goes forward, right? But excellent pedaling is another story. You need to apply power around a 350-millimeter circle, with the force perpendicular to the crank arms the whole time. This involves three pairs of major muscles in your legs and hips, as well as dozens of supporting muscles all over your body, all firing in perfect sequence, up to twice a second, for hours at a time, against varying resistance, on rough terrain, in dirty shorts . . .

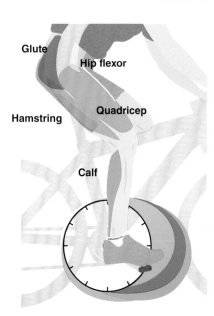

Glute
Hip flexor
Hamstring
Quadricep
Calf

Which muscles do the work

The thickness of each area shows the relative amount of useful power each muscle produces.

Your quads do most of the work at the top of the stroke. Your glutes and calves take over as your pedal approaches six o'clock, then your hamstring sweeps the pedal back to nine o'clock. Your hip flexors help lift the pedal to the top for another go-around.

Adapted from Ericson, et al. 1986. "Power output and work in different muscle groups during ergometer cycling." *European Journal of Applied Physiology and Occupational Physiology*, 229-235.

As you can see, a lot goes on between your little toes. Because a perfect stroke is so complex, it makes sense to break it down and attack one segment at a time. Picture the pedaling rotation as the face of a clock. Pedal strokes vary among riders, depending on their body types, riding positions, cadence, and even which type of riding they're doing. The following photos show Gunn-Rita Dahle on a trainer in Boulder, Colorado, during a break from competition. In 2004, she won the World Cup, World, and Olympic cross-country titles, so I guess you can say her stroke will give you some good guidelines. Note: You need clip-in pedals to pedal this way.

Down: 1 to 5 O'clock

The majority of your pedaling power comes from driving the pedals downward. But this is not a simple downward push. The downstroke involves three directions: forward, down, and backward, each using a different set of muscles.

- Early in the afternoon (before 3 o'clock), use your quads to push your feet forward.
- Later in the afternoon, use your glutes to push your leg downward. There's a lot of power here.
- As you get near the bottom, use your calves to extend your foot and start sweeping the pedal back toward evening. Typically, the higher your seat, the more you extend your foot (Gunn-Rita runs a pretty high seat). With a very low seat (as in downhill racing), your heel might stay beneath your toes.

Back: 5 to 7 O'clock

If you find yourself pushing down at the bottom of your stroke, you are wasting energy and wearing out your pedals (just kidding on the pedals).

- With your toes pointed down a bit, scoop backward with your hamstrings.
- Pretend you're scraping dog crap off the bottom of your shoe. Traditional wisdom says to pretend there's mud on your shoe, but dog crap is more motivating.

Up: 7 to 10 O'clock

The muscles that pull your feet up are too slow to lift one foot fast enough to get out of your downward foot's way. When you spin fast, your pushing leg actually lifts your pulling leg. The best you can do is lighten the load.

- Keep pulling with your hamstrings as you pass the bottom of the stroke. As you pass 9 o'clock, start pulling straight up with your hip flexors. Doing this correctly requires concentration, but you can really feel the added power and smoothness.
- As you stroke upward, lift your toes.

Forward: 10 to 1 O'clock

If you pay attention to your form, you can begin your power stroke way up here, which means you carry more momentum into your downstroke and create more power and better times for all.

- As you sweep upward past 10 o'clock, drive your knees up and forward with your hip flexors.
- Your heel should drop a bit as you reach the top of the clock. With a low seat, your heel will be way below your toes. With a high seat, your heel might remain above your toes.
- As you pass high noon, begin pushing forward with your quads. Be ready for your rear tire to break loose from all that power!

PEDALING FITNESS

Your pedaling performance is determined by your genetics and the type of training you do. I (Lee) have a perfectly average aerobic capacity, but I work pretty hard on overall strength, riding technique, and peak power. I'm all about climbing slowly and then rocking the downhill: pumping the bumps, railing the turns, and sprinting the transitions.

Last winter I was invited to an indoor training session at the Boulder Center for Sports Medicine. In the PowerMax class, eight riders sit on trainers wired to power meters, with the ride profile and everyone's speed and wattage displayed on a big screen. What a recipe for brutality! Everyone in the group was a high-level cross-country/road racer, and they were 8 weeks into their 13-week programs. I showed up with base fitness and hairy legs.

Not surprisingly, those guys crushed me on sustainable power. But when it came time to sprint, I generated almost twice their power. I was pretty proud of myself—but after the intervals they were churning out the watts, and I had to stop for a while.

How very humbling. My fitness was totally suited to my style of riding, but it was useless against theirs.

Training Tips From a Pro

Lester Pardoe is a coaching specialist at the Boulder Center for Sports Medicine. He is a certified coach in speed skating, hockey, triathlon, and cycling, and he works with many of Boulder's elite endurance racers. Once a world-class speed skater on ice, Lester now prefers riding bikes on dirt. Lee sat down with Lester before a PowerMax indoor cycling workout at the Center. He shared these basic insights about improving your pedaling fitness:

Are you riding or training? This is the first question to ask yourself. Riding is just riding; training is riding with a specific purpose. If you just want to ride, that's awesome. Have fun—but realize you'd probably be faster, and might have more fun, if you start training with more specific goals.

Most people do their easy rides too hard. "If you watch the Tour de France riders with their heart rate monitors, you can see they spend most of their time at 120 bpm," Pardoe says. "They can't pin it for 21 days." You can't pin it every day either. When it's time to rest, you should really rest.

Most people do their hard rides too easy. When it's time to go hard, you should go *really* hard. Lester's PowerMax workouts are all about intervals: long and hard, short and *very* hard. They all tax your body in different ways, and they are the key to improving your speed. Look at it this way: If you never pin it in training, how do expect to pin it in racing? Or on that Sunday ride?

Create a wide window of speed. The bigger the difference between easy and hard days, the better. Many riders tend to ride at the same medium pace every day, which makes them very fatigued but only medium-fast. Instead, go very hard on some days and very easy on others. This gives you the challenge—and the recovery—to help you get faster.

Beware group rides. These are why a lot of us ride—and what we train for—but be careful. You'll be spurred to ride harder or longer (or both) than you should, especially if you do a few of these a week. As Pardoe says, "I'll be out on a ride here in Boulder, and this guy has the rainbow jersey—and he won it—and I know it's his intensity day. If I try to keep up with him, I'll put myself in a hole."

Be patient and consistent. "Don't jump in where you were before, or where you want to be. You have to start where you are," Pardoe says. "You don't want to take a big step forward and then two steps back. You want to take lots of small steps forward."

Start with lots of low intensity. At the beginning of your season or when you're getting back into riding, do six to eight weeks of easy, long rides and gradually make them longer. This improves your overall fitness and helps you lose extra weight. When you step up the intensity, you'll feel that much better.

But maintain your speed. You've built up your power and speed over the season, so why lose it all over the winter? Every 7 to 10 days during your low-intensity phase, do one-half to two-thirds of your speed workout. By maintaining the intensity but reducing the volume, you can maintain last season's speed while you build next season's base. Bonus: This is usually more fun than churning out base miles.

Don't ride hills all the time. Remember, you do want some easy days. "It's hard to do easy miles on a mountain bike," Pardoe says. "It's just too fun to pin it."

Ramp it up; then notch it down. If you're building up for an epic ride or race, gradually build up your time and distance; then reduce it before the event. Using a 120-mile (193 km) ride as an example, most riders will do a longer ride each week: 60, 70, 80, 90, 100, and then 120 miles. Instead, try building up and then reducing your volume three weeks out: 60, 70, 80, 90, 100, 80, 60, and then 120 miles. You maintain your endurance, but you get better recovery, and you come into your event fresher and stronger.

Exercises

Here are some exercises to improve your stroke and break up the monotony of your life. Do each one for 20 seconds to a minute, with easy spinning between. Remember, these are skill drills, not intervals. Focus on technique and save the puking for later. Do these on a trainer or safe road, and be sure to warm up. Oh, and eat your veggies.

One-footed pedaling. Pull one foot out and pedal with the other, trying to maintain tension all the way around the stroke. You'll be amazed at the dead spots and herky-jerkiness. Dang, you really are a horrible pedaler! You'll also be amazed when muscles you've never used start jumping in to smooth things out.

High resistance. Put it in a huge gear and pedal slowly, at around 50 to 60 rpm. The resistance will force you to recruit all your muscles to keep things turning, and the slowness will teach your brain to fire off the right messages in the right order. This is also a fantastic power workout.

High rpm. Put your bike in an easy gear and spin as fast as you can without bouncing off your bike—100, 120, 150 rpm, whatever you can do. This puts a polish on your perfect stroke.

You can hit all three exercises in one session. In the off-season, emphasize one-footed pedaling. As you build strength entering the season, emphasize high resistance. As you reach the racing season, emphasize high rpm.

Coaching specialist Lester Pardoe: www.bch.org/sportsmedicine/bio-tester-pardoe.aspx

Make Mad Power With These Tips

Master the most powerful segments first. Your downstroke usually takes care of itself. Pay attention to pushing hard, but not past the bottom of the circle. Next, concentrate on sweeping your pedals across the top. This is the second strongest part of your stroke, and it greatly lengthens the amount of time you actually apply power. Once you get the top dialed, think about bringing your pedals up. Lastly, think about scraping the dog poop off the bottom of your shoes. If all you do is push across the top and down to the bottom, your stroke will be powerful and free of dead spots.

Go for a smooth handoff. Your muscles shouldn't hand off a baton and then wait around for their next turn. Strive for smooth transitions from segment to segment, muscle to muscle. This is supposed to be a circle, not a rhombus.

Spin. High cadences (more than 80 rpm) are easy on your legs and give you plenty of snap.

Behold the master: Nobody knows seated climbing better than Lance Armstrong. Here he sits in the pack at the start of the Colorado State Championship XC race (which he won). Eyes up, head up, torso up, arms relaxed.

Loud legs, quiet body. Use only the muscles that carry you up the hill. Any other tension is wasted. After you stop hunching your shoulders and death-gripping your bar, try relaxing your quads on the upstroke.

Stabilize your core. Your abdominal muscles create a stable connection between your torso and hips. If you leave your core loose, you lose power in the sway between your hips and shoulders, and you might give yourself a bonus backache. When you use your lower abs to help pull your legs up, their tension will help stabilize your core. With your lower abs tight like this, your upper belly can still balloon out for breathing.

Breathe with your belly. Try to breathe slowly and deeply, and let your belly expand as you draw air with your diaphragm. You should look like you have a little pooch—if you don't have one already!

Pedaling is pedaling. These ideas apply whether you're laboring up the 401 trail in Crested Butte, hammering a roller at the Olympic cross-country course, blasting out of a starting gate, or going for the recumbent land-speed record.

Do it right, before it's too late. If you've been pedaling bikes for 10 years for five hours a week at 80 rpm, you've turned more than 10 million strokes. If you've done them all poorly, you have some very bad habits to overcome. From the standpoint of creating a great stroke, short and sweet is better than long and sloppy. If you get so tired your stroke turns into a rhombus, call it quits for the day or go in-line skating to finish your workout.

In the Saddle

Seated pedaling carries you up long hills and across expansive flats in the most efficient way. Pedal from your plastic perch whenever possible, and keep these notions in mind:

Use your seat. As you push your pedals forward across the top of your stroke, push your butt back against your saddle. When you push the pedals really hard, pull lightly on the bars to help hold you steady and transmit that power to the ground.

Maintain traction. Move back on your saddle when your rear wheel slips and forward when your front wheel wanders. If you're climbing a steep, slippery pitch, keep your butt back for rear traction and pull your shoulders forward to keep weight on the front tire. When you begin a steep pitch, it's safest to start with your weight way back on the bike to keep the rear wheel tracking. If your front end wanders, just steer it back on track and nudge your weight forward.

Give 'em a rest. Shift forward or back to use different muscles. Move forward to emphasize your quads. Move back to work your hamstrings and glutes. By shifting the work around, you can stay strong as long as King Kong.

Out of the Saddle

Your back is getting sore. You want to carry speed over a short rise. Your buddy just took off for the trail sign. Sometimes you gotta stand up and make some extra power. When your butt leaves the saddle, your perfect pedal stroke tends to leave as well. Don't let it.

Dance on the pedals. You've no doubt heard television announcer Phil Liggett wax poetic about Lance Armstrong's standing climbfests in the 2003 Tour de France. When Lance stood, his stroke stayed as perfect as when he sat. He pulled his pedals up, swept them across the top, and pushed them down in one constant flow. If you pause at the bottom of your stroke, Lance will come to your house and kick your ass. Don't pause. Keep 'em turning.

Pull it. Counteract your massive power strokes by pulling the bars and rocking your bike from side to side. Women can dramatically improve their power by learning to use their upper bodies this way.

Even more abs. Use your core muscles to stabilize your torso and transmit torque from your shoulders to your hips. Don't fall into the trap of building strong arms and legs and ignoring the bridge that connects them.

Aligning your body over the bottom bracket improves your balance and increases your power—especially on a steep hill with good traction.

When it gets extra steep, pull your bars and push your pedals in opposition with each other. This increases your power and levers your rear wheel into the ground. Controlling your ultra-light front end takes some finesse.

Use your hips. Most riders are very quad-dominant. The more you can recruit your glutes and drive from your hips, rather than your knees, the more power you'll make.

Upshift. Your standing power will crush your sitting gear like a bug. If you click it up a notch, you'll maintain traction, preserve form, and go faster—which is always good. Bonus speed trick: On a climb with steep corners and great traction, try standing and upshifting around the turns.

Stand up straight. When you have enough traction, try to stand erect, with your hips forward and your shoulders directly above your hips. This way, you don't waste lower-back effort to pull your torso up; plus, you put max power into your pedals.

No, crouch. When traction isn't so hot or the terrain is rough, crouch on your bike. Move up and down as you cross obstacles and scoot forward or backward to maintain traction.

Get some dynamic traction. The trails in Laguna Beach, California, have some really steep, slippery, technical sections that only a few people can ride. You have to be in the right gear—not so hard that you can't spin it and not so easy that your back tire burns out. To clean a steep, slippery climb, crouch down and forward with your head and shoulders above your bars. With each power stroke, pull strongly and smoothly on the bars. This unweights your front wheel and levers your rear wheel into the ground for extra grip. Bonus: Pulling hard lets you pull a taller gear than usual, which gives you an extra-long, extra-smooth power stroke. And everybody likes that.

Sprinting

On long climbs you gotta spin as efficiently as possible. No sense working any harder than you need to, eh? But sprinting is all about max power. Whether you're charging off the line, blasting over a rise, or passing a foe, there's more to sprinting than just pedaling as hard as you can.

The right gear is more important than ever. Sprints happen soon and hard. When you have time for only a few strokes, you'd better make them count.

Attack it all at once. Commit 100 percent to turning those pedals and getting up to speed as quickly as possible. Try to reach your max rpm in as few strokes as possible. Try for 10; then 5.

Push down like a maniac. Perfect circles can wait 'til after you get up to speed. For now, concentrate on the downstroke. Coach Greg Romero did a study with one

Do what Coach G says. Nobody sprints better than BMX racers, and Greg Romero coached two Americans to medals at the Beijing Olympics. Watch how he drives his hips forward and extends his body into the pedals. (Olympic Training Center, Chula Vista, CA. www.bmxtraining.com.)

of his BMX racers, and his findings showed that the rider actually lost power when he worried about his upstroke. That rider was faster with flat pedals than when trying to pull up with clips.

Go for the triple extension.   This tip comes from Coach Greg Romero, who helped Jill Kintner and Mike Day earn their BMX Olympic medals in 2008. Simultaneously fire your hip, knee, and ankle. Drive your hips forward and try to get your shoulders as far as possible from your feet.

Use your whole body.   As you extend your legs, brace your torso and pull your bars back toward your hips. This is just like the top of a deadlift. Hmm . . . no wonder so many BMX/4X/DS racers swear by deadlifts.

Don't shift too soon.   Wait until you're about to wind the gear out; then shift. Repeat.

Set up your bike like a BMXer.   Compared with a stretched-out cross-country setup, a shorter stem, higher bars, and low seat give you room to sprint your best. Not only is a high seat not in your way, the BMX-style cockpit lets you extend your torso, hips, and legs for maximum power.

Spin to Win

One of the age-old questions is, *Should I spin easy gears or grind hard ones?* Well, that depends.

Everybody has unique leg strength, knee health, and pedaling skill. Some of us spin easy gears, and some of us pull harder gears. (The strongest of us spin hard gears.) Look at Jan Ullrich and Lance Armstrong: Ullrich churns the butter while Armstrong whips the cream, yet both guys are insanely fast in the climbs and time trials.

Each of us has our own personal power band, the rpm range in which we pedal smoothly and powerfully. When the gear's too easy, your legs bounce up and down like you're chopping wood. When the gear's too hard, you bog down like a woolly mammoth in tar.

The broader you make your power band, the better. You want to be neither a stump-pulling diesel tractor nor a high-revving two-stroke motocrosser. You want to be a finely tuned Chevy small block: plenty of pop off the line, smooth midrange for extended power, and gobs of high-end speed.

For steady power, a high cadence places the burden on your aerobic system and lets your legs spin easy. At the same speed, fit riders last far longer at 90 rpm than they do at 60 rpm. Experiment to find your optimum cadence. In deep sand, stay on top of a small gear. On wet moss, filter your power through a tall gear. You might spin fast and light at the beginning of a ride and then slog slow and heavy as you get tired.

As your stroke gets smoother, your cadence will increase. When you first start riding, it takes all your concentration to churn along at 60 rpm. After a few years of concentrated practice, you can buzz along at 100 rpm and sprint past 120 rpm.

When it's time to accelerate, wind those legs as fast as they'll go. If you can make power from 60 to 120 rpm, you can double your speed in the same gear. Shifting means changing your grip, backing off the pressure, and risking a case of chain-fu. So less shifting is better shifting—as long as you're making good power. How many racing engines make their power at low rpm? None. They spin to win—just like you do. Here's your homework:

1. Learn to spin as fast as possible. Top BMXers can spin over 200 rpm. No wonder they don't need gears.
2. Experiment to find your optimum cadence.
3. Use a gear that keeps you at your optimum cadence.

According to Olympic BMX coach Greg Romero, if you're not rocking 180 rpm, you're not spinning yet. He says AA Pro Jason Richardson has been clocked at 255 rpm. Now that's spinning.

Shift Like a Champ

Mountain bike drivetrains can be confusing. With 27 gears and four levers, where do you start?

Shifting 101. Use your rear shifter to fine-tune your gear ratio and keep yourself spinning in your power band. Save front shifts for major terrain changes.

THE PLACE TO PRACTICE SPIN . . .

. . . is in your house, in front of the TV, on an indoor trainer. Rollers give you the highest-quality practice, but clamp-in trainers are much easier to use.

Spin at a moderate pace while you find out who will be America's Next Top Model.

During commercials, pin it! Stay in a low gear and spin as fast as you possibly can. Count strokes for a full minute; then rest and see what Tyra is up to.

The faster you can spin on your trainer, the quicker and smoother you'll be on the trail.

- ○ Big ring: Downhill and fast, flat riding
- ○ Middle ring: Short or mellow climbs and slow, flat riding
- ○ Small ring: Long or steep climbs

Keep your chain straight.   You can theoretically run your chain all the way from your small ring to your small cog or your big ring to your big cog, but doing so invites chain skippage, extra friction, and faster wear. You can hit all of your ratios without crossing your chain.

- ○ If you're in your big ring and you want to downshift from your fifth cog to your fourth-largest cog, drop it to your middle ring and sixth cog.
- ○ If you're in your middle ring and you want to upshift from your seventh to eighth cog, grab the big ring and fourth cog.
- ○ If you're in your middle ring and third cog, and you want a slightly easier gear, drop to your small ring and fifth cog.
- ○ If you're in your small ring and you want a gear taller than your fifth cog, grab your middle ring and third cog.

If this is all too much for you to comprehend, leave it in your middle ring. Your rear gear range will get you through most situations. As a matter of fact, many strong downhillers run single rings with chain guides on their cross-country bikes so they can charge like demons and not worry about losing their chains. Coast the fast descents, and, if you must, walk the steep climbs.

Keep it tight.   For a given gear ratio, use the biggest ring and cog you can without crossing your chain. This tightens your chain and spreads the load over more teeth. A violent sprint can tear a chain right off a small ring.

Shift before you need to.   High-end rear derailleurs can handle a lot of pressure, but even the best front shifters can crumble under your awesome power. Surge for half a crank, back off a bit, make your shift, and then get back on it.

These gear combos . . .

. . . give you all ratios

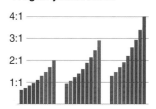

Front: 22, 32, 44t
Rear: 11, 13, 15, 17, 20, 23, 26, 30, 34t

SHOOT YOUR TROUBLES

Problem: No matter what you try, you can't hang with your buddies up the hills.

Solution: Train smart and ride with clean technique. If your buddies still beat you up the climbs, sorry. They might be genetically better climbers than you. But that's OK. You can learn to wax them on the descents. Keep reading.

Problem: The beginning of every ride hurts. A lot.

Solution: Whoa, Tiger! You can't just pin it from the parking lot. Start slowly and gradually increase the intensity. As you warm up, mix in a few short, intense bursts to wake everything up. Make sure you're sweating and ready to rock *before* you hit the first steep climb.

Problem: Your quads are getting really tired, but your glutes are just hanging there.

Solution: Move back on the saddle and concentrate on pushing forward from your hips. This emphasizes your glutes—the strongest muscles in your body—and provides a bit of rest to your four best friends.

Problem: You're struggling and feel really uncomfortable on a climb.

Solution: Pay attention to your form. Open your upper body, lighten your hands, and spin smooth circles. This can make a huge difference. That said, if you're going super hard or you're out of shape, it's gonna hurt. Welcome to cycling.

Problem: When you climb out of the saddle, your triceps get tired from leaning on the bars.

Solution: Move your hips back so your weight moves exclusively to your feet. For extended climbing, rest your hands neutrally on the bars. For max power, pull on the bars with each downstroke.

Problem: Your chain falls off on downhills.

Solution: Descend in your big chainring and one of the middle to larger cogs. Remove links until your chain is barely long enough for your big ring/big cog combo. If the tighter chain doesn't do the trick, think about installing a chain guide.

Problem: You feel tired and weak.

Solution: You *are* tired and weak. Get off your butt and train! But don't overdo it, or you'll dig yourself a deeper hole.

You've heard the old adage "Work smarter, not harder." We encourage you to train so you can pedal harder, but you'll enjoy free speed by learning to pedal smarter. Just as you shouldn't hurl yourself off cliffs hoping you'll learn to land, you shouldn't mash your cranks hoping you'll become a great pedaler. Pay attention to your pedal stroke. A great spin is a bike rider's greatest asset.

CHAPTER 4

Brake Better to Go Faster

When Lee teaches clinics, he starts with riding position; then he goes straight into braking. Braking is arguably the most important riding skill. Proper braking keeps you safe, and it makes you faster overall.

Here are some good reasons to slow down:

○ Maintain a legal, socially responsible speed. We can't overstress the importance of obeying those 15 mile-per-hour speed limits. But seriously, don't be an idiot. Share the trail, share the world, man.

○ Maintain control, especially in rough conditions. If you're going so fast you can't see straight, it's OK to slow down (a bit). Slow and in control equals good. Fast and random equal bad.

○ Set up for a corner. The faster you enter the corner, the harder it is to make the corner. Twice as fast is four times as hard. So slow down—unless you enjoy skidding into poison oak.

Become a master of brake science with these tips:

Reduce your perceived speed.   Most of us brake when we feel like we're going too fast, even when we aren't going fast at all. To take the edge off that "oh my . . ." feeling, look farther ahead. It's that simple. The threats won't seem as immediate.

The less time you spend braking, the better.   When you get on the binders, bad things happen. Tires skip. Suspensions stiffen. Wheels bash. Muscles tighten. When you brake, brake hard; then get back to coasting and pumping. Brakes are like pints of Ben & Jerry's ice cream: fun at the right times but bad news when you use them all the time.

Cover your brakes (with one finger).   Unless you're hammering up a climb, you should ride with your index fingers on the brake levers. When it comes time to slow down, squeeze the levers *with your index fingers only.* Modern brakes have plenty of power for one-finger braking, and this allows the rest of your digits to hold on to the grip. See brake lever setup in chapter 1, page 24.

This close-up was shot during an actual corner. Lee's index finger is resting on the end of his Hayes Stroker Trail brake lever, ready for whatever comes up.

Give it the finger, but which ones?   If you have strong, well-set-up brakes, your index fingers should do the trick. Use your thumb and other three fingers to hold on.

Brake in a straight line.   Your tires must be perpendicular to the ground. If you brake with your tires leaned, they'll either stand up or slide out. Neither is cool.

Brake on good ground.   Look for smooth spots with good traction. It's better to slow down on sweet loam than on wet roots. I (Brian) have been down hills that were so steep and had such good traction that as I slowed down, gobs of dirt fell on me. Trying to slow down in slippery muck just sketches you out and wastes valuable finger fu.

Use both brakes.   Whenever you use the brakes to slow down (rather than turn), use both brakes evenly. Squeeze gradually to give yourself time to adjust your position. Keep reading.

Don't fear the front brake. We know a lot of you do. As long as you're braking properly, and you maintain a balanced position, it's virtually impossible to go over the bars.

Drive your weight into your feet. This is key! As the forward braking force builds up, rotate down and back so all the force goes into your pedals—and none of it goes into your grips. This gives you great traction with both wheels, and it frees the front end to roll smoothly over bumps.

This right here is some tasty braking: hips shifted down and back, all weight in the cranks, arms loose and the fork and shock being crushed equally. Watch the tires work.

Ease into it. If you pull your brake levers suddenly, you're likely to skid your rear tire, which hasn't been cool since the second grade. Squeeze the levers slowly to gradually build up the braking force while you simultaneously shift your hips back to drive the net force into your pedals. This is all about fluid timing. Ease into that hard-braking position, squeeze hard, and get it done; then, as you release the brakes, bring your body forward to your neutral attack position.

Practice braking as hard as you can without skidding. Experiment with body position and lever pressure. Know how long it takes to slow down on a variety of surfaces. The more confidently you can haul yourself down quickly and safely, the faster you'll ride and the less time you'll waste lightly dragging the brakes. Remember: The most powerful braking happens at the point just before a skid.

Never lock your front wheel. You need your front wheel to steer, and when it's skidding, it's not steering. If the front wheel starts to lock, ease off the brake until it starts to roll again.

Modulate or die. Rocks, roots, holes, sand, gravel, and mud give your front wheel lots of opportunities to get stuck or lock up. When it gets rough or loose, you must constantly modulate the brake—on where it's smooth or sticky, off where it's rough or slippery. If you're about to roll off a big rock, brake hard before the rock and then let your wheel roll freely over it.

Load your tires. By doubling the weight on your tires, you can double your traction and cut your stopping distance in half. Bounce up a bit to unweight your tires; then push your bike down and forward as you apply the brakes. Really cram your tires into the ground. You'll be amazed at how hard you can brake without skidding.

Stay in control. On a steep downhill, releasing the brakes for a few seconds can mean the difference between "la, la, la . . ." and "$^%&%!!! ." Look ahead and brake before trouble spots: tight turns, big rocks, and so on.

IT'S ALL ABOUT THE TIRES

If you want ultimate braking power, do the following:

✓ Use a tire with a big, well-spaced center knobs and a soft rubber compound.

✓ Mount the tire so the biggest edges dig in. If your center knobs are ramped, that means your tires will roll faster and brake better, but they might lose a bit of climbing traction.

✓ Run relatively lower air pressure to increase the contact area.

THE FOUR STEPS TO PERFECT BRAKING

1. Start in a low attack position.
2. As you gradually squeeze the levers, rotate back so your weight stays in your feet.
3. Drop your heels to drive all the force into your pedals. Brake hard. Get it done. Your hands should stay light.
4. As you gradually release brake pressure, rotate forward. Your weight should always be in your feet, and your hands should always be light.

Note: You can brake very hard on rough terrain and still maintain light hands. The key is balancing the forces into your feet .

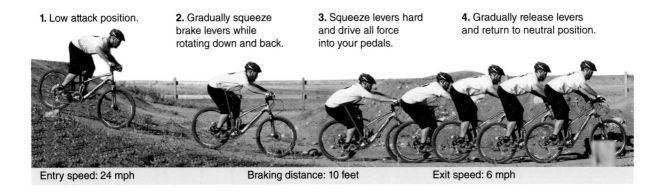

1. Low attack position.   **2.** Gradually squeeze brake levers while rotating down and back.   **3.** Squeeze levers hard and drive all force into your pedals.   **4.** Gradually release levers and return to neutral position.

Entry speed: 24 mph   Braking distance: 10 feet   Exit speed: 6 mph

Know Your Stopping Distance

To brake in the right places and times, you need to know how much space you need to slow down or stop. Your braking sense will develop with experience, but it never hurts to seed your brain with some unpopped kernels:

It's all math, baby!   Stopping distance is a product of tires, suspension, brake power, ground surface, weight distribution, and speed. And let's not forget skill.

Bike setup.   When it comes to gripping the ground, high-pressure semi-slick tires are rebellious teenagers, and low-pressure knobbies are first-day preschoolers (they grab onto dirt like it's their mommy). Long-travel bikes with active suspension designs hook up best, and disc brakes just plain rule. Any setup change will affect your braking, so dial your bike the way you like it and ride, ride, ride!

Beware awesome brakes.   Although we believe there's no such thing as too-powerful brakes, today's disc brakes can be dangerous in the wrong hands. If you are stiff and static (which most of you are), powerful brakes will skid the rear tire very easily, which means you're no longer in control. If you're too far forward (also common, especially on steep and rough terrain), they can even launch you over the bars. When you upgrade to the 8-inch (20 cm) rotors, be careful at first—and really learn to drive the braking force into your feet.

Know your suspension.   Rear suspension generally increases traction and reduces braking distance, but some designs get stiffer when you apply the stoppers. This can make your otherwise friendly bike feel downright abusive. Your wheels will skip, and you might take a bit of a pounding. If you have such a bike, (1) avoid braking in bumps and (2) really focus on keeping your hands neutral.

Rolling friction.   In soft, deep dirt, your bike plows like a lazy horse, so you don't need to brake all that much. As in powder skiing, you can point it downhill and let all the little particles modulate your speed. On hardpack, your bike rolls faster than an AMF Triumph TNT bowling ball, so all slowing must come from your brakes (or bashing into pins—not cool).

Braking traction.   At 10 miles per hour (16 km/h) on dry concrete, it takes about 4 feet (122 cm) to stop. Wet concrete ups the distance to 6 feet (183 cm; a 50 percent increase). Sand drops the distance to 5 feet (152 cm). Sand provides way less braking traction than wet or dry concrete, but its high rolling friction does a lot of scrubbing. Ice is the worst: low traction plus fast rolling equals a stopping distance of 29 feet (9 m).* You can optimize traction by shifting your weight backward the right amount, and you can double or triple your traction by loading your tires as you brake.

Speed kills.   When you plug speed into the equation for braking distance (or cornering or crashing), you see that it has a huge effect on the outcome. If you cut your traction in half, you double your braking distance. No big deal. If you double your speed, you *quadruple* your stopping distance. So the faster you go, the more important it is that you plan ahead—and the more important it is that you load your tires for maximum traction.

* **Calculations inspired by the Science of Cycling Web site,** © www.exploratorium. edu/cycling/brakes2.html.

On the downhills, spend as much time as possible coasting, pumping, and basically ripping. This is more fun and actually safer than dragging your brakes and apologizing your way down the trail. When it's time to slow down—before a turn, before a crazy rock section, before a Marin County ranger—slow down with gumption. Brake hard. Get it done. Then get back to ripping.

Control Your Excess Braking

Do you pedal just for the heck of it, when you don't really need to speed up? Of course not. So why do you brake for no reason?

Blame fear. Most of us scrub speed whenever we feel nervous. Those levers are like our little blankie; they comfort us and tell us we're in control. The thing is, while we're on the brakes, we usually have less control. Dragging them makes your bike unruly. Grabbing them makes you crash.

This is a really bad place to grab your front brake. That's why Marla Streb is fisting her left grip.

Try to brake only when there's a real reason to slow down. If you're nervous with your speed, don't drag the brakes. Instead, brake hard to slow way down; then let your bike roll. When you feel sketchy again, shut it back down.

Riding problems seldom arise from not braking often enough. They usually come from braking too often. In sketchy situations, you're just a twitch away from an unfortunate washout or an over-the-bars calamity.

If an obstacle pops up on the trail, you should be looking far enough ahead to react to it; if you hit a patch of ice or something, braking is the last thing you want to do. If you drag the brakes because you believe you should be doing *something*, try pumping the bumps or even pedaling instead.

Write this on your handlebars: *Brake less. Pump more.*

Remember: Improper or excessive braking is the number one way to mess up your bike's handling:

- Unless you are a kung fu braking master, you become tense and unbalanced. But this can be fixed with practice.
- Braking eats up part of your "traction pie," which leaves less adhesion for cornering.
- With your wheels unable to spin freely, your bike bashes into bumps instead of rolling and skimming over them.

○ Some suspension designs lock out under hard braking. When this happens, you bash into bumps even harder, which is not good.

Stick this to your refrigerator: Brake hard to slow down; then get back to coasting and pumping.

Battle Braking Bumps

Right now, thousands of riders are braking for corners. Their skipping tires are scooping up dirt and piling it into humps. What begins as brown corduroy grows into huge whoops that randomize bikes and beat brains out. Braking bumps form where most people want to brake, and the harder you brake on them, the worse off you are. So what to do?

Here it is: Do not brake on braking bumps. Just because everyone else braked in the same place doesn't mean you have to. There are lots of better places to brake:

These braking bumps are gnarly. The funny thing is, you don't have to brake for this sweet berm.

1. **Outside the bumps.** Consider this the hot tip. You brake on fresh ground, plus you get a wider entrance to the turn—both good things.

2. **Inside the bumps.** When there's no room on the outside, you can brake on the inside of the bumps and then dive into the corner. This makes for a tight turn, but it can be better to fly past huge bumps, brake hard, and then deal with your "acute" turning situation. (Ha! A geometry joke!)

3. **Before the bumps.** If you insist on following the bumpy line but would rather skim over the little bastards than bash into them, brake before the bumps and coast loosely over them. This will cost you speed, but you'll gain comfort. This works fine for leisure riding.

4. **After the bumps.** That's right: after. Most riders brake too soon and too long, and you end up with big bumps way before the corner and little to no bumps near the corner. Skim over the main bumps, pinch those 8-inch (20 cm) discs, and then fold into the corner.

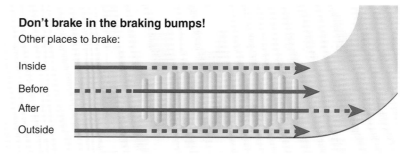

Don't brake in the braking bumps!
Other places to brake:

Inside
Before
After
Outside

When the only decent braking spots have bumps, you have no choice but to grab the levers, stay loose, and use your suspension. Pay attention to the bumps and try to brake hardest where it's smoothest.

ROCK THESE BRAKING DRILLS

Braking is a skill like any other. No, it's actually more important than the others. As your braking fu gets better, try these drills, taken from Lee's coaching:

○ Coast down a hill; then start braking at a set point. See how short you can make your stopping distance. Start on pavement and work up to loose dirt.

○ Try to stop *on* the hill. How quickly can you do that?

○ Sprint down a long flight of stairs and try to stop at the bottom step. Now do it with neutral hands. (Hint: It's all about body position.)

When you can brake hard on a bumpy surface—while maintaining tea party fingers—you'll be ultra confident on steep, rough descents.

SHOOT YOUR TROUBLES

Problem: Your rear tire skids too easily.

Solution: Squeeze the levers slowly. Make sure you shift your weight back so your weight is in your feet and your hands are light. Heavy feet, light hands!

Problem: Your front tire skids. (With your front tire, any skidding is bad skidding.)

Solution: If you're squeezing both brakes evenly and your front wheel is skidding, your weight might be *too far* back. You can tell by the pulling sensation on your fingers. Shift your weight forward until your hands are neutral—neither pushing on the palms nor pulling with the fingers. If the trail is too loose for hard braking, ease off both brakes.

Problem: On rough terrain your front wheel gets stuck and pitches you forward.

Solution: Use the brakes in the smooth sections, and absolutely, positively stay off them while your front wheel rolls over the rough parts.

Problem: When you do lots of serious downhilling, your knuckles ache. The backs of your forearms might burn as well.

Solution: Adjust your brake levers closer to your grips so you don't have to reach as far.

Problem: On long descents, your forearms are pumping and your eyes are rattling out of your head.

Solution: Shift your body down and back, so all the force drives into your pedals—not your grips. Relax!

Your brakes are the most powerful control mechanism on your bike. Just think of it: You can haul down more than 200 pounds (91 kg) of speeding meat and metal with just a little pressure from your index fingers. Now that's power. But your binders are far more than on/off switches for your rolling wheels. A light touch gives you complete control over your speed: You can slow down for a rock, stop in front of an alligator, or set up for a series of corners.

CHAPTER 5

Carve Any Corner

The sun is shining and so is your new XTR crankset. It's a beautiful day after a rain, and the soil is as tacky as a fresh motocross track. You and your friends rail along your favorite singletrack. You fly down a straight, float atop the braking bumps, hit the brakes, and then fold into a flat, sweeping left. You **carve** so hard, sweat flies sideways in front of your glasses. Sweet.

Corners separate fun trails from boring ones and great riders from so-so ones. To corner well is to enjoy the best trails in the world.

Master the Basics of Every Turn

You could fill an entire set of encyclopedias with all possible combinations of turn radius, camber, and elevation, but you can break every turn into four steps: the setup, the entrance, the turn itself, and the exit.

Set Up the Turn

Successful cornering depends on good lines, and lines begin before you reach the turn.

Look as far as you can into the turn. If you're noodling along on a twisty singletrack, you'll peek 10 feet (3 m) around a redwood trunk. If you're hauling the mail down Vermont's Mt. Snow downhill course, you'll scan along the tape 100 feet (30 m) ahead. Check out the surface and the worn lines. Decide where you want to enter the turn and where to start braking.

Get on your line. Your corner has already begun. Line up on the inside, middle, or outside, depending on the line you plan to follow (see Follow the Right Lines, page 85).

Judge your speed. It takes practice to learn how hot you can bake different corners. The worse the traction and the tighter the radius, the slower you have to go. The better the traction and the wider the turn radius, the faster you can go. But beware: As your speed increases, the turning g-forces increase exponentially. That means that twice the speed makes a turn four times as hard to make. Err on the slow side unless the ground is tacky or the turn is banked.

Slow down while you're still going straight. Brake late and hard so you spend more time at speed. Enter the turn slowly so you can accelerate past the apex and exit with max speed.

Enter the Turn

Now it's time to initiate your corner. You'll lean into sweeping turns delicately, as if you were opening your grandmother's photo album. You'll fold into tight turns as if you were slamming a phone book shut . . . bam!

Let off the brakes. Most riders dive into corners, get nervous, and grab a shipload of Shimano. Their bikes stand up and follow a tangent into the poison oak, or they slide out. If you wake up tomorrow and decide to lay off your brakes in corners, your riding will improve instantly and dramatically.

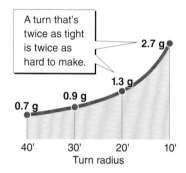

Tight turns are harder to make

Side forces in a 20 mph turn

A turn that's twice as tight is twice as hard to make.

2.7 g

1.3 g

0.9 g

0.7 g

40'   30'   20'   10'

Turn radius

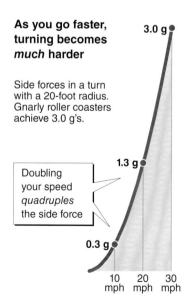

As you go faster, turning becomes *much* harder

Side forces in a turn with a 20-foot radius. Gnarly roller coasters achieve 3.0 g's.

3.0 g

1.3 g

Doubling your speed *quadruples* the side force

0.3 g

10 mph   20 mph   30 mph

Get into your attack position. Now you're perfectly centered and balanced. The lower you get, the more arm range you have.

Lean into the turn. The faster and the tighter the turn, the more you have to lean. See Lean to the Right Degree on page 88.

Look where you're going. In the California Motorcycle Safety Foundation's classes, they teach the "big head turn." As you begin the turn, scan along the trail toward the exit. Go ahead and notice important details, but keep your eyes moving through the turn. Scary obstacles want you to stare at them. You must resist. When you turn your head, your body unconsciously leans that way, and the bike follows right along.

Be patient. If you're out riding a new trail, don't dive straight into the insides of corners. It's safer and usually faster to enter wide and have a look before you initiate your turn. (Check out the lines section on page 85.)

HOW BIKES TURN

At very low speeds (subwalking speeds), you steer your bike by turning your handlebars in the direction you want to go. At high speeds, you must lean your bike in the direction you want to go. Leaning is much more reliable than steering. When you steer your wheel, your tire basically bashes into irregularities in the ground and deflects in the direction you want to turn. When you lean a tire, it rolls around the turn like a rubber-edged ice cream cone. Steered tires want to slide. Leaned tires want to rail.

When you lean your bike, the handlebars turn by themselves. This amount of turn is integral to your bike's geometry—and it's perfect. If you prevent this turning, your bike will tend to go straight. If you turn any more, your front wheel will tend to plow.

So what should you do? Keep your hands neutral and let your bars do what they want. They know better than you do.

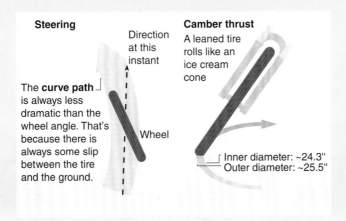

Steering

Direction at this instant

The **curve path** is always less dramatic than the wheel angle. That's because there is always some slip between the tire and the ground.

Wheel

Camber thrust

A leaned tire rolls like an ice cream cone

Inner diameter: ~24.3"
Outer diameter: ~25.5"

Textbook form from Joey Schusler at the 2009 SolVista Nationals: body low, hips turned, hands light, eyes out.

Make the Turn

While you're carving your corner, your job is to maintain traction and hold your line. Remember that cornering is dynamic: You'll cross different surfaces, and you'll hit things. If you try to rigidly maintain any one position on your bike, you will get deflected, and you'll follow a tangent into a cactus. Instead, keep your arms and legs loose and project your head and torso in the direction you want to go. Let your body move so your bike can stay in its groove.

Lower your center of gravity. How many Formula One cars have you seen with lift kits? None, that's how many. Squat as low as you can. Lower your head to your bars. If your seat is low, drop your hips as low as you can. If your seat is high, slide your butt back and drop your shoulders so your torso spreads above the seat.

Distribute your weight. Stay balanced between the front and rear of your bike, but:

○ If you feel the front end pushing (sliding out), lean forward to increase front-wheel traction.

○ If you feel the rear end starting to slide out, lean backward to help it catch. That said, if your rear tire really lets go, lean forward to make your front tire dig in. As long as your front wheel keeps tracking, you'll probably make the turn.

Lay off the brakes! If you're overbaking it, you can use some rear brake to slow down and maybe skid the rear end around. But don't touch the front brake, no matter what. If you do grab a fingerful, your front wheel will wash out and you'll crash, or your bike will stand straight up and you'll blow the corner. Either way is a bummer.

Load it. You can dramatically increase traction by pressing your bike down while you carve your turns. Press slowly and gradually for long, mellow turns, and pump violently for abrupt turns. Many great riders, especially downhill and slalom racers, seem to bounce in and out of tight turns. As they enter a turn, they hop slightly to unweight the tires, and then they cram their tires into the apex, achieving max load and max traction.

In a series of turns, load the turns; then use the light moment between them to swing your bike in the other direction. It feels exactly like powder skiing: heavy right, light middle, heavy left, light middle . . . on and on down the trail.

Loading a turn Learn this move. It's your key to cornering faster in all conditions.

1. Drop your weight as you approach your turning point. **2.** As you make the turn, press into the ground for increased traction.

Light between turns   This trick helps you transition between close corners. Technical singletrack will never be the same.

1. Load the first turn.   **2.** Unload. Steer and lean into the next turn.   **3.** Drop into the next turn and repeat. Stoked!

Exit the Turn   The end of your corner is just the beginning of the next thing. If a straight follows, wait for your bike to straighten out and then start pedaling. If another corner follows, you should already be setting up for it. A clean exit is the most important part of a corner, and it depends on everything that came before it.

SLOW, LOOK, LEAN, ROLL

That's what the Motorcycle Safety Foundation teaches its road-riding students.

1. Slow down as you approach the turn.
2. Look through the turn for the best line.
3. Lean into the turn.
4. Roll the throttle.

Since we don't have that throttle thing, let's slow, look, lean, carve.

Follow the Right Lines

Good lines make for smoothness, speed, and ease. Bad lines make for jerkiness, slowness, and struggle. When you go through a corner, try to make your line as wide as possible. This reduces the violence under your tires and lets you carry maximum speed to the exit of the turn.

You can choose from three basic approaches, each with its good and bad points.

Dive Inside

With an "early apex" or "early entrance," you enter fast on the inside and dive right into the corner.

Good: You carry max speed into the turn. You can protect the inside line from some badger who's trying to pass you. (See the passing section in chapter 13, page 216.)

Bad: You must make a tight turn after the apex—on ground you haven't seen. You tend to overshoot the corner or stall on exit. This is the line for eager juniors: They rush into the turn all excited and then blow their speed.

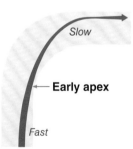

Slow

← **Early apex**

Fast

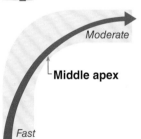

Moderate

└ **Middle apex**

Fast

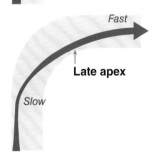

Fast

↑ **Late apex**

Slow

Early apexes will ruin most turns except those that open up as you go through them (they're called increasing radius turns). If you have room to drift outside on the exit, an early apex works fine. When a fast section leads through a turn and then into a slow section, like a rock garden, go ahead and carry max speed directly into the inside of the corner. Your slow exit speed won't hurt you because you have to slow down for the rocks anyway.

An apex for every radius
There are a zillion variables, but these lines tend to be fastest in these types of corners.

Constant radius corner	Increasing radius corner	Decreasing radius corner
Middle apex	Early apex	Late apex

HOW TO BRAKE HARD WHILE RAILING A FLAT TURN

Don't.

It's extremely difficult to brake hard while simultaneously railing a flat turn. There just isn't enough traction, not to mention skill. If a unicorn suddenly appears in your corner, first straighten out; *then* brake hard. If you've been practicing your braking drills, you'll be under control before you strike the magical beast.

Carve a Smooth Arc

With a middle apex, you enter from the outside with moderate speed, carve past the middle of the turn, and exit wide. In a consistent turn with good traction, a middle apex will carry you faster than any other line.

Good: This is the mathematically perfect line. You carry the most speed through the entire turn.

Bad: You can't see the exit very well. Poor traction and unseen obstacles can give you trouble.

Square It Off

With a late apex, you slow down, enter wide, initiate your turn, and then accelerate to the exit.

Good: You can see farther through the turn before you commit to a line. You go relatively straight on the exit. You can start pedaling earlier and carry max speed out of the turn. This is the line for cagey veterans: They know when to take it slow, and they save their pop for when it counts. When there's no room to drift outward on the exit, a late apex is the only way to go.

Bad: Nothing.

Although a middle apex is often faster, a late apex is safer. Use it on strange trails, in sloppy conditions, and when you don't mind someone sneaking by on the inside. When a straight follows the corner, square it off early and start pedaling as soon as you can.

Don't be afraid to change your mind—or your line. If you see a rock to avoid or a bank to use as a berm, go for it!

Series of Turns

You zoom along the bottom of Mt. Charleston near Las Vegas. The apron of high desert sweeps for miles in every direction. Joshua trees stand everywhere, like people with their hands in their pockets. The trail winds among them, a big-ring slalom with no end in sight. You're on autopilot: left . . . right . . . left . . . right—but you don't notice the tight chicane ahead. You sweep through the left; then—whoa!—you've already blown the right, and you smash into those swordlike leaves.

Twisty trails can force you to alter your normal lines. You see, the best line for the first turn frequently messes you up for the next one. The last turn in the series is the most important; compromise the others to set yourself up properly.

When in doubt, enter wide and square off the first turn. For example, in a left-then-right series, enter on the far right, cut across the first apex, and then exit as far left as possible to set up for the right turn.

In a series of very tight turns, aim your head and body in a straight line and let the bike turn under you. Think of yourself as a head floating down the trail.

In a series of connected turns, try to send your head straight and make your bike do the work.

The last turn is the most important

Late apex in first turn allows smooth middle apex in second (constant radius) turn.

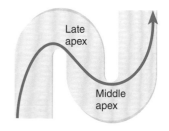

Late apex in first turn allows late apex in second (decreasing radius) turn. Time to pedal!

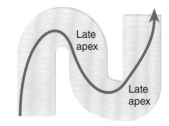

Head floating down the trail

Your tires use the banking for traction.

Your head and upper body go as straight forward as possible.

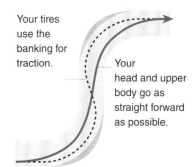

Lean to the Right Degree

To rail turns, you have to fling your body to the inside of your tires, teasing gravity and momentum into a stalemate. The tighter and faster the turn, the more you must lean. If you're falling to the inside, you're leaning too much. If you blow through the turn, you aren't leaning enough.

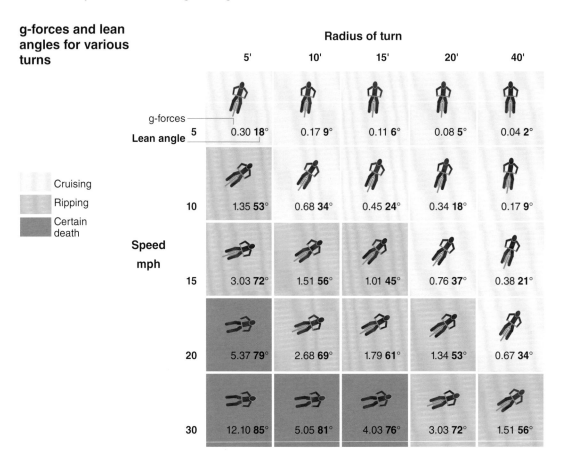

g-forces and lean angles for various turns

Radius of turn

Speed mph	5'	10'	15'	20'	40'
5	0.30 **18°**	0.17 **9°**	0.11 **6°**	0.08 **5°**	0.04 **2°**
10	1.35 **53°**	0.68 **34°**	0.45 **24°**	0.34 **18°**	0.17 **9°**
15	3.03 **72°**	1.51 **56°**	1.01 **45°**	0.76 **37°**	0.38 **21°**
20	5.37 **79°**	2.68 **69°**	1.79 **61°**	1.34 **53°**	0.67 **34°**
30	12.10 **85°**	5.05 **81°**	4.03 **76°**	3.03 **72°**	1.51 **56°**

g-forces
Lean angle

☐ Cruising
▨ Ripping
▨ Certain death

NERDY—AND USEFUL

At the last national downhill at Snow Summit, California, the course crossed the ski run, cut along the side slope, and then jumped back onto the ski run. The side-slope turn was off-camber, loose, and sketchy, so going fast was nervous-making, but the exit was uphill, so the faster the better, right?

Luckily, I (Lee) flatted in the last practice and had to walk down the section. I noticed a rut had formed, and its bank was sloped at least 45 degrees.

Ah hah! Knowing the turn radius, the bank slope, and the math, I knew I could go as fast as I wanted through that turn.

And I did.

The chart on the facing page shows the g-forces and your lean angle for a variety of turns and speeds. Did you know that when you rail a berm with a 15-foot (4.6 m) radius at 15 miles per hour (24 km/h), you're pulling 1 g and leaning 45 degrees? Well, you are. This might seem like nerdiness for nerdiness' sake, but this knowledge can be useful. If you're not sure how fast you can go through a turn, stop and check out the banking. If the angle of the berm (or rut or little ridge) matches your speed and the radius of the turn, then go for it with confidence. Of course, you can go faster than the banking allows, but you'll need gobs of traction.

For every combination of radius and speed, there is only one lean angle that balances turning forces with the force of gravity. You can achieve the same amount of lean in a few different ways, and they work best in different situations.

Lean your bike and body together.   When your lean angle matches the angle of a berm, you can press directly through the tires and just plain rail the corner. Leaning with your bike works in flat corners, but only when the ground is as sticky as that Clif Shot dribbling from the corner of your mouth.

Lean your body more than your bike.   Less bike lean presses more meat into the ground, which you'll appreciate while you turn on a wet bridge, claw around an off-camber sweeper, or haul the mail through a slippery berm. Bonus: The extra pedal clearance lets you get on the gas sooner . . . braaap!

Lean your bike more than your body.   This position gives you extra traction and stability in flat and off-camber corners, or anytime your lean exceeds the angle of the ground. Weight your outside pedal. That levers your tires into the ground, so slipping doesn't happen. In almost every turn, this is the best, safest, and fastest way to go. Practice cornering this way. It'll never steer you wrong. This is the best cornering position for any turn whose traction might let you down.

Leaning your bike and body together.

Leaning your body more than your bike.

Leaning your bike more than your body.

The safest default. Bike leaned more than your body, eyes and hips pointing where you want to go. Big smile.

The safest default is leaning your bike more than your body. You can never go wrong that way, for these reasons: (1) You get more bike lean and cornering force. (2) You set a harder edge by driving down into the pedal. (3) If the bike bounces or slips, you're above it where you can control the situation, rather than going down with the ship.

The Truth About Countersteering

Contrary to popular belief, **countersteering** is not turning your wheel the opposite way while you skid around a turn, nor is it riding in circles on your kitchen counter. Countersteering uses gyroscopic forces and the geometry of your bike to lean you into a corner. High speeds require it. Here's how to countersteer into a fast left turn:

- ◎ Turn your wheel slightly to the *right*. For a brief instant, the bike will steer right.
- ◎ The bike will almost immediately lean to the left. As soon as the bike leans, you'll begin to turn left.
- ◎ Because of the way steering geometry works, the wheel will flop over to the left and help you make your turn. Voilà, you're turning left.
- ◎ The bike will hold its lean angle without any input from you. Try loosening your grip on the bars. See? You're still carving. For more lean, nudge your bars to the right. For less lean, nudge 'em to the left. Be sure to let the wheel flop where it wants to. Try this in high-speed turns. You'll be stoked.

The Motorcycle Safety Foundation teaches its students to push left to go left. As you lean your body into a left turn, press forward on your left handlebar. The countersteer and lean will complement each other, and you'll soon be railing like a pro bikercrosser.

Countersteering into a left turn

You need speed.

1. Turn bars slightly to the right.

2. Bike will lean to the left.

3. Relax. The bars will turn to the left. You're carving!

PEDALS PLANTED OR LEVEL?

Outside Pedal Down

✓ For long turns

✓ For flat and off-camber turns

✓ Anytime you need to set a hard edge

Note: Never turn with your inside pedal down, unless you're going, like, 0.1 miles (or kilometers) per hour.

Pedals Level

✓ Short, quick turns. (It takes too long to switch from side to side.) Besides, you want to pump these turns.

✓ Rough ground. You don't want your outside pedal digging into roots and such. Trust us.

Inside Foot In or Out?

A dropped foot can help you through long, sketchy corners. Leave your outside foot on the pedal and plant your butt on the seat. Take your inside foot and skim it along the ground. This lowers your center of gravity a bit, and it puts more weight on your rear tire. Your rear suspension works under your mass, and your bike tracks like crazy. Even if it isn't helping all that much, you feel safer with your foot out, don't you?

You might compromise your first pedal strokes, but if you carry mega speed through the corner, who cares?

Moto Style

To focus extra weight on your front wheel in an extra-sketchy turn, extend your inside foot forward, up near your front wheel. This shifts traction to the front end, and, if you do need to dab, your foot doesn't get pulled back behind you.

Curtis Keene spends his winters on a moto, and that really shows in his cornering style. Braaap!

As you can tell from this chapter, cornering can get pretty complex. If you practice these key moves, we promise all of your turns will be sweeter.

1. **Low attack position.** The lower you are, the more you can lean your bike, and the tighter you can turn. Lowness also gives you the range to load and pump the turn. Oh yeah.

2. **Look through the turn.** Yeah, yeah, we know this is obvious. But everyone forgets. Scan through the turn, through the exit, and try, as soon as possible, to find the next turn.

3. **Lean your bike.** Stay balanced over the pedals. Push the inside grip down into the turn. Let the bars flop however they want (they know what to do). Make sure the saddle is to the inside of your butt crack. The tighter the turn, the more you must lean your bike.

4. **Turn your hips.** Driving from your hips, not your shoulders, turn your upper body toward the exit of the turn. Imagine there's a flashlight in your belly button. Point it where you want to go. This adds a ton of power to your turn.

Remember

✓ Low, look, lean, turn

✓ Low, look, lean, turn!

✓ LOW, LOOK, LEAN, TURN!!!

A tricky turn made easy

All corners are different. This one has a gradual lead-in, a rocky belly, and an off-camber outside line. These four basic steps make most corners easier.

1. Low attack position.

2. Look through the turn.

3. Lean your bike.

4. Turn your hips.

Rail Berms

Berms intimidate many mountain bikers who didn't grow up on BMX tracks, but they provide the ultimate turning experience. The Sea Otter Classic slalom course has some of the best berms ever. You blast down the start ramp, finesse a couple of grassy gates, hammer straight down the fall line, and fall into this huge 100-degree left. You pull so many g's it feels like the flesh is melting off your face. You get a few pedal strokes on the way out, and then—pow!—you hit a triple jump and rail through a perfect 180. If you ride that course, you will smile for the rest of your life.

Berm
Positive camber; bank

You don't need race-sculpted berms to enjoy the benefits of positive camber. Look for worn lines, ruts, little banks—anything you can press your tires against. A smooth, nicely arced berm practically rides itself.

Lay off the brakes.   You can carry more speed through a berm than any other kind of turn. As a matter of fact, if the banking is steep enough, you can safely go faster than your brain will let you.

Lean it like you mean it.   Steep berms allow deep lean angles. For every berm, there is a "perfect" speed at which your lean angle presses your tires directly into the ground (see the chart on page 88). For example, a turn with a 15-foot (4.6 m) radius and a 45-degree bank would be perfect at 15 miles per hour (24 km/h). With this perfect lean, you don't even need tire traction; you could run Teflon and still rail the corner. When you go so fast that your lean exceeds the berm's banking, you have to make up the traction difference as if it's a flat turn. That's why it's always a good idea to lean your bike beneath your body.

Go as high as you need to.   Most berms are flattest at the bottom and steepest at the top. Try to match your lean angle with the banking. If you're going slow, ride low. If you're going fast, ride high. Bonus tip: The fastest riders create a narrow, overhanging track along the top of a berm. If you have enough speed to ride that line, you'll rail like a Hot Wheels car. The berms at the Encinitas YMCA were oververtical. You could ride them as fast as you wanted. Heck, it seemed like you couldn't ride them fast enough.

Keep pedaling! This can be hard to fathom, but if the berm isn't too rough, you can sit and pedal the whole way. French downhill legend Nico Vouilloz did that all the time.

Mind your lines. In a perfect, constant berm, you don't need to worry about early, middle, or late apexes. Just follow the bank around the turn. That said, you can exit fast by squaring the turn high near the beginning of the turn and then accelerating down toward the exit (see the passing section in chapter 13, page 216 and chapter 7 on pumping). Definitely take a critical look at your berm. If it's steep on the entrance and flat on the exit, enter it high and drop down on the way out. If it's flat on the entrance and steep on the exit, enter it low and let your speed carry you up the bank.

Pump track designer style: Lee knows the angle of the bank matches his lean angle (he measured; it's about 70 degrees), so he pushes straight through the bike.

World champion racer style: Brian is going so fast through this berm that his lean angle (about 74 degrees) exceeds the steep banking. So he treats it like a flat turn and leans his bike more than his body. Basically sick.

Carve Flat Turns

Flat turn
Zero camber

A Hot Wheels car can rail a berm. Flat turns require skill. Tires scraping across the ground like to slide, and they require finesse to stay on track.

Run great tires. In the middle of a slippery turn, the difference between a $20 and a $50 handlebar means nothing. The difference between a $20 and a $50 tire means everything. The right size, casing, pattern, and compound provide more traction, which is important. What's even more important is your confidence. Believe in your tires, believe in yourself.

Lean your bike more than your body. Weight that outside pedal while you're at it.

Load it. As you initiate a tight turn or square off a wide turn, unweight your bike and then cram your tires into the ground.

Most flat turns aren't entirely flat. Look for a rut, a tire track, or anything you can use as a mini-berm.

This corner gets tighter as it goes around a blind hillside. Get low, lean your bike—lean your bike more—and look as far ahead as possible.

PICK THE RIGHT PEDALS

The functional and emotional differences between flat and clip-in pedals are most obvious in the corners. Which type of pedal is better? That depends on you.

Your confidence. If you are nervous about sliding out, or you're pushing so hard that you're *going to* slide out, then flat pedals will help you hang it out with greater confidence. If you feel good that you'll make the turn, or if you rarely take your foot off the pedal, you're probably better off clipped in.

Your style. If you tend to keep your feet up and railing, road bike style, stick with the connection of clips. If you're more likely to put a foot out, moto style, rock the flats. Unless you unclip often, there's no real advantage to cornering on flat pedals.

Your mood. We both switch depending on the kind of riding we're doing: clips for trail, flats for pump and jump. Learn nuance and confidence on flats; then apply those skills with the power and control of clips. Remember: A great rider can rip on pretty much any bike, with any setup.

Pro DHer Curtis Keene tried clip-in pedals for a couple seasons, but he says he's just more confident with flats. He rocks flats for DH, dirt jumping, trail and even road—and he probably climbs faster than you.

AN E TICKET IN YOUR BACKYARD

Pump tracks are awesome for lots of reasons, and number one is the berms. You can learn to rail corners and pull mega g's right in your backyard—and you can do it whenever you want. If repetition is the mother of skill, pump tracks are the parents of corner rippage.

See the pump track chapter, page 119.

High and outside: Lee enters a berm at the Lyons Bike Park, which he designed and built right in the middle of town. When you can rip the pump track on your trail bike, trail riding takes on a whole new radness.

Survive Off-Camber Turns

Off camber
Negative camber

Everything that applies to flat turns applies to off-camber turns, only more so. When you combine your positive lean with the ground's negative lean, you get a traction nightmare.

Many corners are built off-camber to aid drainage. Set your bike on edge and crush your suspension and tires through that outside pedal. Remember: twice the down force equals twice the traction.

Go slow. With the ground pointing away from your tires, a skid is closer than ever.

Do a late apex. Hit the apex very high and let yourself drift lower as you exit. If you expect the drift, it won't be so scary. A rut or berm frequently forms on the exit, where your predecessors finally caught traction. Use it!

Get even lower, stay even looser, and look even farther ahead than in flat turns. The sketchiness will tempt you to tighten up. You must resist. You are a corner-carving machine. Make it happen, baby!

Lean your bike even more. Really set an edge. And you might as well load the tires while you're at it.

Try to turn where it's not actually off camber. Look for any flat or, even better, banked surface where you can square off the turn.

Conquer Switchbacks

Switchbacks' sharpness, steepness, and exposure turn flowy riders into wigged-out stickmen. But remember: **Switchbacks** are nothing more than tight, steep corners.

Slow WAY down for downhill switchbacks.   As you drop through the turn, you want to reach a happy speed, not scare yourself into an unfortunate braking incident.

You almost always want a late apex.   For a downhill left switchback, slow down, enter to the far right, square the turn against the bank (see, it's like a little berm), and drop through to the exit. Early apexes can be deadly—that outside exit line tends to be a cliff.

Do everything right.   Low, look, lean, turn—it's all more important than ever.

Use the ruts.   When a rain channel cruises around the outside of a wide switchback, rail it just like a berm. When the rut carves a tight line across the inside, drop your rear tire into the rut and track your brakeless front tire around the outside of it. When the rut runs around the outside of a tight switchback, let your rear tire follow it and steer to the inside. A little rear brake keeps your rear meat in the track (only on closed courses, of course).

Pull out a foot.   Sometimes it pays to drop your inside foot and whip your bike around a super-tight corner. Steep exits bring you right back up to speed. In flat exits, you'll lose some time finding your pedal. The San Juan Trail in southern California has dozens of steep switchbacks. When we follow people down and they pull their feet into the turns, they might gap us a little, but we're back on their tails within two strokes.

Default switchback lines

Downhill

Uphill

Negotiating a tricky switchback
This turn is so tight the bike will barely roll around it without hopping the rear end. One approach:

1. Enter as wide as you can.   **2.** Get low and lean into the turn.   **3.** Trust your bike and look to the end.   **4.** Use the whole trail if you have to.   **5.** Lean even more to finish the turn.

This loose, off-camber right demands one of Steve Peat's patented skid setups.

Nose wheelie!　On a slow, tight switchback with decent traction, you can do a nose wheelie and kick the back end around. You don't have to swing it the full 180 degrees; you need just enough to help aim you into the turn.

Climbing switchbacks.　Switchbacks occur only on steep hills. Follow the widest line possible to reduce the grade and give your rear tire room to track inward. Build momentum with a couple of hard cranks, and keep the power going as you round the bend. Shift your butt to the edge of the seat, and lean the bike below you. If you can't pedal because of ruts or roots, make sure you gain tons of speed on the entrance. Don't touch your brakes!

Skid Into Loose Corners

Don't skid on public trails. Use these techniques only on race courses—and then only sparingly. If you can rail a corner without skidding, that's usually fastest. Basically, if a turn has a berm, rail it. If there's enough traction or space for you to carry momentum through a turn, then carve it. Skidding only makes sense in slow, slippery corners that you want to square off. Use the skid to aim your bike in a new direction, and then resume your rolling.

As you zoom down the right lane of a gravelly **doubletrack**, a flat left turn approaches. If you arc through the inside of the turn, your front tire will surely wash out. The solution: a skid setup. Remember: This is about steering, not slowing down. Bring your bike to a reasonable speed before you reach the corner.

1. Nail the rear brake to break the tire loose. Note how far outside the main line Peaty chose to begin his turn.
2. Get the bike skidding sideways (note the lean).
3. Lean forward to make your front tire track though the turn. Do not touch the front brake!
4. When the rear end swings around to where you want it, release the brake. Your rear tire will catch, and you'll shoot into the corner. Sa-weet!

Be ready for your tires to slip. If the traction were good, you wouldn't be doing a skid setup, would you? When the skid happens, stay off the brakes and steer where you want to go.

Other fun stuff:

○ Try a little **kickout** to help set up the skid.
○ You can skid into the beginning of a corner and then release the brakes and rail the rest of it.
○ You can kind of half-skid, half-carve when you're going fast.
○ Controlled skidding is tricky. Practice in a safe place. Use flat pedals.

Pump Berms for Free Speed

When you encounter a tight turn with a steep bank and an abrupt transition, you can pump it as if it's the trough between two **rollers**. When you think about it, a berm is basically a hole on its side. For extra speed and traction, try dropping into the turn, pumping the transition, and then getting light on the exit. When you feel the bike unweight, that's your cue to start pedaling and set up for the next turn. See chapter 7 for more details on pumping.

Pumping a berm, pump track-style on the trail bike.

Deal With Drift

Mountain bike tires slip. They squirm. They **drift**. They skid. They skip.

When you haul ass on persnickety surfaces, that's what happens. You'd think we'd be used to it, but most of us freak out when traction runs out and the tires get loose. It doesn't take many cliff drops and cases of poison oak to develop a case of drift phobia.

No matter how boffo your braking, how luscious your lines, how potent your pump, you will eventually drift in a turn. The good news is, you don't have to be afraid. You see, your tires *never* grab the ground completely. Anytime you ride around a curve, the rubber alternately grips and slips. On pavement, the knobs might squirm 1 millimeter every tenth of a second. You don't even notice that. On sand over hardpack, they might slip an inch (2.5 cm) every second. No biggie. On embedded rocks, they might skip a foot (30 cm) every few seconds. Umm . . . yikes! Although a front-wheel side trip feels wild, remember that as long as you stay low and loose and you let the bike do its thing, your tire will regain traction, and you'll continue through the corner. Whether this happens 10 times per second or once per minute makes little difference.

Grip-slip-grip is natural. Get used to it. Be ready for it.

1. At the 2009 SolVista Nationals, Shawn Palmer enters this flat turn with a foot-out moto style.

2. The bike drifts, he dabs his foot and he shifts forward to make the front end stick.

3. The rear end is still loose, but the heavy front end is tracking. All is good, and the brakes were never touched.

RALLY SLIDE

Here's a little trick for ya: Say you want to slide into a left turn. Skid your rear tire to the left (toward the inside of the turn); then whip it around to the right and enter the turn. This left-right swing adds more energy to your entrance.

Scrutinize the corner. If you see gravel or marbles, don't be surprised when things get jiggy. Same with speed. Hauling the mail into a flat or off-camber turn is just asking for funny business.

Aim for a tighter line than you need. This gives you room to drift. You can always open up your turn, but tightening will make you crash. Bonus: You're probably not the first person to slide through this corner. There might be a bank—or at least a pile of dust—where everyone else finally caught traction. Use it.

Lean your bike and keep your weight balanced over your pedals and tires. This literally keeps you on top of the situation. Breaking loose while you're leaned far inside is like kicking the bottom of an upturned broom.

IT'S OK TO LOSE CONTROL

(At least for a moment.)

Find a flat, slippery, obstacle-free corner. Ride the corner faster and faster until your wheels start to drift. As long as you stay loose and low, you'll find that your tires will regain traction and you'll be just fine.

Most of the time. Rock the pads and flat pedals.

Balance the slippage. You want both wheels to go together (this is that two-wheel drift you always hear about). If one wheel starts to slide more than the other, subtly shift your weight to that wheel. When you maintain a long drift, it feels like your bike is walking sideways.

If you're turning right and your front wheel suddenly lets go, steer with the slide (to the left) until it catches; then gently turn the wheel back to the right.

If the rear lets go, keep your weight on the front tire. As long as your front is tracking, it'll pull the rear into line.

Stay loose. Yes, for the ten-thousandth time. The more you fight the slide, the more you'll slide and the dorkier you'll look. Your bike must be free to find its way. After some practice, gravelly corners will feel as predictable as pavement.

FRENCH CORNERING DRILL

✓ Find a corner with an uphill exit.

✓ Practice riding it every which way: at different entrance speeds, along various lines, unloaded and loaded, and so on.

✓ Measure your success by how far you coast up the hill. The higher the better—remember how you did that one!

SHOOT YOUR TROUBLES

Problem: When you start a turn, you go kind of straight—until the end where you try extra hard and crash.

Solution: This is very common. First make sure that you enter the turn in your low attack position. Lean the bike and *let the bars turn* (going straight comes from not letting the bars steer naturally; that final crash comes from steering them too much).

Problem: You feel yourself falling to the inside of a turn. Heck, you might actually hit the deck.

Solution: You're leaning too much for your speed and the tightness of the turn. Lean less or go faster. We say, *go faster.*

Problem: You blast straight through the turn. You might feel yourself tensing up and hitting the brakes as you follow a tangent into a Joshua tree.

Solutions: Most of the time, merely leaning the bike more will do the trick. Just pitch your bike into the corner, and it'll probably come around. If that doesn't work for ya, try slowing down and following a gentler arc. Also, always, always, *always* look where you want to go, out past the exit of the turn.

Problem: Your front wheel washes out.

Solutions: Chances are you're nervous and leaning back on your bike (the natural instinct: push your brain away from danger!). Enter the turn with weightless hands. If your front tire starts to go, gently shift your weight forward onto the bars until your front tire resumes tracking. As long as your front tire is doing its job, your rear tire can do what it wants.

Problem: You have trouble making flat and off-camber turns.

Solutions: Lean your bike more and weight the outside pedal. Pick smoother lines. Load your tires for temporary extra traction.

Problem: In berms, you find yourself steering up the banks to stay on course.

Solution: You're going too slow! Either speed up or ride lower in the berm, where it isn't so steep.

Problem: You freak out whenever your tires break loose.

Solution: Either slow down so you don't drift, or practice drifting in a controlled situation. This is a natural part of mountain biking; we suggest you get used to it!

Corners have the most variation in mountain biking. The possible combinations of radius, camber, elevation, surface, speed, and lines stagger the imagination. Corners separate world-class trails from merely fun trails and great riders from merely good riders. When you can pick great lines, carry the right speed, and maximize your traction, you'll rip on the best trails the world has to offer.

CHAPTER 6

Wheelie and Hop Over Anything

If we lived in a two-dimensional world, we could get along fine without lifting our wheels off the ground. But riding in a two-dimensional world would be awfully flat, wouldn't it?

Mountain biking is all about that vertical dimension. Ripples, roots, rocks, ravines—they force us to go over or around. If you can't lift your bike, you're stuck going around. That's entertaining, but the real thrills begin when you can take the bird line: straight over.

Notes to beginners: Learn these moves step by step—first the wheelie, then the rear wheel lift, and then the bunny hop. Start with small obstacles on forgiving ground. Wear your helmet, gloves, and pads.

Lift That Front Wheel

Boys learn to lift their front wheels around the time they learn their ABCs. They goof around in front of their homes, tugging and tugging until—voilà—they've popped their very first **wheelie**.

We have no idea what the girls were doing at this time (our wives were hanging with Barbie), but most of them missed the wheelie lesson. So you end up with these excellent women who can arrange million-dollar deals and rail singletrack, but who can't pop wheelies for the life of them. They are strong and free, but any curb stops them in their tracks.

Traditional wisdom says most women aren't strong enough to lift their bikes. Bah-hooey to that. Ninety-eight-pound boys routinely manual 40-pound downhill bikes, and plenty of women are stronger than them.

You wheel-on-the-grounders might be asking why you need to pop wheelies. The reasons outnumber the shoes in our wives' closets: jagged rocks deflect your wheel, bumps slow you down, and curbs thwart shopping trips, to name a few. When you can lift your front wheel over obstacles, you retain speed and control in all sorts of situations.

SET UP FOR SUCCESS

Some simple bike changes will accelerate your wheelie, manual, and hop mastery. In order of ease and importance:

Drop your seat. The lower your saddle, the bigger and more fluid your movements.

Switch to flat pedals. This is the only way to guarantee you're not pulling on the pedals.

Shorten your stem. Moving your bars higher and closer gives you more range and better balance.

Sitting and Pedaling Wheelie

You're climbing a nice singletrack with excellent traction. A 3-inch (7.6 cm) root crosses the trail. Bashing into it will slow you down or knock you off line. If you can get your front wheel over that bugger and keep pedaling, your rear tire will crawl right over it.

GET YOUR WHEEL OFF THE GROUND

This is all about shifting your weight back. You can achieve this by pushing back with your arms, pedaling hard, or both.

1. Start in a neutral position: butt on the seat, arms slightly bent.
2. Pull your shoulders down and forward. Your power pedal should be at around 2 o'clock.
3. Explosively push your torso upward and backward with your arms. At the same time, uncork a powerful pedal stroke. If you are nice to puppies, your front wheel will pop up.
4. Keep your arms straight and your weight back. Don't bend your arms! Keep pedaling.

A wheelie is a great way to get your front tire onto a ledge.

1. Neutral position.   2. Crouch forward.   3. Crank and push yourself back.   4. Keep leaning and pedaling

Center of gravity

KEEP IT THERE

Pedaling around with your wheel in the air isn't very useful on the trail, but it looks cool. Learn to balance sitting wheelies before you move up to coaster wheelies.

Keep lifting your front wheel until you find the balancing point. The magic spot will feel weightless, like you are neither working to keep the wheel up nor falling on your bum. It's all about getting comfortable with the balance. Here are some tricks to help you stay on top:

Find the balance.   Once you get to the magic spot, keep pedaling nice and easy. If you feel yourself falling forward, pedal harder. If you feel yourself falling backward, brake a little. If you start falling to one side, lean to the other side.

Choose the right gear. A really low gear gives you a fast pop but short loft time. A higher gear gives you less pop but longer loft. Find your happy medium. When your kung fu is good, you'll use your normal, low climbing gear. You can get it spinning very easily, for great explosion, and you keep it spinning to maintain lift.

Pedal all the way up to it. It's easiest to approach your wheelie point already pedaling and then give it some extra juice when the time is right. After you get the hang of this, you can try jabbing the pedals from a coast. Warning: The lift is a bit more violent, and low-quality rear hubs tend to hesitate before they grab (and they might skip under your awesome power).

Never stop pedaling. Keep turning the pedals after you pop your wheel up. It's easier to give a little more or less gas if your foot's already turning the circle.

Light brakes. If you jab your rear brake, your front wheel will slam to the ground so fast you won't be able to stop it. All you need is a tiny bit of lever pressure. If you find you keep giving it too much brake at once, try lightly dragging the brake as you ride. This is like your constant pedaling: It's easier to give a bit more or less when you're already giving some.

Stay loose. We can't say this enough. Sit lightly on the saddle so you can slide forward or back, right or left. Feel free to sway your knees in and out. If you're using flat pedals, you can tilt your foot to the side or even hang it out like an outrigger.

Coasting Wheelie, aka Manual

When you're coasting downhill or on flat ground, this is the best way to get your front wheel over trouble. You'd be amazed at what your rear wheel can roll over after your front is already clear, especially with suspension. Remember to stay loose and keep your speed reasonable.

GET YOUR WHEEL OFF THE GROUND

This is *not* about pulling on your handlebars. It's about shifting your weight back. The more fluidly you can move from the front to the back of your cockpit, the easier this is.

1. Start in your attack position. The lower you are, the farther back you can get.
2. Shift your weight forward, onto your bars. Your entire body rotates forward around your bottom bracket. Really load the fork and front tire.

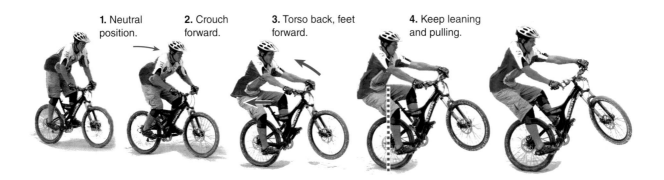

1. Neutral position. **2.** Crouch forward. **3.** Torso back, feet forward. **4.** Keep leaning and pulling.

3. Feel the pressure in your hands; then push your body backward. Straighten your arms all the way. Your entire body rotates backward around your bottom bracket until your center of mass is over the contact patch of your rear tire. For extra lift, push your feet forward.

4. Let your body's momentum pull the front end up. The farther back you go, the closer your center of gravity gets to your rear tire's contact patch, and the longer you can keep your wheel up. Don't go too far, though, or you'll "loop out," which means "fall on your bum."

If you can get your front wheel onto a sidewalk, you can let your rear wheel bash right over the curb. Go slow and stay loose, and soon you'll experience real freedom.

KEEP IT THERE

Because you can't use pedaling power to cheat your front end upward, you have to maintain balance with perfect body position and sharp reflexes. Expert manualers can balance forever over all sorts of terrain, from rocks to bumps to stream crossings.

Here are some tips to help you find some balance in your life:

○ Straighten your arms and lean all the way back to the balance point.

○ If you need to raise your front wheel, push your hips backward or pedals forward.

○ If you need to lower your front wheel, pull your hips forward or your feet toward you.

○ It's all in the hips. Leave your arms straight.

MANUAL TIPS

Preload.   When you go from your neutral position to your crouch, drop your weight quickly and then immediately push back upward. The rebound of your bike's tires, frame, and suspension will add to your explosion.

Timing.   You want your wheel to be highest when it reaches the obstacle. Lift too soon and you hit on the upswing. Too late and you hit on the downfall. Perfect timing depends on your speed, the height of the obstacle, and how fast you lift your wheel. Pop lots of wheelies, and perfect timing will come.

Learn on a hardtail.   On a full-suspension bike, you have to not only maintain your balance over the rear wheel, but also compensate for the moving suspension.

A manual comes in handy any time you can't (or don't want to) roll off a ledge.

Front wheel too low.

Solution:
Move hips backward.

MANUALING A DOUBLE

Manualing across the gap between two rollers (or rocks) is more about pumping than manualing. See pumping in chapter 7.

Pro bikercross racer Petr Hanak secures yet another hole shot. Keeping his front end high lets him carry more speed than if he rolls both wheels through the trough.

Wheelie Sideways

An hour into your singletrack climb, you enter a super-tight switchback. You know your bike won't track through the deep rut carving through the apex, so you ride past it, pick your wheel up, swing your bike around, and set your wheel down at the top of the turn.

1. Look and lean into the turn like normal.
2. Explode with power and pick up the front end. Burst forward out of your saddle. Keep your arms pretty straight and drive your hips forward (like in a deadlift). Keep leaning into the turn!
3. Set it back down and enjoy the rest of your ride.

Lift Your Rear Wheel

To get over big, sharp rocks and impress everyone on Rodeo Drive, you gotta give your rear end a lift.

Basic Rear-Wheel Lift

1. Start in your attack position (the lower, the better), and shift your weight back. Load the rear end of your bike. You should feel the pressure build up under your feet.

2. Lunge forward. Push back against your pedals and pull with your arms.

3. Let it come up. Drive your weight onto the bars, and lighten your feet to let the rear end rise.

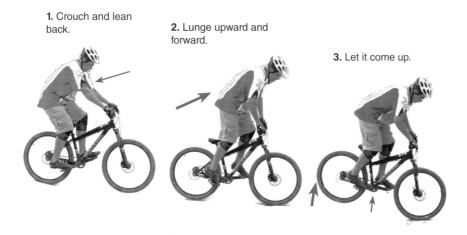

1. Crouch and lean back.

2. Lunge upward and forward.

3. Let it come up.

Exaggerate.   This is all about weighting and unweighting. While you're learning, lean all the way back; then hurl yourself all the way forward. Make it count.

Cheat (if you need to).   With clip-in pedals, you can easily pull the rear wheel upward. This is fine and good (if you're a sissy), but it's best to learn without relying on clip-ins. Flat pedals will teach you better form, and you'll be able to hop higher in the long run.

To lift your rear wheel onto a ledge, drive your hips forward and push down into the pedals. (Yet another reason to master the full range of your cockpit.)

Kick It Out

In a kickout, you keep your front wheel on the ground and hop your rear wheel sideways. This trick was a big deal in the first grade, and it remains useful.

Kick your rear wheel out to avoid a rock in a turn. Do a kickout as you enter a flat, fast turn; when you set your rear tire down, it catches traction and shoots you into the corner. Neat.

If you can lift your rear wheel straight up, a kickout is easy. Say you want to kick out to the left:

1. Start in your low attack position. Always.
2. Steer and lean to the left. As the bike starts to turn, shift your weight back to load the rear end.
3. Lunge forward and to the left. Keep your body relatively still, and swing the bike beneath you.
4. Let the rear wheel swing wide. Note that these are flat pedals. The pop comes from the rapid load and unload, not from pulling with your feet.

The hot tip for this tight S section: Pump over the big rock, plant your front tire, then swing your rear tire around.

Get Over Small Obstacles

When an obstacle fits below your chainrings, you can slowly cross it by lifting first your front and then your back wheel over it. Use this technique while you ride slowly over any small object: a branch, a rock, and even the dreaded curb. Let's use a couple of two-by-fours as an example:

1. Start in your attack position, and load forward. As you approach the lumber, crouch down and forward.

2. Lift the front wheel. Immediately shift your body back (see the wheelie section on page 104).

3. Lunge forward. As soon as your front wheel touches down, push explosively into your pedals and propel your body forward. After you push, lighten your feet to allow the pedals to come up. If you're clipped in, you can actually pull the bike upward, but that's cheating.

4. Air that rear wheel. As your body continues to lunge forward, shift your weight to your bars. Even if your rear wheel doesn't clear the obstacle, it'll be light enough to roll over easily.

5. Settle back into attack position. Absorb the landing. You did it!

1. **Load the spring.** As you approach, crouch down and forward.

2. **Lift the front wheel.** Quickly push your torso away from the bike and pull on the bars with straight arms. (See the wheelie section.)

3. **Lunge forward.** As soon as your front wheel lands, push explosively on your pedals, then slightly unweight your feet to let the pedals come up.

4. **Lift your rear wheel.** As your body continues to lunge forward, bend your knees to let your pedals (and rear wheel) come up.

5. **Touchdown.** Rock and roll. You did it!

Hop Over Large Obstacles

If the obstacle is too big to fit beneath your chainrings, you have to lift both wheels over it. This is a bona fide **bunny hop**. When you can hop over an obstacle without slowing your flow, you'll enjoy a whole new level of fun and freedom. Logs won't stop you. Rocks will make you smile. Curbs . . . ha!

Don't try to lift both wheels at the same time. It's not very powerful, and it's very hard to time correctly for a real-life obstacle. Proper hopping is a two-step process: (1) Rock back into a manual and (2) explode off the rear wheel. This is the most powerful, consistent way to get over stuff.

1. Enter in your attack position—the lower you are, the more lift you can generate—and load the spring. Shift your weight forward. Bring your chest close to your handlebars. The faster you compress, the more rebound you'll get for your hop.

2. Lift your front wheel. Shift your weight backward and get your front end up (review the coasting manual, page 106).

3. Lift the rear wheel. Timing is essential here. At the moment your weight presses into your rear wheel, push explosively down into the pedals and spring upward. If you get light on your pedals, and you live a righteous life, your rear wheel will levitate.

4. Have a good attitude. Let your bike arc through the air. It should be level as you cross the obstacle. For max height, bring the bike close to you.

5. Smooth landing. Extend your landing gear. For small and medium hops over pine trunks, let your front wheel land first. Absorb the landing with your arms, then your legs. For huge hops over park benches, land rear wheel first (for more on drops, see chapter 8, Drop Like a Feather).

1. Load the spring. **2.** Shift backward to lift your front wheel. **3.** Press the rear wheel and let it rebound upward. **4.** Have a good attitude. **5.** Smooth landing.

When low speed won't let you clear the obstacle, let your wheels bounce off the top. Here are some assorted bunny hopping tips:

Timing. The faster you're going, the sooner you should start your hop. If you take off too late, your rear wheel will clip the log on its way up, and then you're in for a bucking good time. When you're hauling full-speed mail, you might start your hop 20 or more feet (6 or more m) before the obstacle.

Suspension. A suspension bike takes longer to load and unload, so you have to begin your hop earlier and time your compression and releases more slowly than with a hardtail. The same hop requires more effort with suspension than without. The softer and longer travel your suspension, the longer and slower the load. Imagine bouncing on a big, droopy trampoline.

Seat height. Lower it! You need the space to shift fore and aft, and to explode upward. With a remotely adjustable post, you can quickly lower your seat for a single, dramatic hop; then raise your seat and resume hammering.

Cockpit length. The shorter your top tube or stem, the easier you can shift your weight back, and the more effectively you can drive your hands and hips together.

Pedals. Clip-in pedals let you easily pull your bike up with your feet. We recommend that you learn to hop the real way—with flat pedals. The harder you push your pedals down, the harder the earth returns the force, and the higher you go. It's just like hopping on your feet.

Hopping onto ledges. This is just like a regular hop, only there's no fall. Land on top with your wheels level. Keep your torso as low as you can, and really pull the bike up into your body. Smooooth . . .

A good, reliable hop lets you flow through some hard-edged situations. Lyons Bike Park, designed and built by Lee for just this sort of moment.

Hopping onto a ledge

It's just like hopping over a big obstacle, except it ends at apogee.

1. Preload forward.

2. Rock back into a manual.

3. Explode off the rear wheel.

4. Pull the bike upward.

5. Suck it up as much as you can.

HOP AS HIGH AS YOU CAN

You can do it anywhere, and it's great practice.

✓ Expand your range of motion.

✓ Dial in your timing

✓ Increase your explosiveness.

✓ Turn up your confidence.

✓ Have fun.

Next time you encounter a folding chair on the trail . . . it's ON!

Pro freestyle rider Zach Lewis shows perfect form over a folding chair. Zach's explosiveness lets him jump pretty much anything.

Hop Sideways

You're hauling the mail down an eroded doubletrack, and a deep rain rut crosses your line. No problem: Do one of your sweet high-speed bunny hops, with a twist. This trick is also handy for hopping from the street onto a sidewalk, or over a random wooden plank.

1. Just before your hop, steer and lean in the direction you're heading.

2. Hop like a maniac. With your body in the air, swing your bike to the other side.

3. Straighten your front wheel and set your bike down. Because you'll be turning as you land, lean a bit to the inside.

Hop in Place

Here's another cute trick. Hop up and down a few inches, and make constant little corrections as if you're on a pogo stick. When you get the hang of this, you can hop forward, backward, side to side, and even in a different direction.

○ Do it anywhere to practice your balance.

○ On the trail, it gives you time to check things out and hop over to a new line if you need to. If you overshoot a switchback turn, you can stop, hop a 180, and continue on your merry way.

Pedal Hop

Say you need to cross a deep gully, but you're going too slowly to hop across it, and there isn't enough space to pedal up to speed. It's time for the **pedal hop**, a trials move with trail appeal. This is also a handy urban move.

As always, you need to be in the perfect gear—not too hard and not too easy.

1. Approach low and forward. Time your power pedal so it tops out at the edge of the gap.
2. Explode up and forward. Push the pedals and pull the bars. Drive your hips all the way forward. Hello, Mr. Stem.
3. Push your bike in front of you. This will give you extra distance.
4. Absorb the landing.

If you accelerate fast enough and pull hard enough, your rear wheel will launch you like a rocket. (Note: The forward explosion in step 2 is useful anytime you lunge onto a ledge. Keep reading . . .)

Lunge Onto a Ledge

You follow the white dots up a slickrock face in Moab, Utah. The traction is incredible, so you have no excuse to get off and walk. You reach a foot-high (30 cm) ledge. Your buddy just seems to lunge up and over the thing. Here's how you can do the same. For those of you who live in soggier climes, feel free to lunge over rocks, roots, and water bars.

This move is easiest when you can pedal the whole way. If the rise is so sharp you'll stab a pedal, you have two choices: (1) Time your pedaling so you arrive with pedals level, or (2) give it a burst of speed and coast—you'll have to lunge forward much harder without the added pedal oomph.

This move has huge ramifications for technical climbing. Stop bonking those water bars—flow right over 'em!

1. Approach in a neutral pedaling position, eyes tracking beyond the obstacle.
2. Lift your wheel with a wheelie (see page 104).
3. Set your front tire on top; then immediately lunge forward with a power stroke. This gives you propulsion and lightens the rear tire.
4. Suck the bike upward to clear the ledge without lifting your whole body.
5. Push the bars forward and go back to your neutral position. Sweet!

SHOOT YOUR TROUBLES

Problem: When you try to lift your front wheel, it only pops up for an instant, even when you yank as hard as you can.

Solution: Sharply push your weight backward and pull on the bars with straight arms. You don't lift your front end with your arms; you lift it with your body mass. At low speeds, snap your pedals to help get the front end up. Keep your finger on the rear brake lever in case you start to loop out. Don't bend your arms!

Problem: You still can't lift your front wheel the way you want to.

Solution: You *think* you're shifting your weight way back, but you're still too far forward. Push your hips *way* back, well behind your seat, behind your rear hub, to the back of your rear tire. Cover that rear brake.

Problem: Your rear wheel seems stuck to the ground. All the grunting and groaning in the world won't lift it.

Solution: Load and unload your pedals very sharply, in time with your suspension. The harder you push downward, the more your bike will rebound upward. Dramatically and convincingly shift your weight backward, then forward. If you're running clips, go ahead and pull your pedals up (cheating!).

Problem: When you try to bunny hop, your rear wheel doesn't fly as high as your front.

Solution: Master the basic rear-wheel lift before you step up to hops. Really accentuate the one-two, front-rear timing. Push and pull on your bars and then load and unload your pedals. Also, work on your explosive power. The higher you can jump off the bike, the higher you can hop on the bike.

You wouldn't enter an archery contest without arrows, and it's just as silly to ride trails without knowing how to wheelie and hop. These get-over-stuff skills are some of the most important in your quiver: When a log appears on the trail, whip out a bunny hop. When you hurtle into a rock garden, bust into a manual. As you race through a rhythm section, hop the first roller, manual the next two, and jump the last three. Heck, you never know which arrow you'll need.

Pump Terrain for Free Speed

Every rider knows at least two ways to gain speed:

1. Pedaling
2. Coasting downhill

Those methods are both time proven and effective, but did you know there's another way to gain speed, one that requires neither a turned pedal nor an extended downslope?

There is, and it's called pump.

The speed you get from pumping isn't exactly free, but it's a fantastic deal. Not only do you go faster, but you also ride smoother and in more control—and you have way more fun.

What Is Pump?

Put simply, pumping is the act of getting light on the fronts of bumps and heavy on the backs of bumps.

When you roll up something, you slow down. The heavier you are, the more you lose speed.

When you roll down something, you speed up. The heavier you are, the more you gain speed.

The point of pump is to minimize your weight when you roll up, and to maximize your weight when you roll down.

Where Can You Pump?

You can pump anywhere the terrain rolls up and down—a BMX track, a skate park, any trail, and, of course, a pump track.

Pump the back of any hump: a roller, a rock, a root, a log, a water bar.

Always scan ahead, looking for things to pump. This makes you much more active—aggressive in a controlled way—and it does wonders for your riding.

You should be pumping every significant bump on the trail. These rocks are just like a pump-track roller.

Why Should You Pump?

Pumping lets you ride faster and use less energy. You gain speed in places where it's too rough or tight to pedal. And you gain seconds over your buddies or competitors who are just getting beaten up.

Pumping also helps you stay in control. Even if you're already going fast, getting light on the fronts and heavy on the backs keeps you from hitting things. You're more connected to the terrain, and you're much less likely to bounce wildly.

HOW YOUR BIKE AFFECTS YOUR PUMP

You can (and should) pump on any mountain bike. But realize that every bike pumps differently.

Hardtails require greater precision on your part, but they reward you with the most pump power.

The more suspension you have, the more leeway you get, but the more energy you waste pushing into the fork and shock. You can pump a long-travel bike like the champion you are, but it takes big moves and real aggression.

The lower your seat, the more leg range you have, and the more pump you can generate. No matter what you ride, lower the seat!

The shorter your stem, the more arm range you have, and the more pump you can generate.

Remember that every bike is a spring like a diving board or trampoline. Learn your bike's timing. Learn to push through the suspension and really connect with the ground.

The ideal pump bike, from a pure pumping standpoint, is a stiff little dirt-jump hardtail.

Features of an ideal pump-track bike
You can master pump on most any bike, but a dirt-jump hardtail like this Specialized P.3 is ideal.

Short stem, riser bars
Short, nimble cockpit

Very low seat
Lots of room to move

Stiff, short-travel fork
For max pump

Flat pedals
Freedom and skill

Short chain stays
For easy manualing

One speed
All you need

Low-knobbed tires
Fast on hardpacked dirt

Also, pumping is fun. It allows you to feel sweet flow on even the roughest trails. Have you ever heard great riders talk about how sweet a certain gnarly trail is? We guarantee, if they're ripping it smoothly, they are pumping.

Watch any video of a great rider (especially that Lopes guy) riding interesting terrain. You will see him pump every chance he gets.

The Continuum of Pump

There are several ways to achieve the almighty pump. Pick the right technique for the terrain and your speed.

Front-wheel pump.   To gain the most speed, lean forward and, as soon as you reach the top, push the front of the bike down into the backside. Follow up your arms with your legs.

Both-wheel pump.   When you get up to speed, it becomes hard to push the front end down quickly enough to get full backside. Relax into the middle of the bike (attack position!), and push down with your legs. As you'll recall, this pushes with both wheels. This is a good, safe default for most riders in most situations.

Rear-wheel pump.   If you rock the pump through multiple bumps, you'll soon reach a speed at which you can't push your front wheel into the gap. It's time to pump-manual. Let the front wheel carry across the gap, and focus all of your pump on the rear wheel. Done right, this is very powerful and very fast. Be sure to set the front wheel on top of the next bump—then get another great backside.

No-wheel pump.   This is actually a two-wheel pump, but it's delayed just a bit. We all reach a speed at which we can't even push the rear wheel down into the trough. At that point it's time to jump. Clear the gap completely and be sure to land at the very top of the backside. From there, push down hard and be on your merry way.

Gaining Speed Over a Single Bump

This is a very aggressive move best saved for lower speeds and kung fu masters. Anytime you lean this far forward, you're really relying on your skills, strength, and confidence.

1. **Push down.** The harder you preload the bike into the ground, the lighter you'll get on the frontside—and the heavier you'll get on the backside. The faster you're going, the earlier you have to push. Even at this low speed, Lee is preloading two bike lengths before the roller. That's a lot farther than you thought necessary!

2. **Pull up.** Little known fact: Pulling over the front is just as important as pushing down the back. Remember: You're a wave of energy, and this is all cyclical.

3. **Pull yourself forward.** As your bike rolls up a steep rise, you have to pull yourself toward the bars to stay over your feet (you remember that). If you want to really connect your front wheel with that backside, you have to pull yourself even farther forward. Sternum over the stem!

4. **Push with your arms.** Your front end is super heavy, and your arms are super bent. Cram that front wheel down the backside. It's like bench pressing 300 pounds (136 kg)—as fast as you can.

5. **Push with your legs.** This is the finishing move, and it's the source of your real power. Look: You're now preloaded for the next roller. Keep rocking that cycle!

Pumping to gain speed

| 1. Push down. | 2. Pull up. | 3. Pull yourself forward. | 4. Push with arms. | 5. Push with legs. |

Maintaining Speed Over a Single Bump

Consider this Standard Pump 101. It's safe, relatively easy, and very effective in a wide variety of situations.

1. **Push down.** Preload hard and early. If you just rode over a roller, that backside pump becomes this preload. Remember: The harder you push, the harder you can pull, and the harder you can push (and the cycle goes on).

2. **Pull up.** At mellow speed on mellow bumps, you can let the bike come up to you. At high speeds on bumpy bumps, you need to pull it toward you—as if you were hopping over the frontside to the backside (which you will be doing someday).

Pumping to maintain speed

| 1. Push down. | 2. Pull up. | 3. Stay centered! | 4. Push down (mostly legs). |

3. **Stay centered!** As you pass over the top of the bump, you should be in your perfect low attack position—perfectly balanced over your feet, with your hands weightless. This helps ensure that your bike is following the sine wave, but your head is not.

4. **Push down.** At turbo speed, your leg power overwhelms your arm power. Stay centered. Drive downward from the hips. Pick up for the next roller.

Pump-Manualing Across Two Bumps

This is one of the coolest-looking, sweetest-feeling moves in mountain biking. Unlike flat-ground manualing, which is all about leaning back, pump-manualing is all about pushing the rear wheel down.

1. **Absorb the first roller.** The slower you're going, the more you need to lean back.

2. **Keep the front wheel high.** Let it carry right off the top of the roller. Resist the temptation to lean back or pull with your arms. Just stay where you are (near center) and . . .

3. **Push down with your legs and pull back with your arms.** This is the crux move. *Do not* lean back. *Do not* bend your elbows. Instead, drive downward from your hips, and row the handlebars back to your hips. This levers the rear wheel down and generates awesome power.

4. **Set your front wheel on the second roller.** Pro trick: Start pulling yourself forward. This keeps you centered over the bike (rather than falling off the back), and it helps you connect with the backside.

5. **Absorb the top of the roller.** Get low, stay centered, all that stuff.

6. **Push down the backside.** A sweet manual is only decoration unless you get a great pump on the way out. Push hard and prepare to manual the next pair.

Pump-manualing between two rollers

| 1. Absorb roller slightly rearward. | 2. Keep front wheel high. | 3. Push down with legs, pull back with arms. | 4. Set wheel on roller. | 5. Absorb top of roller. | 6. Push down backside. |

Pumping a Turn

Pumping a turn is like pumping a hole that's been turned sideways. The first half of the turn is like the backside of a bump; the second half of the turn is like the frontside.

All the good stuff happens in the beginning of the turn. Get heavy in the first half; then get light in the second half.

1. **Enter low, just like when you absorb a roller.** As with rollers, the lower you get, the more pump you can access.

2. **Extend into the belly of the turn, like pumping the back of a roller.** When the turn starts turning, you should start pushing. Try to be fully extended at the midpoint of the turn. The harder you push—and the better you time it with the arc of the turn—the more pump you'll get, and the easier step 3 will be.

3. **Absorb the exit and set up for the next turn.** The exit of a linked turn is like a virtual roller, and it should be treated as such. Pull hard. Pull yourself low. Swing your bike into the next entrance. Once you enter the cycle, keep working it. Singletrack will never be the same.

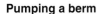

Pumping a berm

3. Absorb the exit (like another roller) and set up for the next turn!

2. Extend into the belly of the turn, like pumping the back of a roller.

1. Enter low, just like you're absorbing a roller.

Applying Pump on Real Trails

It's easiest to learn pump on a BMX track or pump track. The rollers are smooth, the shapes are obvious, and you can repeat the same move over and over without distractions.

Once you program your mind and body to pick up for every front and push down every back, your trail riding will change forever—and for the better. One day you'll be riding a trail you've ridden a hundred times, and all of a sudden, you'll see a red dotted line going right over those big rocks, instead of around them. That's OK: Go for it!

Even if you don't actively gain speed, you'll gain control, confidence, and braaap!

Pumping a natural roller

4. Extend fully for max pump.   **3.** Push front end down backside.   **2.** Bend low and absorb high spot.   **1.** Extend legs into low spot.

And Keep in Mind

Look for your opportunities.   Actively seek pumpworthy lines. The fronts of holes and the backs of humps, rocks, logs, and roots all beg to be pumped. Great riders seldom coast along; they constantly wring speed from the terrain. The more actively you scan the trail ahead, the more pump you'll get, and the better you'll ride overall.

Unload the fronts.   Beware frontsides. At best they slow you down. At worst they buck you into oblivion. Before you pump the back, you have to get over the front. You can unload, manual, hop, jump, or skip. Do whatever suits your fancy, as long as you have enough range of motion to push down the back—and as long as you don't bash into the thing full force.

Pump small things.   You don't need a long ramp. All you need is a little slope, a rock, or even a tiny root. Anything is better than nothing.

Pump rough things.   If you try to pedal through a jumbly rock garden, you'll stab a pedal and catapult onto your noggin. If you try to coast, you'll bog down and fall on your shoulder. We say bah-hooey to both of those options. Instead, try to pump the backsides of the bigger rocks. A rock garden threatens a hundred ways to kill you, but it promises a hundred places to catch backside.

The rougher it is, the more you have to pump.   Like we said, even if you're not actively trying to gain speed, the act of pumping keeps you riding the wave of the terrain. You won't hit things so hard. You won't get bounced around so much. You won't want to go back to work on Monday.

Pump on uphills.   You can use the pump on any downslope, even if it's on a climb. Say an uphill trail dips into a creek bed and then climbs the opposite bank. Pedal your arse off as usual; then pump the slope down into the bed. Unload as you zoom up the rise, and you'll be golden.

THE GNARLIER IT GETS . . .

. . . the more aggressively you have to pump.
   The faster you're going, and the bigger the front- and backsides, the harder you hit things and the farther you fly off things. To stay in control when things get silly, get low and aggressively work the terrain. The more you work it, the less it works you.

The best way to stay in control in big rocks: aggressively disconnect from the frontsides and connect with the backsides. Lee pushes for all he's worth.

Pumping aids technical climbing

| **1.** Enter in neutral climbing position. | **2.** Pull over front of bump. | **3.** Push into back of bump. |

Make clean technical climbs. The notion of light frontsides and heavy backsides works as well uphill as downhill. Next time you're clawing your way to a technical section, purposefully unweight as you go over rocks, roots, ledges, and water bars. If you can get some backside, too, so much the better. You'll be amazed at how much better, and easier, you climb.

Become the wave. Imagine that every trail is a sine wave. The wave might be small and choppy or big and swoopy, but every trail has an overall shape and flow. As a rider, you are a sine wave of energy. When your wave gets into phase with the terrain's wave, you'll be smooth. When your wave pre-acts the terrain—staying one step ahead, as with aggressive pump—you'll be *fast*.

Think 3-D. At the highest level, pumping integrates bumps and turns into one constant, multidimensional sine wave of love. Learn to pump bumps; then learn to pump turns. Relax and have fun. At some point you'll feel those skills start to converge—and then it'll be on like Donkey Kong!

Wax your buddies. Once you learn pump, *you* can be the rider who rails through crazy sections that just about kill everyone else and says something nonchalant like, "That was sweet."

Remember: A nice backside will take you far—in life and in bike riding.

PUMP TRACKS: THE HOTTEST THING SINCE SINGLETRACKS

Over the past few years, pump tracks have exploded from an unheard-of training method to fixtures in thousands of backyards, bike parks, and even city parks. Pump tracks are fun, safe, inexpensive, and relatively easy to build. Here are the essentials:

What: A pump track is a continuous loop of berms and rollers that can be ridden—no, *ripped*—without pedaling. Pump tracks are sprouting up all over the world; they fit anywhere and serve all sorts of riders.

Why: For land managers, pump tracks safely attract and entertain riders who feel threatened by jumps, drops, and skinnies. For riders, pump tracks are fun, offer a great workout, and build new skills. Once riders learn to pump terrain, every bump on every trail becomes a way to increase speed and control.

Who: Everyone. Kids play. Experienced riders learn new skills. Hard-core riders try new combos. Families and friends hang out. Lee has been busy building pump tracks around Colorado, and they have become magnets for the local riding communities. No one is left out. Everyone has fun. And if your kids want to try cross-country, that wouldn't be so bad!

Where: You can fit a sweet track pretty much anywhere: in a backyard, next to a BMX track, or next to a parking lot. Any shape will do as long as you have at least 600 square feet (20 × 30 feet) (56 sq m; 6 × 9 m) to work with. The biggest tracks are about 150 × 150 feet (46 × 46 m) . Most tracks are about 50 × 50 feet (15 × 15 m). A very slight grade (1 to 2 percent) is ideal for drainage; a 10 percent grade is the max. You can dig up the endemic dirt, but it's best to import topsoil; the track packs harder, drains better, and lasts longer.

How: Start with the outside loop. Build the berms first; then space rollers evenly along the straights. Every surface should slant up, down, or sideways—you can't pump flat ground! Keep everything smooth and gradual so beginners don't strike their pedals (test this by pedaling around the track). Add one or more crossover lines to multiply the options. Use the slope or drains to keep water from pooling on the track.

In the beginning, water the track before every ride. Over time the surface will become hard, fast, and super fun.

For more pump track guidelines and design samples, check out Lee's book (or e-book) *Welcome to Pump Track Nation: How to build the best pump track on Earth—Yours* on www.leelikesbikes.com. Lee designs and builds pump tracks and dirt-jump parks for individuals, companies, and parks.

Zach Lewis rocks some airy style at the pump track he and Lee built in Keystone, Colorado. He built speed for this jump without pedaling.

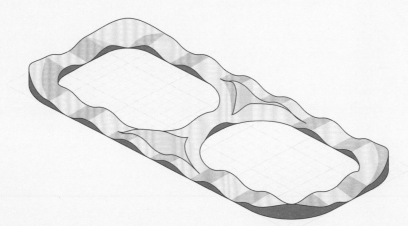

International standard pump track design, from www.leelikesbikes.com.

SHOOT YOUR TROUBLES

Problem: You feel your head and torso rocking back and forth through the bumps, even when you're going slow.

Solution: First, loosen up. Second, make sure your hands are following the terrain. If a bump is 12 inches (30 cm) tall, your hands have to move at least 12 inches (the height of the bump plus the compression of your suspension).

Problem: Your head and torso are staying level, and everything feels smooth, but you still can't gain or maintain speed.

Solution: Add some leg. Lee has taught hundreds of riders how to pump, and 90 percent of them have trouble controlling their legs like this. Make sure you're fully extended in the space between the bumps, and fully compressed (as low as you can get) on the tops of the bumps.

Problem: You keep hitting your seat.

Solution: Lower it. Even farther. If your bike's seat won't go low enough, consider a different seatpost—or a different bike.

Problem: Your low-speed pump feels good, but when you get going fast, you start hitting things and getting out of whack.

Solution: This is a good problem to have. As you go faster, you have to be more proactive. Pick up your front wheel before you reach the frontside, and push down the backside as hard as you can. This becomes a cycle: The harder you push, the earlier you can pull; the earlier you pull, the harder you can push.

Problem: You are a strong climber and a good all-around rider on your bike of choice, but you just can't seem to loosen up and rock the pump.

Solution: This is another common problem, especially among longtime XC riders. You need a change of venue. Get yourself a DJ hardtail or BMX cruiser. It will feel strange at first, but that strangeness might just open your body and mind to this whole new style of riding.

Pump isn't just a way to gain speed without pedaling. It's a whole philosophy of riding. It's the act of melding yourself with the terrain, of following its contour, of using its shape to your advantage. Without pump, mountain biking is fun. With pump, mountain biking is the most awesome thing you've ever done. Whichever your riding style, do yourself a favor and learn to pump. You'll enjoy this great sport at a whole new level.

Drop Like a Feather

You're flying down the A-Line trail at the Whistler Mountain Bike Park in British Columbia on your little slalom bike. The trail has a sweet rhythm: left, jump, right, jump, left, jump, right, jump. Up ahead, a few riders stand on the trail, looking down. Oh, yeah, you remember: It's that big rock drop. You slow down, cut to the right side, and take off. The crushing gravel and pounding bumps disappear in a rush of wind and weightlessness. You fall, fall, fall to a little downslope, land with a squish, and set up for the next left. Aah . . . good living on the front line of the mountain bike revolution.

Dropoffs have been part of mountain biking since the beginning, but today's trails and riding styles incorporate more and bigger drops than ever. Normal riders take vertical lines on cross-country trails, stunts are popping up everywhere, and the neighborhood kids are hucking off 50-foot (15 m) cliffs. When you learn to take off safely and land smoothly, you'll have more freedom and fun anywhere.

Land Smoothly

Elliott Hoover boosts a big one on his hardtail, proving, once again, that technique will get you farther than suspension. Note his low, level torso.

So you can bottom your 9-inch freeride bike off a curb? Don't be too proud of yourself. Smooth landings are where it's at. Save your body, save your bike, save the world.

Minimize the drop. If you're just out riding, find a line that drops less and aims you downward toward the landing instead of flipping you skyward. When you reach your takeoff, crouch your body as low as possible so your body doesn't have to fall as far. Get your bike back on the ground as soon and as smoothly as possible. There's nothing cool about breaking bottom-bracket spindles and ankle bones.

Keep your front end up until your rear takes off. Dropping one wheel at a time is dangerous business: If your chainring catches the lip, you pitch forward. If your front wheel falls into the landing crater, you flop over the bars. If your rear rolls forward while your front drops straight down, you become a human catapult. The bottom line: Until you're completely airborne, keep your front wheel level with or above your rear wheel. Word.

Use speed to your advantage. The faster you go, the more easily you keep your front end up until your rear end drops. If you go fast enough, you hardly have to do anything to match your bike's attitude to that of the trail. Speed lets you clear gnarly rocks and bad landings. Flat landings feel smoother when you land with momentum than when you land slowly and stick to the ground.

Match your landing to the slope. On flat landings, get your rear wheel down first. This minimizes your free fall and lets you absorb the landing with your legs. On downhill landings, get your front wheel down first. Steep landings are so smooth you'll wonder when you're going to land. If you do land rear wheel first on a downslope, your front end will slam down, and you'll be bummed.

Big is cool, but don't be a fool. If the drop is lower than your knee pads, you can usually roll right off it, no big deal. But when drops grow taller than your wheels, you gotta start paying attention to your form, and you should definitely look before you leap. As Mr. T would say, "Don't jack the height until you're droppin' right."

Fast Drop to Downhill

Whether you know it or not, you probably do drops all the time. You might not session 20-foot (6 m) cliffs, but as you fly down trails, you spend a lot of time out of contact with the ground: You haul over holes, blip beyond boulders, and soar beyond slopes. Really, a "drop" happens anytime you carry enough speed to arc above the ground.

YOU DROP MORE OFTEN THAN YOU REALIZE

A fast, ledgy descent is a series of small high-speed drops. If you have speed:

- ○ Get low to minimize the drop.
- ○ Keep your bike level off the edge. If you're going super fast, all it takes is a slight rearward shift.
- ○ Extend your landing gear.
- ○ Absorb the (gentle) landing.
- ○ Repeat.

When you have speed, you can keep your wheels out of the rocks (and the horse poop).

The art of dropping is the art of controlling the attitude of your bike and landing smoothly. When you master this art, you can hop over objects at speed, skip rough sections, and maintain momentum when the ground drops out from beneath you. By the way, a drop is basically the second half of a jump. When you can land smoothly from a takeoff, you're ready to propel yourself skyward.

Cool. When you encounter drops on your favorite trail (or cliff), try not to jump upward. Stay low and rely on speed. The faster you go, the easier this is.

If you can manual consistently, you are ready to try small high-speed drops.

1. Approach the takeoff in your low attack position. Get low. Lower.
2. Preload forward as if you were going to do a manual, which you are.
3. As your wheel reaches the edge, shift back into a manual.
4. Keep your front wheel up until your rear wheel leaves the takeoff.
5. Come back to center and match the angle of your bike to the angle of the landing.
6. On a steep landing, land front wheel first, just as if you were landing a double jump.
7. Absorb the impact (if any) and be on your way. Braaap!

Dropping into a turn. Steep trails frequently drop over outcroppings and then fold directly into tight, rutted turns. Anytime you drop directly into a turn, take the drop as you normally would; then immediately center your weight so you can corner well. If you hit the turn with your weight still in the back seat, your front tire will wash out.

Fast drop to downslope   While this might look scary from the ladder, a little confidence and speed makes it feel easy.

Slow Drop to Flat

Dropping off a rock, ladder, or loading dock at low speed is actually a lot harder than soaring off an outcropping at Mach 5. This move is both old-school trials and new-school North Shore. It requires you to lift your front wheel and keep it there, and then absorb a blunt landing.

Practice on a low curb from a standstill. As you get the hang of controlling your bike's attitude, step it up a little at a time. You want to avoid the thing where your front wheel falls to the ground and your rear wheel or chainring tags the edge of the drop, sending you over the bars for certain.

Use this approach anytime you don't have enough speed to quickly clear the takeoff. The slower you go, the more you have to pop your front tire up and accelerate to keep it up.

If you can pedal wheelie consistently, you are ready to try small low-speed drops.

1. Preload forward.
2. Shift back into a pedal wheelie.
3. Accelerate all the way off the edge.
4. Keep the front end up!
5. Extend your legs and land rear wheel first.
6. Suck up the impact. Right on!

When you you're going slow and you don't want to roll down a ledge, wheelie off the edge and keep your front end up until you land. Note the body position: right over the bottom bracket.

HOW FAR CAN YOU DROP ON YOUR BIKE?

Well, that depends on the steepness of the landing and your smoothness as a rider. If you're a meathead, you can destroy a freeride bike on a 2-foot (61 cm) flat drop. If you're a kung fu master, you can finesse an XC race bike down an 8-foot (2.4 m) steep drop.

At a press launch for a major bike company's (not Specialized) 4-inch (100 mm) trail bike, they said the bike was designed to withstand a 4-foot (1.2 m) drop to flat. How they quantified that is anyone's guess, but that seems like a good guideline. If you're smooth.

Lee coaxes his carbon Stumpjumper about six feet down to a steep, smooth landing. Slowing down was the hard part!

Half-Pipe Drop-In

Your buddies are killing the mega half pipe at your local skate park. From where you quiver atop the ramp, the coping seems dangerously abrupt, and the walls seem impossibly steep. You've never seen anything like this on a trail. If you creep in, you'll catch your rear wheel on the coping. If you fly straight off, you'll land flat bottom—14 feet (4.3 m) down. It's time for a drop-in. Uncork this baby on half pipes, quarter pipes, and other types of skate ramps. It also has its place on extra-abrupt on-trail transitions.

1. Ride across the platform, almost parallel to the edge. Get both tires as close to the edge as possible. The closer you get, the less likely your rear tire will clip the coping, and the longer your transition to flat.

2. Turn in and pop your front wheel over the coping. Push your nose down as if you were landing a double, but even more so.

3. Hop your rear wheel over the coping. Make sure you clear the edge. If your rear tire clips, you're looking at a 10-foot (3 m) flat landing—on your head.

4. Get your tires onto the ramp as soon as possible. Extend your arms and legs. Land with both wheels at the same time or with your front wheel barely first. Ride it out, baby!

SHOOT YOUR TROUBLES

Problem: You land hard and bottom your bike. Despite what you might think, this is not cool. Not cool for your bike. Not cool for your body.

Solutions: First of all, make sure you have the right spring rate and sag (see the suspension setup section on page 36). Then: (1) start the drop with your weight as low on the bike as possible; (2) extend your limbs to get your wheels on the ground as soon as possible; and (3) absorb the landing with your arms' and legs' full travel. Important: Don't increase the amplitude until you can land smoothly 1,000 times out of 999 tries.

Problem: On low-speed drops, you land front wheel first in a gnarly nose wheelie, which quickly leads to head-first landings.

Solutions: Get more pop with your pedals and keep accelerating until both wheels leave the takeoff. Lean back more. If your form is perfect and you're still a nose-heavy nose-lander, try a shorter stem and taller bars. Don't mess with drops until you can drop off a curb perfectly 1,000 times out of 999.

Problem: On high-speed drops to downhill landings, you land with the rear wheel first and your front wheel slams hard.

Solution: As always, relax. When you leave the takeoff, match the angle of your bike to the angle of the landing. Your arms will be relatively straight, and your legs will be bent. When the front wheel touches down, straighten your legs to contact the ground; then absorb the landing.

Problem: When you drop into a half pipe or something similar, your rear wheel clips the edge.

Solution: First, good luck with your recovery. That 10-foot (3 m) drop to flat is gonna hurt. Second, as you enter the half pipe, really hop upward and push your front wheel downward. This will help rotate your rear wheel upward.

Whether you ride urban, trails, or full-on freeride, enjoy all kinds of drops. Clunk to flat, sail to downslope, and aim into a vertical wall. When you get the hang of those crazy landings, do you know what comes next? Jumping!

CHAPTER 9

Jump With the Greatest of Ease

ou zip along one of your favorite singletracks. A drop falls to your left and a rock outcropping looms ahead. You've always followed the main line around the rocks, but today you're carrying more speed than usual. As you approach the rocks, your mind's eye draws a dotted line straight across them. You're feeling the flow and you let it happen. There's an instant of heavy g's as you pump the face of the first rock, a moment of weightlessness as you fly over the outcropping, and then a gradual reweighting as you roll down the backside and rail into the turn. Aah . . . if you could bottle that feeling, you'd be rich.

Jumping isn't just for crazy kids. Maybe you want the smoothest way over a rock section. Maybe you hit a water bar and find yourself flying, and you want to know what to do. Or maybe you want to have fun on a local slalom course. Whether you're a roadie, a cross-country rider, or a downhill racer, it pays to be at least somewhat comfortable with flight. As they say, "To air is human. To land safely is divine."

Learn to Jump

In the first edition of *Mastering Mountain Bike Skills,* we said the best way to learn jumping is to start as a kid. Kids are unencumbered by fear, and when the inevitable crashes happen, they bounce without injury (or fear).

Although it's always best to start these things young, Lee has since taught many adults how to jump, and he believes any good rider can become a solid jumper. Crashes are not inevitable. If you follow the right progression, jumping becomes a natural outgrowth of the more fundamental skills.

Prerequisite Skills

Before you take to the air, you *must* be smooth and consistent with these skills:

- **Attack position.** The attack position gives you the balance and range of motion to boost powerfully, fly gracefully, and land smoothly.
- **Hopping.** Hopping teaches you to load and unload your bike. The higher you can hop, the more boost you can get off jumps. It also teaches short flight skills.

This table is perfect for learning. You can land as short as you want without consequences. Not that Bobbi Watt has any problems.

- **Dropping to flat and downslopes.** This skill lets you practice your landings independent of takeoffs.
- **Pumping.** Pumping is perhaps the holy grail of all riding skills. It teaches you to load and unload in time with the terrain, and it trains you to let your bike follow an arc while you stay centered over your pedals.
- **Doing all this with flat pedals.** With clips, you can do a lot wrong and still make it. Flats force you to load and unload correctly, and to keep your feet flowing with the bike.

Make sure your fundamental skills are dialed. Start small and work your way up. Never, ever, ride with stress. If you feel freaked out, go back to a smaller jump. The more confident you feel, the more successful you'll be, and the faster you'll learn.

Location, Location, Location

There are two reasons beginners might want to avoid popular jumping spots:

- The dudes who build jumps care more about huge air and tricks than providing you with a nice, safe jump to learn on. They build stuff big and steep, with gaping holes between takeoff and landing lips. We don't know why, but they always put weird stuff into the gaps: tools, jagged pieces of metal, appliances, that kind of stuff. These guys focus on takeoffs and landings. What's in between means little to them.
- There are usually a bunch of characters hanging around, most of whom are better jumpers than you. If you are self-conscious at all, either you'll feel lame and stay out of their way or you'll feel pressured to try things you're not qualified to do. It's sort of like the adage, "Don't look at supermodels. They will only make you feel fat."

BMX tracks are good places to learn because the jumps are rounded and safe to roll over. It's hard to get a lot of practice, though, with the limited sessions and all the kids asking for your autograph.

Build Your Own

You need a nice beginner's jump.

- **Height:** Two to three feet (61 to 91 cm), with a 1-to-3 height-to-length ratio.
- **Takeoff:** To make a mellow jump, make your lip transition smoothly from flat at the bottom to 30 degrees at the top. Neutral jumps are usually around 45 degrees. Trick jumps are 60 degrees or steeper.
- **Top:** Flat and about 8 feet long to start. You want your entire bike to fit.

THIS ISN'T AS HARD AS YOU THINK

In my teaching, I (Lee) have seen lots of great all-around riders freeze up and become useless when they try to jump. It's like they're two different people: Awesome Jones on trails, Weak Willy on jumps.

The fact is, all-around trail riding is more technically demanding than pure jumping. Whatever you're riding, try to ride it with the same confidence.

A perfect beginners' jump

This tabletop might appear too mellow, but you'll be *stoked* when you start clearing it.

Takeoff angle: 30°
Height: 3 feet

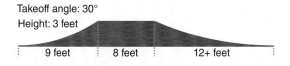

9 feet   8 feet   12+ feet

- ⊙ **Landing:** Almost twice as long and way less steep than your takeoff. This sort of landing gives you less backside pump, but it gives you a bigger target. Save the pinpoint landings for later.
- ⊙ **Approach and run-out:** Long, clean, and smooth. You should have nothing to think about except your jump.

On your first tabletop jump, you can work on your launching, flying, and landing without worrying about coming up short (smashing into the face of the landing ramp) or impaling yourself on an old shovel handle.

You can start with a single jump and a flat landing, but the ground will be a lot lower than the top of your tabletop, and those landings will hurt. Plus, jumping is all about the feeling you get when you land on the backside. The first time you clear the top of your table, you will be stoked beyond all recognition.

Preflight Checklist

Don't try to be a bloody tough guy. Not "bloody" in the British expletive intensifying sense, as in "Steve Peat bloody knows how to party." We mean "bloody" in the vital-fluids-spewing-from-your-body sense.

- ❑ **Helmet.** (Preferably full-face.)
- ❑ **Gloves.** Your hands are involved almost every time you crash. When you scrape your palms off, you will miss them.
- ❑ **Pads.** In order of importance: knee, elbow, hip. Heck, there's nothing wrong with full armor.
- ❑ **Flat pedals.** Flats allow more foot jive for balance, and, of course, they facilitate quick dismounts. They also force you to load and unload correctly.
- ❑ **Low seat.** This helps you pump takeoffs and absorb those Evel Knievel landings.
- ❑ **Confidence.** Your base skills should be dialed, and you should know what you're doing. If you can't see and feel yourself doing a jump successfully, step it down.

Jumping basics   A smooth landing comes from a relaxed flight and the perfect takeoff. Sound easy? Keep reading.

Takeoff: Pump the lip just the right amount.

Landing: Smooth, baby, smooth.

Flight: Stay loose and let the bike move.

Takeoff

What you do on the lip determines what happens to you in the air. If you absorb the face of the jump, you stay low. If you press into the face, you go high. If you just sort of ride into the jump, you get bucked over your bars.

Catching good air is all about balance and timing. Here's how to pump a jump to catch moderate air. (Note: This is just like bunny hopping, except you are more neutral front to rear.)

1. Coast in a neutral position. Center yourself over your pedals, arms and legs slightly bent. Pedals should be level.

2. Crouch down as you approach the jump. This is all in your legs. Let your arms follow.

3. Your crouch should be lowest when you reach the bottom of the face. Note how the front tire is on the face and the rear tire is just reaching it.

4. From your low position, immediately begin to spring upward. Don't hang out in a crouch. Bend down and then immediately pop back up like you're bouncing on a trampoline. This is the crux move.

5. Push down with your legs as you ride up the face. The harder you cram your bike into the face of the jump, the more lift you'll get. Push all the way up the face. Big jumps require a longer, slower push than tiny jumps. For max lift, straighten your legs all the way as you reach the lip. This should be almost all leg power; your arms follow.

6. As you leave the lip, bend your arms and legs to let your bike rise into your body. This gives you added clearance, and it helps to keep you loose in the air.

RELAX, IT'S JUST BIKE RIDING

Remember that jumping requires the same skills and movements as pumping and hopping. When you hit that jump, do it with the same relaxed focus as you would have hopping a curb. If you can't hop a curb, you have no business jumping. If you do go for the jump, keep these points in mind:

- If you feel yourself tensing, wiggle your knees and elbows a bit.
- Make your hands as loose and light as possible. (Lee finds that the less he uses his arms, the smoother he jumps.)
- Gaze over the takeoff toward the landing.
- Have a "soft" focus. If you're hyperfocused on the lip itself, you'll either stop on it (because you're not ready for what comes next) or you'll be stiff and off balance (because your focus is on the ground, and that's where your body will want to go).

Flight

In the beginning, just stay over the center of your bike and stay loose, even if you feel off balance. If you relax, your body will balance itself automatically. If you stiffen, you'll stay off balance all the way until you hit the ground.

When you first start out, it's hard not to be a dead sailor—a stiff and styleless mannequin. To practice proper lack of tension, loosen your grip and move around on your bike. Turn your bars here and there. Do anything but be stiff. Tricks are cool because you have to relax to do them. Eventually, you'll need something to do in the air—mess with your tear-offs or adjust your clutch lever like a motocrosser.

After you get the hang of this, try bringing your bike up into your body. When you pop off the lip, bend your elbows and knees and let your bike come up toward you. This will help you get extra air and give you more range of motion for pumping the backsides of jumps (see the sections on dirt-jumper style and rhythm, pages 148 and 153).

Stay balanced over your pedals and let your bike follow a natural arc through the air. This is just like pumping over a big roller (except that the top of the roller is missing!).

Curtis Keene is neutral and relaxed as he boosts this monster double at the SolVista Nationals. Braaap!

TIME YOUR JUMP

When you first get on a diving board or trampoline, you bounce up and down to get a feel for the springiness. You time your jumps so you sink all the way down with maximum downforce and spring back up with maximum upforce. If you jump up too soon, you get ahead of the upward push, and you don't go very high. If you jump up too late, you get kicked harshly in the feet. It's the same on bike jumps.

Proper timing depends on a jump's size, your speed, and the springiness of your bike.

	Jump size	Bike speed	Bike suspension
Slow pump	Big	Slow	Soft
Fast pump	Small	Fast	Firm

Landing

To begin with, you should land on the flat top of your tabletop jump.

Land with your back wheel first.   This is like landing a flat drop. Don't drop the bike. Reach your feet downward, set the rear wheel down, and then bend your knees to absorb the impact. When your front tire lands, use your arms to absorb that impact (see the section on dropping to flat ground, page 135). You should land like an airplane, only smoother and quieter. But go ahead and make that tire-screeching sound if you want. As you get comfortable, hit your jump with more and more speed.

Spot your landing.   Look where you want to put your wheels; then put them there. This gives you a specific place to aim for and helps your body prepare for a nice landing rather than brace for a random impact. Life lesson: How confident can you be when you have no idea where you're going?

Hold it close.   If you're holding your bike high and close to your body, you get to choose when you extend your landing gear. If you're extended and stiff in the air, you land whenever physics dictate. OK: You've spotted your landing, and you're flying in the right position. A sweet landing is easy.

Backside!   Pretty soon your front wheel will start to reach the backside of your landing ramp. The landing will feel much smoother. This is very cool. Be careful not to land with the rear wheel on the end of the flat and your front wheel high in the air. Your front wheel will slam onto the backside really hard, and you might get pitched over the bars.

Try to land with your front wheel first or with both wheels at the same time. While you're in the air, extend your arms to touch the front wheel down on the backside. You're only a touch of speed away from a perfect landing.

This is a perfect landing: Front wheel then rear wheel, in exactly the same place. Brian is super low and ready to pump the heck out of this backside.

Perfect landing.   Your front wheel will land right at the top of the landing ramp, and your rear wheel will land in exactly the same place. When you get it right, you'll hardly have to absorb the impact. The steeper the landing, the smoother it'll be. After a really steep landing, you can spend the whole day thinking you're still in the air. It's that smooth.

Warning: Jumping is addictive. Small jumps lead to big jumps. Consider yourself warned.

Rigid or Suspension for Jumping?

BMX bikes jump effortlessly. Their tightness returns all the energy you put into the takeoff. Hardtail mountain bikes are more forgiving, but the front suspension and bigger frame and wheels take the edge off the spring action. Suspension bikes are the most forgiving of all, but they suck up a lot of your energy.

PROS OF RIGID

- ○ You can jump higher and faster with less effort.
- ○ You get a better pump in rhythm sections.
- ○ You learn more precise timing.
- ○ Smaller, lighter bikes are easier to whip around in the air.

PROS OF SUSPENSION

- ○ Your timing doesn't have to be as perfect.
- ○ You get a margin of error in case you come up short or land flat.
- ○ Suspension bikes can provide more traction in turns—if your jumps have turns.

The bottom line: If you're afraid of hard landings, jump with suspension. If you want to become a great jumper, jump with a hardtail. If you really want to become a master, learn on a 20.

Dial Your Jumping Style

All jumps are different. They're big, small, tall, short, steep, gradual, on fire, and everything in between. You can hit them with mega speed, or you can botch a turn and arrive too slow. In the real world of dirt jumping, you must alter your style to suit the situation.

The two basic ways to hit a jump are max-air dirt-jumper style and ultra-low racer style. Most jumps require a mix of the two techniques. Learn both and dispense as needed.

Matt Vujicevich pumped this double hard and got plenty of air in return for his effort.

Curtis Keene sucked up this same jump and stayed nice and low. Same entrance speed, different result.

Get Max Air—Dirt-Jumper Style

This slows you down but gives your bike max loft. Use this technique when you feel like you need to reach for a landing, on really tall, steep dirt jumps where you want to fly high and be a trickster, or on short, lippy jumps where you have to go pretty slow and pump high to catch the backside.

1. Compress your body deep into the lip. It should feel like you're bouncing on a trampoline, trying to get max height.
2. Press against the lip as it pushes your bike upward and backward, creating maximum compression between you and the ground.
3. Explode upward at the very top of the lip. It should feel like a mammoth broad jump.
4. Keep your body high and extended on takeoff.
5. Lift the bike up into your body for extra air, and to give you room to adjust.

Mess around. Notice how different timing and oomph affect your height and distance. You'll be amazed at how slow you can go and still clear lips. Compete with your friends to see who can clear a jump the slowest.

Dirt-jumper style

Max pressure into transition. | Explode off lip. | Fly! Be free! | Extend to catch backside. | Must . . . go . . . higher.

You lose speed.

24 mph   18 mph

Stay Low—Racer Style

Sometimes you want to keep your momentum, barely clear the landing, and then get back to business. This isn't just a racing technique: Use it when you're going so fast you might overshoot a jump, or when you need to land quickly and nail a corner. Here's how to suck up a jump at speed.

1. Let your bike roll into the lip, but keep your body high. If there's a small dip before the lip, keep your body high and push your bike into the hole.
2. Coast up the lip without pressing down. With dirt-jumper style, you want max tension between your bike and the face of the jump. With racer style, you want as little tension as possible.
3. "Suck up" the lip. As you reach the top and the lip pushes your bike upward and backward, pull the bike into your body. It's the opposite of the dirt-jumper explosion. It's more like an implosion. Don't force any energy into the ground; absorb it all with your body.

4. Keep your body low and compressed on takeoff.

5. Get as low as you can in the air. Pull the bike close to you, and be ready to push it into the landing.

Play around with this. See how fast you can go without overshooting the landing.

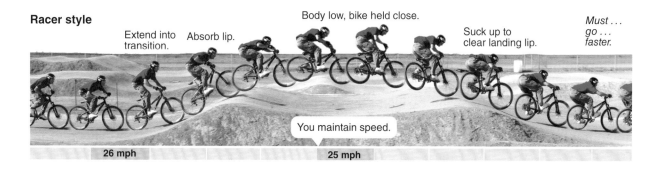

Racer style

Extend into transition.

Absorb lip.

Body low, bike held close.

Suck up to clear landing lip.

Must . . . go . . . faster.

You maintain speed.

26 mph

25 mph

Save Yourself

You might be going too slow, or maybe you didn't pump hard enough. Either way, you're coming up short. There are some things you can do.

Come up short like a pro

Pro MTB/BMX racer Chris Powell demonstrates a perfect case at the Olympic Training Center in Chula Vista, California. His head goes in a straight line and he loses almost no speed. The key, believe it or not, is being very active and aggressive—as if you're proactively pumping the landing.

1. Extend into the landing.

2. Right before you hit, starting pulling the bike upward.

3. Suck up the landing as much as possible.

4. Actively push into the backside.

20" BMX bikes allow more range of motion (and better casing) than any mountain bike.

Lower your landing gear. If you're not going to make the landing, you'll know it as soon as you take off. This is the one situation in which picking your nose is a bad thing. Lift the front end, drop the rear, and actively absorb the impact, much like sucking up a lip.

Pick up your bike. If you feel like you're not going quite fast enough to clear the jump, use your best dirt-jumper style and pump the heck out of the face. As you leave the lip, pull your bike up with your arms and legs.

Double-pump it. You're flying along and it's clear you won't quite make the landing. This all happens in the fraction of a second.

- Lift your bike just a bit.
- Push it down.
- Violently pull it back up. The up-and-down dynamic gives you more upward mojo than a single lift.

Lift your rear wheel. Say your front wheel is going to clear the backside, but you need a little something extra to get your rear wheel over the lip.

- Grip the bars really tightly.
- Rotate your hands forward as you push forward and down.
- Lift your feet as the rear end comes up.

Abandon ship. If things look messy, get rid of your bike and try to land on your feet. Tuck and roll. Keep your arms and legs inside until the ride comes to a complete stop.

GOING HUGE

How far you can jump a bike has yet to be determined. In the first edition of this book, we said that with the right jump, the right speed, and the right landing, there's no reason you can't go over 100 feet (30 m). In February 2006 Jason Rennie was towed up to speed by a Yamaha YZ250 and jumped 133.6 feet (41 m).

When I (Brian) did that huge jump for *ChainSmoke 2*, it was a little scary the first time. The actual jump wasn't that tall—the takeoff was 3 feet (about 1 m); then it dropped 5 feet (1.5 m), and there was a long tabletop with a long landing. The thing was, I was going so fast. I knew I wouldn't get hurt if I came up short, but I knew it would be harsh. When I hit it the first time, it popped me higher than I expected and I flew 87 feet (27 m). The next few times I didn't go as fast, and I went only 75 or 80 feet (23 or 24 m) to backside. It was actually pretty easy once I got used to the speed.

Handle All Sorts of Jumps

After you master a variety of lips, jumping styles, distances, and landings, you're ready to step up to the fun stuff. These advanced jumps require solid all-around skills, so if you haven't done your homework, expect to be grounded.

Sail Over Doubles

Doubles are a total mind trip. Technically, they're identical to tabletops. You pop off the takeoff ramp, you fly through the air, and then you land on the backside. The fact that there's a gaping hole between the lips should make no difference to you. But it does. Right now in the world, 1,389 riders are intimidated by doubles that would be pieces of cake if the gaps were filled with nice, smooth dirt. This is a classic case of being afraid of what *might* happen.

When you jump in the real world, you usually jump over something: a rock, a stream, a big hole with a shovel in it. You should learn to judge takeoffs and landings so you don't have to worry about landing in random, terrible places. Don't tackle a double until you can perfectly backside a tabletop of the same persuasion. You should not hurl your carcass off a lip unless you believe you'll actually reach the landing. Start small and slowly work your way up.

If the takeoff and landing are at the same elevation, jumping a double is exactly like jumping a tabletop with the same shape. That said, here are some things to keep in mind:

- **Spot your landing** and then scan forward from there. Do not look into the hole. Stop it!
- **Get your back tire over the lip,** especially when the front of the landing ramp is sharp and steep. Conundrum: If you prepare yourself for clipping the lip, you'll drop your feet and you *will* hit the lip.

Elliott Hoover boosts a *biiiig* double at a Boulder, Colorado, DJ spot.

○ **'Tis better to overshoot** than to undershoot. Most riders "feel out" a double by landing short; then they gradually work up to a smooth landing. This is bad a for a few reasons: (1) You're dealing with hard landings; (2) you risk an over-the-bars experience; and (3) you erode your confidence. We say it's better to go for it the first time. Err on the side of distance. If you overshoot by a bit, you can always back off. This is much smoother—and more confidence-boosting—than starting too short.

○ **Nail step-downs:** When the landing lies below the takeoff, you don't need as much speed or pump to land cleanly. You have extra vertical speed by the time you fall to the landing, so coming up short hurts more than usual.

You maintain speed over step-downs. Note the backside boost on the landing.

DON'T BE AFRAID

Although step-ups can be visually arresting—there's nothing like hauling mail into a 6-foot-tall lip—well-built ones are actually pretty safe. By the time you reach the top, you've exhausted most of your momentum. If you come up short, it's usually a very soft impact.

This step-up at the Lyons Bike Park is actually a great learning jump. Its lip is tall but consistent, and its top is very forgiving. It's a favorite of little DJ kids *and* their XC dads.

○ **Step up to step-ups:** When the landing towers above the takeoff, you need extra speed and pump to clear it. Rhythm sections contain **step-ups** because they give you extra-jumbo backside. Step-ups are visually arresting—all you see is a wall of dirt—but the landings are actually smoother than **step-downs** and normal doubles. If you hit a step-up just right, you can set your bike softly on the landing, like a mother bird landing in her nest. How nice.

Carry extra speed into step-ups because the vert lip will slow you down.

Pump Rhythms

If there's one thing you should learn on your bike, it's jumping rhythm. When you get it right, it feels perfectly smooth, and the rhythmic weight-then-weightlessness is one of the most exquisite feelings on earth.

A **rhythm section** is usually a series of closely spaced double jumps. As you come down one landing, you transition immediately into the next takeoff. You must rhythmically pump the transitions to create speed for the jumps. Rhythm is a puzzle. You must get the first piece in order to get the second. If you screw up one double, the next is very hard to make.

Warning: Don't mess with rhythm until you've mastered pumping rollers and jumping double jumps. You should be able to handle a variety of lips, steepnesses, and speeds. Things go wrong quickly in rhythm.

Curtis Keene enters a sweet set at The Shells in Redwood City, California.

TIPS FOR SIMPLE RHYTHM

- ○ **Land as high as possible** on the landing ramp, front wheel first, followed by your rear wheel on the same spot. Do this with German precision.
- ○ **Press down** into your pedals as you reach the bottom of the face. You will feel an amazing acceleration. On a steep landing, it feels like the gas is wide open.
- ○ **Stay sharp.** Adjust for varying distances, steepnesses, and speeds. The most interesting rhythms require all of your jumping kung fu. Let's see what you've got.

Pumping rhythm   After you land the first jump, a good pump will more than double your speed for the second one.

2. Push your front end down. Get low and back.

3. As you reach the bottom of the landing slope, straighten your legs to push your bike into the transition.

1. Stay neutral and relaxed in the air.

—10 mph—   ——23 mph——   —9 mph—

Combine Rollers and Jumps

When you approach a set of rollers—or any takeoff and potential landing—consider the depth of the gap, the lippiness of the takeoff, and your speed. The deeper the gap, the more you want to jump over it. In order to jump, you need a certain amount of lip. If the lip is steep, you can hit it pretty slowly and pump it dirt-jumper style. If the lip is gradual, you need lots of speed. If you don't have enough speed to clear the gap, go ahead and manual across—and pump the backside for free speed while you're at it.

TO SUM IT UP

Deep gap + steep lip + fast approach = jump

Shallow gap + gradual lip + slow approach = roll or manual

Rhythm sections on BMX and bikercross tracks include various combinations of obstacles: single rollers, multiple rollers, tables, step-ups and step-downs. These rhythms are ultra-fun. They allow myriad approaches, from simply rolling all the way through to combining jumps and manuals in a stunning display of biking prowess.

IT'S ALL ABOUT THE PUMP

You can gain that last bit of speed by sneaking in a half-crank of the pedals, but that can upset your balance and force you to jump with your opposite foot forward. Rather than pedaling through jump sets, focus on pumping the landings, rollers, and berms. As a matter of fact, many "new-school" dirt jumpers rarely pedal within jump sets.

BMX Rhythm This section at Dacono BMX in Dacono, Colorado, looks simple but gives you plenty to play with.

Jump Hips

The only thing cooler than jumping is turning while you jump. You can't actually arc sideways while you're in the air, but you can rotate your bike so you land facing a new direction. Do this when a jump sits in a turn.

1. Look where you want to go and turn your bike across the lip of the jump.

2. Throw your head and body into the turn.

3. Turn your bars the way you want to go, and let the rear end swing around to the angle you want.

4. Straighten your bars to match the landing and suck it up, baby!

Get a Transfer

In a **transfer jump**, you jump to the side but land in basically the same direction you took off. You can use this to jump from line to line on a trail, or to jump from one line of jumps to another.

1. Ride across the lip in the direction you want to go. As always, look ahead.

2. Fly straight toward your target. Whee!

3. As you approach your landing, push down on your inside grip and turn your bars outward. This and a little body English will whip your rear end around and lean your bike a bit. You're setting yourself up to make a little turn down the backside of the jump.

4. Right before touchdown, turn your bars into the landing. This will straighten your bike and set you up for the next thing. Sweet.

KNOW YOUR PACKS

The cool people refer to rhythm sections as "six-packs" or "ten-packs" or whatever-number packs. A **six-pack** is three doubles, for a total of three lips and three landings.

Jump Into Turns

For the ultimate in three-dimensional fun, hit a double and land in a berm. It's easier than it seems: Handle the corner as if there's no jump and handle the jump as if there's no corner.

1. Set up for the turn as you leave the jump.
2. Fly toward the outside of the corner. You might need your hip or transfer skills. A little countersteer helps lay the bike into the turn.
3. Land with your wheels perpendicular to the ground. If you land in a left-hand berm, pitch your wheels out to the right, as if you're already railing the corner. You *will* be railing it in a second.
4. You're dropping into the berm with a lot of force, so you might as well pump it for some extra exit speed (see the section on pumping berms, page 99).

Lay Your Bike Flat

Few things are as stylish as laying your bike over in a nice, flat tabletop. In addition, tables let you pitch your bike over to land in a turn. Here's how to lay your bike down to the left:

Do a tabletop to the left

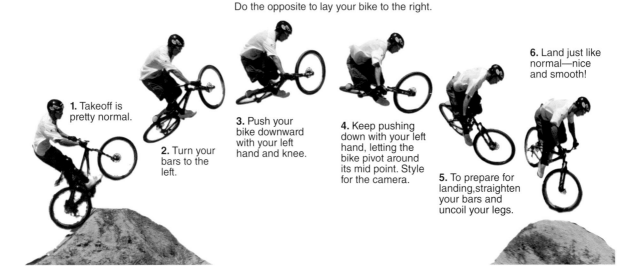

Do the opposite to lay your bike to the right.

1. Takeoff is pretty normal.

2. Turn your bars to the left.

3. Push your bike downward with your left hand and knee.

4. Keep pushing down with your left hand, letting the bike pivot around its mid point. Style for the camera.

5. To prepare for landing, straighten your bars and uncoil your legs.

6. Land just like normal—nice and smooth!

TABLE TIPS

- ○ Hip jumps make it easy to **flatten your bike**, because you're already slipping sideways through the air. It's hard to get your bike out, flat, and back again while you're going straight.

- ○ You can get your bike flatter when your front foot is on the bottom side. If you jump with your right foot forward, you'll rule at laying your bike to the right. You'll suck at doing it to the left. Sorry.

- ○ Keep a very loose grip, to allow your bike to move freely. Let your top hand turn on the grip. It might end up 180 degrees from where it started. That's OK. And stylish.

Turn-Down

If a tabletop is a stylish dirt jumper, the **turn-down** is his racer brother. A turn-down keeps your body low and gets your front wheel on the ground early. It works best when you're hipping or transferring, and you're going so fast you'll overclear the jump. To see an ultra-high-speed turn-down in action, watch James "Bubba" Stewart on a motocross track.

Say you want to turn-down into a left:

1. Turn across the face of the jump. This gets your body lower than if you ride straight off.

2. When your front wheel takes off, turn it even farther to the left, down toward the ground. Ha! See? A "turn-down."

3. Push your bike down. Keep turning the bars and let the rear end whip around.

4. Straighten your bars. Turn the wheel in the direction you want to go; then begin to straighten your arms and legs. At this speed it's easy to overclear the downslope, so really push your bike down to catch the backside.

5. Land front wheel first. The rear end might be whipped around when it lands, but that's OK. As long as you're steering in the direction you're heading, it's all good.

Turn it down   Uncork this baby next time you jump through a turn with way too much speed.

Bump Jump

You can use a square rock or curb as a takeoff to jump over a section. The challenge is, if you bash your front wheel into such an abrupt edge, it'll slow you down or knock you silly. In a **bump jump** you clear your front wheel and literally bump your rear wheel into the object, letting it bounce you skyward. Compared with bashing front wheel first, a bump jump preserves momentum and maintains control. Before you try this move, make sure you have manuals and jumps dialed.

Bump jump   Here's a nifty trick for those of you who have wired manuals and jumps.

Keep Pedaling Over a Jump

The gate drops and you explode with pedal-spinning fury. You and three other hungry racers, that is. A tabletop jump or roller lies between you and the first turn. This is no time to sail through the air—you gotta keep the power on. (This is also super-handy on trails.)

1. As you approach the hump, pedal hard and pull the front end up. You don't want your wheel bonking the face.

2. As your bike rides up the face, suck the bike up into you. Get way low and way back.

3. If it's a short hump, as in this photo, stay back on the bike and keep pedaling. If it's a long table, get over the center of your bike and pedal like normal, but as you reach the end of the table, get back over the rear of your bike.

4. When you reach the downslope, push downward—and keep pedaling!

To pedal over a series of humps, repeat this move: high, low, high, low. Braap braaap!

SHOOT YOUR TROUBLES

Problem: You land way short.

Solutions: Resist the temptation to go faster. Speed without skill creates more problems than solutions. Instead, focus on pumping the lip smoothly and powerfully. If that feeling eludes you, practice slow bunny hops over immovable objects. Once you get the feel of loading and unloading your bike, take it back to the jump.

Problem: You get off balance in the air. You've been known to land crooked, with unpleasant results.

Solution: As soon as you take off, return to your relaxed attack position. This puts you in the middle of your cockpit, with plenty of arm and leg range to make midair corrections.

Problem: You're nervous and tense every time you hit a certain jump.

Solution: Stop riding that jump! Step down to an easier jump. Do it 100 times perfectly, build your confidence, and then come back. But not until you can roll up to it with no trace of tension.

Problem: Your front wheel finds perfect backside, but your rear wheel clips the landing. You still roll down the ramp, but you lose a lot of speed.

Solution: Chances are your legs are too straight and your rear wheel is too low. Have someone watch you. If your front wheel and body are flying like the riders who are making it, then this is an issue of overzealous landing gear. When most of us get nervous, we tend to extend our legs in preparation for a hard landing. You must believe you'll make it. As you take off, let your bike and feet float up into your body. Don't extend your legs until your landing is underfoot, if you know what we're saying.

Problem: You land hard.

Solutions: Try to land on downslopes. Land with soft, extended arms and legs and try to use your full body-suspension travel.

Problem: You can handle tabletops no problem, but doubles scare the heck out of you.

Solutions: First, become hyperconfident on tables of the same ilk before you go for the double action. Second, stop staring into the gap. Instead, look softly somewhere beyond the landing.

Problem: You strain to generate speed in rhythm, you have a hard time moving your bike in the air, or you feel a bit out of control.

Solutions: You probably have too much upper-body tension. This is huge! Totally relax your upper body. Stand on your pedals and let your hands float on the grips. Play a game with your friends: Watch each other, and if your friends see any muscular tension in the air or in the transitions, you have to do 10 push-ups. (Unfortunately, the push-ups might make you even tighter.) If you can relax your upper body, you will immediately notice better flow, more pump, and a whole new level of style in your jumping. Like we said, THIS IS HUGE!

Jumping—as an extension of pumping—is the ultimate expression of bike mastery. It's no coincidence that every great jumper is also an exceptional trail rider. (However, not every exceptional trail rider is a great jumper.) Jumping is fun and addictive on its own, but it also helps you flow better in every situation.

CHAPTER 10

Flow
on Any Trail

When you learn to brake, pedal, corner, hop, pump, drop, and jump, you can get yourself over, around, or through just about any obstacle. That's a fine start. But to *flow* down a trail—to experience the ultimate joy of mountain biking—takes more.

See Better to Go Faster

If you want to smash into a rock, do this: Zip along a trail. See a rock. Stare at the rock. As you get closer, slow down and lower your head to keep the rock locked in your gaze. Because your bike points at the rock, chances are you'll smash into it. When you stare at a rock, you tell your brain, "Rock. Rock. Rock!" Your brain does the only thing it can with that information: It gives you a rock.

To guide you down a smooth line, your brain needs better info to work with.

See as fast as you ride. You can only ride as fast as you can scan the trail. When your eyes slow down and look closer to your front wheel, you have to slow down. When your eyes speed up and scan farther ahead, you can speed up. Keep scanning ahead; never lock your eyes on anything.

Raise your gaze. When you drive a car on a dark country road, your high beams let you see farther and drive faster. Think of your eyes as high beams: Point them as far down the trail as you can. When you swoop through a redwood forest at 10 miles per hour (16 km/h), follow the light soil 20 feet (6 m) ahead of you. When you haul down the Kamikaze downhill, look for the white gravel 100 yards ahead. If you look farther down the trail, you will immediately become a better rider. Know why?

When you elevate your gaze, you literally elevate your perception of the trail. Instead of noticing individual objects—little round rock, big pointy rock, huge wet rock—you sense the overall flow of the trail—left, right, up, and down. A rock waterfall scares most riders at Northstar-at-Tahoe mountain bike park in California. Hundreds of head-sized and bigger rocks jumble down a steep slope. A lumpy chicane crosses halfway down. At the bottom, a 4-foot (1.2 m) slab drops into a flat, dusty turn. Most riders clatter down one rock at a time—bap, bap, bap, bap, bap—barely make the left, flounder through the right, creep down the drop, and then blow the turn. The fastest pros see the section at a higher level: a descent, a transfer, and then the drop. They pump the first pitch, whip their bikes over the chicane, float off the drop, and rail the corner. They project their attention beyond the rocks toward their ultimate goal—that final corner.

The higher you look, the lower your perceived speed—and the faster you can ride. Next time you drive down the freeway, look straight out your side window and try to count the dashed lines in your lane. They

When you approach a tricky section, try to pick a reference point that's beyond the section. It'll help guide you through the gnarl.

whiz by too fast, don't they? Look a hundred yards (or meters) ahead and notice how the dashes seem to slow down. By looking ahead, you give yourself more time to deal with situations: a tight turn, a rock, a sweet jump.

You're a flashlight, not a laser.   Sweep your eyes over an area a few feet (about a meter) wide that encompasses your line and the obstacles or landmarks around it. Say you're cruising down the National Trail in Phoenix, Arizona. You don't want to be thinking, "Rock right, cactus left. Rock, cactus, drop . . ." Instead, see the ribbon of smooth dirt, and just kind of *feel* the boundaries.

Beware the magnetic rock.   When you see something scary—a rock, a gap in a double jump, whatever—notice it but keep your eyes moving. As you approach the object of your fixation, you unconsciously aim for it, slow down to keep it in view, and fail to plan for the next situation. How many times have you bashed right into that rock you were trying to avoid? How many times have you cleared a rocky climb and then fallen on a smooth section? When you fill your focus with one thing, there's no space to deal with anything else.

YOUR EYE: THE RIGHT TOOL FOR THE JOB

Your most detailed vision concentrates in the center of where you're looking, in a cone about 15 degrees wide. If you're looking 25 feet (7.6 m) down a trail, your area of highest focus is about 6 feet (1.8 m) wide. As you approach the side of your vision, the level of detail goes down, but your ability to track movement goes up. So what does this mean? Use your high-definition vision to choose lines as far ahead as possible. As you approach obstacles, let your peripheral vision do what it does best: keep track of the obstacles and tell your brain when it's time to hop, skip, or jump.

Practice, Practice, Practice . . .

You can (and should) practice good vision every day in every situation. Driving, walking through crowds, pushing a cart through the grocery store—anytime you're scanning ahead and letting your peripheral vision handle the details, you're priming your eyes, brain, and body to rip trails.

What's Next?

Make sure you always, always, always look ahead to the next turn or obstacle. Not the one you're currently riding. The next one.

Focus on where you want to be at the end of the section. Your peripheral vision will handle whatever's between you and your goal.

Under your wheels, out of your mind.   The root crossing the trail isn't going anywhere. Keep scanning ahead and trust your automatic ability to get over it. When you walk up a set of stairs, do you stare at every single step? Of course not. If you do, maybe mountain biking isn't for you. Shoot, maybe *walking* isn't for you.

Connect the dots.   When you read a trail, you design a giant connect-the-dots puzzle. If you stare at individual scary things, your puzzle will have only a few dots, and your path will be herky-jerky. The faster and more fluidly you can process many points, the smoother your line will be.

Look at the things that matter.   Note your turning points, watch out for obstacles you have to ride around, and look for objects you can pump. Ignore everything else. Experienced riders know what they need to pay attention to: boulders, cliffs, and trees. Novices waste effort looking at things that don't matter: gravel, tiny ruts, and small woodland creatures.

Pick Great Lines

Rather than following the "easy" line around the rocks and finally wedging yourself awkwardly into the turn, pump straight over the rocks and drop into a perfect entrance.

A trail is a blank canvas: an area framed by rocks, foliage, course tape, or thousand-foot cliffs in which you render your mountain bike masterpiece. Because your tires need a path only a few inches wide, your choices are nearly endless. This is the most complicated aspect of mountain biking. You have to balance speed, terrain, equipment, skills, risk, and your goals—all while your heart pounds and your eyeballs rattle out of your head. So where do you start?

If you're just cruising, especially for the first time on that trail, go ahead and follow the worn line. The path most traveled weaves around obstacles and provides the smoothest, easiest route from point A to point B. A thousand happy mountain bikers can't all be wrong, can they?

Well, yes, they can. A line that avoids every little obstacle has lots of curves, many of them quite tight. Most riders dive into corners too early, creating slow exit lines. For low speeds and climbing, the smooth line works just fine. But as your speed increases, you have a harder time making all the corners. You can't flip your bike around each and every rock, and your cornering g's overpower the available traction. You could slow down, but that's no fun. Instead, look for straighter lines and smoother arcs. Pump right over the rocks instead of slaloming around them. Line up wide for corners, carve all the way inside, and exit wide, even where roots crisscross the trail. Experiment to figure out what you can ride over without losing speed or killing yourself. As you zoom down a trail, avoid these "threshold" obstacles. Otherwise, go straight down the straights and carve mathematically perfect arcs around the corners. As world champion downhiller Steve Peat says, "Use the whole trail. Don't be a sheep."

The Tunnel Trail in Santa Barbara, California, consists of slabs of jumbled, weirdly eroded sandstone. There's no obvious "easy"

1 + 1 = 3

As a coach, I (Lee) am always being asked, "How do I ride a switchback with a drop in it?"

My answer: Before you can ride a switchback with a drop in it, you have to master switchbacks without drops, and you have to master drops without switchbacks.

After you completely dial these basic skills, *your mind and body will begin to combine them naturally*. As this synergy builds, you'll ride ever-more technical terrain—and you'll have more fun doing it.

A more extreme example: Elliott Hoover rails a berm as he drops. Or drops as he rails a berm.

line—just rock, rock, and more rock. You have to let your eyes scan quickly for the smoothest routes: water gullies, worn-down rock, or scrubbed-off tire tread. Make your best choice, but be ready in case you encounter something gruesome. An average Joe can creep over a foot-high round stone. A pro downhiller can bound over a 4-foot (1.2 m) boulder. As your skills and confidence increase, you'll find yourself sailing and railing over things that now terrify you, flowing straight down the trail like water.

The Power of Pump

When you add the pumping arrow to your skills quiver, you give yourself a whole new range of line choices. You no longer favor little bumps over big ones. Say you have a choice between a turny line filled with **baby heads** or a straight line right over some boulders:

Turny line—You have to slow down for the turns, and the little rocks make your bike feel super sketchy.

Boulder line—You go straight, so no turns. And you can actually gain speed and control on those boulders.

Take it from us: If you master the art of pump on a pump track or BMX track, there will come a day when you naturally take the boulder line—and it's gonna feel awesome.

A LINE FOR EVERY PURPOSE

Cruising: On any well-used trail, a worn path meanders among the obstacles and cuts easy, if not perfect, arcs through the corners. This is literally "the path most traveled." It's usually the safest way down the trail. Perfect for leisure, exploration, and learning.

Racing: Whether cross-country or downhill, you want the fastest, straightest lines your current skills, equipment, and conditions can handle.

Freeriding: This is all about fun. Time is no worry, and it seems like safety isn't much of a worry, either. Depending on your level, you might veer off the main line to drop off a stump, or you might huck off a 40-foot (12 m) cliff. There seem to be no limits, and the regular rules of speed and efficiency do not apply.

Dial In Your Speed

IMBA would like us to say we love mountain biking because it helps us appreciate nature. But when you ask riders what they love most about our fine sport, most say "speed." Whether on foot, skis, surfboard, camel, car, or jet, we humans have an innate need to haul ass.

Swoooosh! **Curtis Keene carries ludicrous speed through some dark woods.**

Fast is definitely more fun than slow, but the real measure of pleasure is perceived speed: the sensations of sight, sound, and movement. Ten miles per hour (16 km/h) on a bike with gravel crunching and trees whooshing past is a lot more stimulating than 650 miles per hour (1,046 km/h) in an airliner with cellophane crinkling and the snack cart squeaking by. Beginners love the howling wind, the skittering tires, and the very notion that they're riding a bike so fast on dirt. Experts tend to focus on the feelings of acceleration and deceleration, swooping in and out of turns, and flying over obstacles. It's the same level of excitement, with a different focus.

Every line has a range of viable speeds. Flat, easy lines have a wide range; it doesn't matter whether you go fast or slow. Steep, gnarly lines have a narrow range of speed—too slow and you can't carry over rough stuff; too fast and you lose control. As a matter of fact, the gnarlier the line is, the more speed you need and the more you must commit. Speed helps you float over the tops of rocks, hop farther over roots, whip through corners, and carry momentum through violent sections. When the going gets really steep and silly, braking screws up your bike's handling, and you can't really slow down anyway. You just have to surrender yourself to the hill.

Speed is like voltage. It pushes you down the trail, through corners, and over rises. It stimulates your senses and gives you a thrill. Of course, the higher the voltage, the stronger the shock. In general, the optimum speed lets you get over obstacles, make corners, react to surprises, and have fun. People who try to haul ass before they master the basics crash often and hard. That's a dangerous, counterproductive way to become a fast rider. Instead, concentrate on being smooth. Speed will come.

Ride With a Reserve

It's a crazy, random world out there.

Say you're out riding 100 percent. You're right on the edge of control, and we'll bet you're having fun. But if something happens—a flat tire, an unexpected rock, a surprise hiker—you have nowhere to go but down.

If, on the other hand, you ride at 80 percent, you still have a 20 percent reserve of traction and mental acuity to deal with the inevitable. You should always ride with some reserve. The right amount depends on the situation.

0 to 10 percent reserve. Timed race run. You want to win, but is a ruptured spleen worth a plastic medal?

25 percent reserve. Weekend ride in a public park. Two words: Sierra Club.

50 percent reserve. Expedition in the middle of nowhere. Two words: wolf food.

75 percent reserve. Riding a dirt road with your arm in a sling, which one of the authors (Lee) admits to having done. Two words: dumb ass.

Commit

Whatever you do, you must do it with confidence. On terrain that you find easy, you can cruise along pretty much however you like: fast, slow, standing on the saddle, or whatever. When the situation calls for only half your abilities, you can get away with using half your wits. But the more a situation tests your skills and confidence, the more committed you have to be. There's a nice paradox here: When you're most nervous, that's when you have to find it within yourself to commit 100 percent. Crazy.

Failure to commit leads to failure to stay on your bike. If you try to corner without leaning, you follow a tangent into the poison oak. If you try to jump too slowly, you land on top of the school bus. If you try to hop a curb without really snapping upward, you ruin your rear wheel, and the cheerleaders laugh at you.

When the line is smooth, you can roll along a nice, easy two-dimensional line around the mushrooms, past the fairy princess's chalet, and up to

CAN YOU SEE IT?

If you can see and feel yourself doing a move—a big jump, a tricky rock section—you can usually do it.

If, on the other hand, all you see is a blank screen (or yourself crashing), you usually *cannot* do it.

When most riders encounter the blank screen, they tense up and make mistakes. If you can't see it, you probably shouldn't try it.

Whatever you're doing, give it! Lee pulls his clavicleless right shoulder even farther out of line pulling out of this 360-berm-to-roller. (Location: Lory State Park, Fort Collins, Colorado—bike park designed by Lee.)

the gingerbread house. The rougher the line, the more three-dimensional your path becomes. You have to hop over moats, manual over smoldering villages, and dive into tight turns. This rapid weighting and unweighting requires you to scan critically for your line and commit 100 percent to throwing your bike around.

Low-Commitment, Low-Risk Riding

Low-commitment riding, aka "cruising," is slow and mellow. Mud might make you nervous. A mellow trail might bore you. Or you might be 50 miles (80 km) from a rest at Everest base camp, and a crash might mean certain death.

- Pick the smoothest, easiest lines even if you have to ride around obstacles. (But honor the pump. Going straight over stuff can be the easiest and safest way.)
- Keep your speed down.
- Pedal softly and efficiently.
- Brake lightly to slow down gradually.
- Steer gently.
- Let your bike roll slowly over rough terrain.

High-Commitment Riding

High-commitment riding, aka "ripping," is fast and aggressive. You might be hauling the mail on a familiar trail. Loose dirt might force you to commit to a steep pitch. Or you might be railing the SolVista national downhill course, and a win would mean free tires for life. (Whoo yeah, some riders risk almost anything for that!)

EXPEDITION MODE

When I (Lee) am on a long ride with an undetermined outcome, especially far away from home, I slide into my "expedition mode."

It's all about efficiency. I pedal only often and hard enough to get up the hills, and I try not to touch the brakes (it's too much work to regain speed). I take straight lines and pump everything with moderate energy. I know I can maintain this pace almost indefinitely, and that I can ride any terrain that comes up. Expedition mode is pretty fast and super fun.

- Pick the straightest lines, even if they go over gnarly stuff.
- Go fast.
- Pedal aggressively.
- Brake hard to slow down quickly.
- Lean and press hard into corners.
- Manual, hop, or jump over everything in your path.

Find a State of Flow

Mountain biking satisfies so many desires. It transforms a gunnysack full of kittens into a ripped, hard body. It carries you through stunning places with exceptional people. Its sights, sounds, smells, and sensations block out all your inner demons. And, of course, the speed and magnitude of it all excite you like nothing else.

You can go for half a dozen rides and enjoy them for half a dozen reasons. Your lunchtime loop keeps you fit, Moab's Porcupine Rim Trail enthralls you, a twisty singletrack whips you like a roller coaster, a huge jump scares the heck out of you.

These are all fantastic ways to enjoy our fine sport, but the ultimate experience happens when your thoughts crawl into your CamelBak and your body flows along the trail without effort or voice. Time changes. Tension disappears. You're focused but not forced. Controlling your bike becomes effortless. You've entered the magical state of "flow."

Dr. Mihaly Csikszentmihalyi describes the feeling of flow in his groundbreaking book, *Flow: The Psychology of Optimal Experience:* "Concentration is so intense

CHOOSE YOUR PILL

You're zooming down National Downhill at Whistler Mountain Bike Park, British Columbia. The trail is steep, tight, and rough, but at least it's made of dirt. You cross a dirt road and drop into Clown Shoes. Before you know it, you're riding a wooden roller coaster—whoa!—which soon funnels to a foot-wide, 5-foot-high log ride. Yikes! You feel like Neo in *The Matrix.* What do you do?

Take the blue pill. *The story ends. You wake in your bed and believe whatever you want to believe.* Stop and walk around the section. You won't gain anything, but you won't lose anything, either. The thing is, how content can you be once you know what's out there?

Take the red pill. *Stay in Wonderland and see how deep the rabbit hole goes.* Sometimes you just have to take the red pill. Dive into the unknown. Have faith in your skills and experience. More often than not, your commitment will carry you through. Your world will never be the same.

BRIAN ON REBUILDING CONFIDENCE

In the spring of 2004, I broke my ankle and I was off the bike for two and a half months. When the bone healed, I started riding XC, and I felt good on regular trails. I didn't feel like I lost much, but when I got on the slalom bike and started sprinting and jumping, that's when I started to feel rusty. I didn't want to crash, and I just didn't feel confident—like, "How will my leg feel if I hit that lip really hard?"

When you get to a certain level, you always keep 75 percent of your skills. You can go out and ride anytime at that level. But it's that last part that separates the good guys from the great guys. At a downhill race in which most pros run 7:00 and the winners run 6:00 or 6:10, the winners could run 6:20s all day long. Those guys have total confidence to go that speed, and their race runs are no big deal to them.

Time is the main thing. I have to have my leg feel good so I can go into situations with total confidence; that way, if I push hard and something happens, I won't get hurt. I know how to do these things; I just have to get comfortable doing them.

Regaining confidence after an injury is a lot like building confidence as you step up your riding. You're not going to go from jumping a 5-foot double straight to a 25-foot double. You have to be smart about it, or the whole process will take a lot longer. When you try something, you have to have the confidence to know you can do it. That comes from experience and knowledge, and time spent on the bike. Over the years, you learn how to react to various jumps, speeds, lips, distances, and so on.

On motos, if we both have 250s, I can tell you to hit a jump in third gear half open, but because your bike strength is unique to you, I can't tell you how hard to pedal. You just have to start gradually and build up your experience and confidence to go bigger.

that there is no attention left over to think about anything irrelevant, or to worry about problems. Self-consciousness disappears, and the sense of time becomes distorted. An activity that produces such experiences is so gratifying that people are willing to do it for its own sake, with little concern for what they will get out of it, even when it is difficult, or dangerous."

Does that sound familiar?

Flow only happens when the demands of the situation intersect with your abilities. The trail isn't so hard that it scares you, nor is it so easy that it bores you. The further the demands lay above your perceived abilities, the bigger the rush. Savor a peaceful cruise down a local trail, enjoy a thrill behind a faster rider down a new path, or transcend all you thought possible by pinning it for an entire cross-country race. You might vomit at the end, but it feels so good, doesn't it?

We say "perceived" abilities because that's what counts. Most of us can climb harder, corner faster, and fly farther than we usually do. When you can let go of your inner mother and flow along in this zone, you'll have max fun and improve your riding.

Unfortunately, we can't just put on a Flow-Tron 2000 helmet and instantly feel that ecstasy. (If we could, we'd never do anything else.) According to the book *Good Stress, Bad Stress* by Barry Lenson (2002), flow is a precise psychological state that requires these elements:

Adequate skills. You don't learn to flow. You learn to ride your bike. When you can corner, hop, pump, and jump without thinking, then you can flow. You might achieve ecstasy in the soft Santa Cruz woods but flounder amid the raspy Phoenix boulders. When you worry about surviving the ride, you do not flow.

Goals. If you ride around—la, la, la—with no mission, you miss the rewards of accomplishing your goals. Set a goal. Spin smoothly, rail corners, stay on your buddy's wheel, or just stay on your bike for a change. If you need a ready-made structure, compete in a race. You have to know you're doing a good job.

Excitement. Too little stress and your mind wanders. Too much stress and you freak out. Go ahead and let some butterflies flutter in your tummy. They tell you you're being pushed, and that a huge stoke awaits.

You know those moments when everything—bike, body, trail and even the trees—comes together perfectly? Curtis Keene does.

The good news is, achieving flow is neither random nor extremely difficult. Here are some tips to help you achieve flow more consistently and in crazier situations.

Break 'em down. Break big tasks into small components. If you're an intermediate jumper and you try to nail a technical 10-pack all at once, you'll end up more broken than satisfied. Instead, try to get a perfect takeoff on the first double; then master the landing. When you get that down, add jumps number 2, number 3, and so on.

Practice. Don't just go out and ride, either. Pay close attention to what you're doing. Systematically build the skills you need to rip. Focus your mind on pedaling perfect circles. Then do a million of them.

Hang with the right crowd. Ride with people at or above your skill level. You will rise or fall to the level of your peers. Beware: If you feel inadequate around superior riders, or if they take you places you aren't ready for, you'll find it difficult to have a good time.

Pick the right tool for the job. You should not be worrying about your bike tracking correctly or holding together. You heard it here first: Go forth and buy!

Conquer your obstacles. Pay attention to the things that prevent or interrupt your flow. Maybe you tense up every time you encounter baby head rocks. Either stay away from them or learn to ride them.

Don't pay attention to yourself. As soon as you realize you're ripping, the ripping pretty much stops. Remember that scene in *The Empire Strikes Back* when Luke stood on one hand with his eyes closed, with Yoda and a bunch of stuff balanced on his feet, and he started to levitate his X-wing fighter? He was definitely ripping. As soon as he opened his eyes and thought, "Yes! I'm a Jedi Master!" it all came crashing down. Don't be self-conscious like Luke. Be confident like Han.

LEE RACES UNCORRECTED

Going into the 2007 Sea Otter Classic, I had a few years of coaching under my belt, and my skills were better than ever. I trained hard over the Colorado winter, and I showed up ready to rock the dual slalom and downhill. Little did I know I'd be taking a special test.

Dual Slalom

We qualified in heavy rain and sloppy mud. This is where age and experience really come in handy. I took my run with Steve Peat. I chased him the best I could, had a great run, and qualified second in semipro. Stoked!

I went through the rounds no problem, but in the round of 8 I got really self-conscious. I started overanalyzing my riding, which slowed me down, and I got eliminated. I was theoretically the second-fastest guy in the class—and my self-conscious lameness really bummed me out.

That night over the campfire, my buddies dispensed some wisdom: My skills were way higher than my speed. In the beginning, you use your skills to build up your speed. That'll get you pretty far. But at some point it's time to pick a speed and let your skills fill in. It was time for me to release it all and go for it.

OK.

Lee practicing the downhill (with eyeglasses).

Downhill

I'd been practicing with pro racer and bro' Curtis Keene, and I was feeling awesome. We timed every run, and I knew what I could do. With all the Pump Track Nation, raw Colorado trails, and the altitude advantage, I was ready to win semipro.

But the universe had other ideas.

"30 seconds."

I'm in the gate, ready to rock. I put on my goggles, and—pop!—the left lens of my glasses falls on the ground. YIKES! I have serious astigmatism. I can't drive without correction. Everything's blurry, and I have no depth perception.

I try to fit the lens back into my glasses. It's muddy. My gloved fingers are fumbling. The guys behind me are fidgeting.

"10 seconds."

I can get this. Everything's fine.

"Beep beep beep beep BEEP!"

Crap. I keep fiddling. There's no way I can ride without my glasses—or is there?

"10 seconds" (for the guy behind me).

Damn.

Then . . . peace. I put my glasses in my pocket and went for it uncorrected.

I sprinted down the ramp, carved the first off-camber turn, and screamed, "I'm pinned! I'm freaking pinned!" I knew the course, and I knew I had to stay neutral. Attack position, attack position, attack position.

The whole race was a blur: the impacts to my feet, the course tape rubbing my elbow (better move over). I don't remember it happening, but there's a photo of me rocking this long tabletop, perfect form, nice and low. People say I was yelling "I am so freaking good at this!"

I was in the moment. I was unencumbered by the details. And I was fully pinned.

My official race time was off the back, but my actual riding time was even faster than in practice. As bummed as I was with the bad "result," I was super stoked with probably the best run of my life.

It just goes to show: If you know the trail and have the skills, fitness, and confidence, anything is possible.

Know Why You Ride

A lot of us ride every day. We ride and ride and ride. When we're not riding, we think about riding. But I'll bet most of us have a hard time explaining why we ride.

Is it for fun? For exercise? For a feeling of freedom? To make a living? Whatever your reasons for riding, that's cool. Just know your reasons.

When you know your motivations, you can design your path to happiness. If you just want to have some fun and burn some calories, then ride safely and enjoy your Sunday rides. If you want to make a living as a pro, then get serious about training and racing. If you need to become a great rider to validate yourself as a worthwhile person, good luck. You'll find that after you clear the jump or win the race or wax your buddies, that hole in your soul will still be there.

FASTER CAN BE SAFER

We all have a natural pace at which everything flows well. To go faster is inviting calamity. To go slower can be just as dangerous.

I (Lee) experience this all the time while I'm coaching on technical terrain. I'm riding the speed I think the rider should be going, plus I'm thinking about him or her and probably talking too. My bike gets balled up, and I get too self-aware, and I bobble. I'm way safer riding at my own pace!

SHOOT YOUR TROUBLES

Problem: As you zip along a trail, you get bogged down on certain obstacles; for example rocks, logs, or inflatable alligators.

Solutions: Practice similar obstacles in isolation. For example, if rocky ledges ball you up, hop the curb in front of your house 100 times a day. As always, keep your eyes moving. Notice the obstacle; then keep tracking forward.

Problem: While your buddies fly through technical sections, you get caught in all the tight corners.

Solution: Try following a straighter line over rocks and such. The less you have to turn, the better (assuming you can get over the rocks and such). When it's time to turn, get low and lean your bike!

Problem: You crash a lot.

Solution: Slow down and take mellower lines! Don't go fast and gnarly until you master slow and easy. If a certain trail or obstacle always messes you up, stop riding it! Take a step back, work on your skills, and then return.

Problem: You slow way down in rough sections where you can't pedal.

Solution: Pump the terrain. As an exercise, see how fast you can ride without pedaling. You'll be amazed at your high speed—and your high heart rate.

Problem: You get tense in certain situations, say, rock gardens or dense woods.

Solution: You're probably afraid for a reason—a crash, a scary clown, whatever. To ease your anxiety, ride these sections very slowly and strive for ultimate smoothness. Start increasing the speed after the scary clown leaves you alone. Remember to pump the terrain. Not only does it work better—but it also gives you something positive to focus on.

Flow goes way beyond the mechanics of controlling a bike. It's a philosophy and a style. It's your way of experiencing the trail, of using your skills and equipment to have the most fun possible. Do you stay low and fast or fly high and stylish? Whichever your inclination, turn off your brain and let your skills come together on the fly. You'll be amazed at what you come up with.

CHAPTER 11

Handle Crazy Conditions

ountain biking gets its soul from the random situations you can find yourself in: steep rocks with wet moss, tangled roots covered in snow, deadly ruts lined with mud, and so on. If you want to stay sterile, ride the skate park or BMX track. If you want to go insane, hit the trail!

When the terrain gets rough, slick, and loose, it's more important than ever to ride in a relaxed, fluid attack position; look where you want to go; and pump wherever possible. If you promise to do that much, feel free to use these tips when the going gets weird.

Unnecessary Roughness

Rocks, logs, roots, ruts, and bumps can be the stuff of nightmares, or they can make your dreams come true. Let's opt for the latter.

Think of a rough trail like a colossal rhythm section. The rocks, logs, roots, ruts, and bumps are merely obstacles to be handled. Depending on your speed, the roughness of the section, and the length of the section, you might roll lightly, manual, hop, pump, jump, or go around. The key is, don't think of roughness as a threat. Think of it as a series of little obstacles that you can handle one at a time. Here are some general tips:

Staying low and looking ahead—Jacqueline Harmony keeps it smooth on the rough downhill course in Angel Fire, New Mexico.

Carry speed. It's a big mistake to slow down too much for rough terrain. Momentum keeps you high on the bumps and carries you all the way through rough sections. Steve Peat says, "Sometimes the best thing to do is just pedal as fast as you can, get off the back of the bike, and try to skim over the tops of the rocks. It's like a whoop section on a motocross track. The faster you go, the smoother it is."

Ratchet it. When you don't have enough clearance for full pedal strokes, ratchet your pedals back and forth for some propulsion action.

If it's small, fly over it. Single stones, lone logs, and small sections should get one of your patented hops or jumps. There's no good reason to run into the fronts of these guys unless you want to jump over something else.

Go light. When you reach a long series of hits that you can't absorb individually, preload and then unload so your tires and suspension absorb the jolts and your bike skims across the tops of the bumps. You have to be extra light when crossing a bunch of random objects—a big tangle of roots, for example. "Oh yeah, you just ping through roots," says Peat. "You gotta be loose, because you *will* get sent this way and that." Flat pedals require some downward pressure to keep you aboard; you can get way lighter with clip-in pedals.

Pump it. When you learn to pump through rough sections, your whole world will change. You can actually gain speed in rough sections that bog most riders down. The key is unweighting and weighting in the right places. All you have to do is unweight (or fly over) the front side of an object—be it a log, rock, or root—and press down on the backside. If there's a section with a bunch of little roots, you can unweight all the way through them; then pump the last one for free love.

"When I get into rocks, I like to get light so the bike can skim over the rocks," says Peat. "But you start to bog down after a little while, so I look for a place to pop up again." In long sections you can float over the beginning, pump in one spot, float

PUMPING A BUMPY TRAIL

Step 1 is learning pump on a pump track or a BMX track. Step 2 is learning to apply pump to real terrain. Some things to keep in mind while you're ripping the rocks:

Treat big things like rollers. Big rocks, logs, and water bars are like single rollers—light on the up, heavy on the down.

Work the overall shape. Even a seemingly random trail has an overall up-and-down flow. Suspension helps you ignore the details and focus on pumping the big shapes. Most riders can ignore bumps less than 4 inches (10 cm) tall. The better you get, and the more travel you have, the bigger the bumps you can ignore.

Let your bike handle the details. You can't pump 1,000 little rocks. Stay neutral and let your bike do its thing. On rough trails, Brian sets his suspension soft so it can handle the small stuff; he focuses on the big moves.

Pump the turns too. The best trails have a perfect bump-turn-bump-turn rhythm. Get light over the bump, heavy in the turn, light over the bump, heavy in the turn. Once you feel this sweet love, you can kiss your career and family goodbye.

When you actively pump a rocky section, your head will float smoothly down the trail, and everything will feel smooth and sweet. BTW: These rocks don't look big from the side, but they look huge from a speeding bike!

Let's think about this "roughness" thing for a minute. What makes a situation seem rough?

Is it the size of the bumps? No, because you can suck up huge bumps.

Is it the spacing of the bumps? No, because you can skim right over close bumps.

No matter what the trail is doing, a situation only feels rough when you're getting beaten up. And what beats you up? Assuming your bike is set up properly, the two main culprits are unbalanced position and excessive tension.

So: Maintain balance and stay loose.

some more, pump again, and so on. As long as your front wheel isn't hitting something while you pump the back wheel, you're golden.

Bonus: This "dive in and pump it" philosophy forces you to aim deep into the section rather than freaking out on the first obstacle. You'll carry more speed and stay smoother this way.

Free your front wheel, and the rest will follow.   You'd be amazed at what your rear wheel can get over if your front wheel is already clear. If you encounter a rock, log, root, or whatever surrounded by relatively smooth ground, manual your front wheel over it, lighten the rear as it rolls over, and then pump the obstacle for speed. When your front and rear wheels hit obstacles at the same time, you'll bog down like a woolly mammoth in tar. So when you enter a tangled mess of yuckiness, unweight your front tire so your rear tire can roll free and fast.

You might as well jump.   Trying to roll over truly rough terrain—for example, steep rocks with big holes between them—is just asking for hard hits, stuck front wheels, and over-the-bars experiences. If you have the speed, it's best to fly. Either bunny hop from flat ground or use an obstacle as an impromptu takeoff lip. Catch a little backside for a smooth landing and some free speed. Remember, never smack into the front of an obstacle unless you're using it to jump over the next obstacle.

Slippery When Wet

Bad traction is bad traction, whether you blame water, mud, ice, sand, cooking spray, or cheap tires. When your tires and the ground have trouble communicating, things are tough on the whole family. When that happens, you need some counseling:

Stay loose and ready for funny business.   "If you go in thinking, 'This is mud. I'm gonna slide around,' you're more ready when it happens," Peat says. "You can't go in thinking you'll be fine. It's mud; you won't be fine."

Keep it as straight as possible.   You can't carve turns on wet roots. Square off your turns on decent dirt and then fly straight through the nasty sections. As long as you're going straight, you don't have to go slower than normal.

Don't make any sudden moves.   The ground has trouble hearing everything when your tire talks too fast. Speak slowly and clearly, if you know what we mean, and wait for the ground to hear what you're saying.

Hit slick objects straight on.   Hit a slimy root with an angle of incidence, and you're in for a nasty incident.

When you do encounter roots at an angle, try to pop your front wheel over them and lighten your back wheel as much as possible. "It's almost like a bunny hop, but you're not really taking off. You're just going light," Peat says. This also works when you hit things head-on.

When you're climbing in slop, stay in the saddle to keep as much weight as possible on the rear tire. As soon as you stand, you'll lose traction and momentum, and it's almost impossible to get going again on a muddy climb. Pull a taller gear than normal to dilute your power impulse and keep the tire from breaking loose.

Pick your pedaling spots. Because you can't find traction on a slick root, you need to accelerate where there's traction and carry speed over the roots.

Whoo hoo! **When it's this slippery, do your best to keep the front wheel tracking, but be ready to get loose and ride it out.**

Snow can be good or bad. According to Peat, when the top is frozen with frost, you get decent traction and roll fast. When the snow is soft, you sink down and bog. Ice is always bad news, unless you have metal spikes on your tires.

Run the right tires. Slickness calls for sticky rubber and pointy knobs. For snow and terrible mud, run spike tires. The guys at Specialized love when it rains heavily in Santa Cruz, California. They put on mud spikes and RAIL through the loamy love.

Bonus move from Steve Peat himself: "If it's slippery and your rear end starts sliding out, lean forward to get your front wheel tracking, and the back will come back in line." This might seem counterintuitive, but Peaty knows what he's talking about.

PUMPING A SLIPPERY TRAIL

Yes, pump makes everything better.

Focus your downforce. When the trail is slippery, it's more important than ever to turn and brake as heavily as you can. With the right timing and power, you can double or even triple your traction.

Skip the yucky spots. Forget trying to ride straight over that tangle of icy roots. Get heavy before and light over. In that heavy moment on the other side—that's when you brake or turn. This is analogous to skiing badly crusted snow. You have to push down to turn, unweight to transition above the crust, push down to turn . . . repeat.

Dealing With Slop

Where Peat lives in northern England, they have mud the way California has dust. Add all his World Cup experience, and you get a guy who knows mud riding. Peaty says you should get used to the sliding feeling and just go for it. In addition to adopting a banzai attitude, you can try a few tricks to improve your control and comfort:

- Wrap a thin, knotted rope around your grips, in case you get mud on your gloves.
- If rain is falling into your goggles or glasses, extend your visor by attaching a clear lens to the end.
- Peat runs Smith Roll-Offs in really bad weather. If water gets below the film, the film can stick to the lens. The solution: Glue loops of fishing line to your lens to suspend the film a bit.
- When water flings forward off your tire and into your face, add a rubber flap to the front of your fender.
- Fasten a strip of tire tread to your saddle to help you translate your body English into bike English.

Soft, Deep, and Loose

Deep sand, dust, gravel, mud, and snow all have a way of mucking up your cornering and bogging you to a sketchy stop. Give those jerks the treatment:

Shift your balance slightly back.   Your feet will be extra heavy, and your hands will track slightly backward against the grips. Weight your front wheel enough so it tracks straight and grabs when you turn the bars, but not so much that it sinks in

and scrubs your speed. If you've skied powder, you already have a feel for this: Lean forward enough to control your skis but not so much that the tips dive into the snow.

If you hit a patch of sand while you're going fast, lean back and unweight your front wheel *before* your bike starts to slow down. Keep that front end light and motor across like a floatplane lifting skyward.

Climbing in looseness is like climbing in slipperiness. Keep your bum on the seat and make smooth power. Spin an easier gear than normal so you don't bog down.

Well balanced and looking through the turn: Cody Wilderman makes this ultra-steep, hyper-loose turn look easy. Snowmass, Colorado.

Cornering in loose dust is like trying to steer a cargo ship. You can do it, but your vessel doesn't respond very quickly. Lean your bike gradually, and wait for it to come around. If you steer too much too soon, your front wheel will plow, which is just like sliding out except your tire usually catches traction and pitches you forward. Take a page from the motocross book, and set your inside foot up near your front tire. Let the tires drift until they carve their own little berms; then BRAAAAP!

Braking in looseness requires an ultra-light touch, especially in front. Make sure your bike is upright. Ease off the front binder at the first sign of plowage. Now the good news: Deep snow, sand, and mud all like to scrub your speed, so you don't have to brake as much as you would on hardpack. (When you ski down the fall line through deep powder, the snow controls your speed. Same kind of thing.)

PUMPING A LOOSE TRAIL

Yes—pumping helps here too. It helps everywhere.

Look for areas that are less loose. Scan way ahead (like always) and identify your "action areas." You might need to stray from the main line. That's OK.

Use the good areas. Get light in the loose spots, and extra heavy in the firm spots. That's where you'll brake and turn.

Load the brakes. If you must slow down in a long, loose section, first unload; then get heavy and really cram your tires into the ground while you brake gradually and firmly. Your fore–aft position had better be dialed!

WORLD CHAMPIONSHIPS OF SNOW SLALOM

While Brian is enjoying his non-winters in Southern California, I (Lee) have to be more creative in Colorado. When the snow has been around too long, we'll set up gates on a sled hill and let 'er rip. No studded tires allowed; this is supposed to be hard.

The way we see it, if you can corner on snow, you'll be a rock star on dirt.

If you can turn on snow . . . Joey Schusler works the skills that make him one of America's fastest downhillers.

It's all the same.   You swim through dust, you wiggle on gravel, and you ping off baby head rocks. The symptoms seem different, but the treatment is identical: Stay loose and expect your bike to act like an idiot.

Cut this out and stick it to your refrigerator: As long as your body stays on track, it doesn't matter what your bike is doing.

Avoiding the Rut

Running water and rolling tires can carve mini-canyons into your favorite trails. These wheel trappers mess up your balance, scrub your speed, and collect rocks and other nasties. They're usually to be avoided, but they can be your friends.

PUMPING AND RUTS

A heavy–light riding style helps you ride a rutty trail without getting stuck in a . . . well, you know.

Cross ruts with ease. Pump them at will. The more dynamically you ride, the more choices you give yourself.

Stay out of rain ruts.   Ruts that run down the trail love to grab you and lead you into terrible situations. On a fire road or doubletrack, there's plenty of room to take a better line. If the trail is super narrow and there's nowhere else to ride, go ahead and take the rut.

Stay out of uphill ruts.   When you climb in a rut and your rear tire scrubs the canyon wall, you lose speed and risk a slide-out. That's if your pedal doesn't smash into the ground first. Climb above the ruts. If your back tire does slide down in there, keep pedaling and get out as soon as you can.

Stay out of narrow ruts.   Narrow ruts keep you from wiggling around for balance. Paradoxically, the faster you go through a narrow rut, the better.

Cross ruts with caution.   When you have to cross a rut, try to hit it at an angle, and don't let your tires get caught in there. If you hit a small rut head-on, you can just get light on your bike. If you need to span a huge rut that runs parallel to your travel, hop over the entire thing. Manualing works for smooth transitions, but if the transition is smooth, you won't be worrying about the rut, will you?

Use ruts in turns.   When hundreds of riders have carved through a soft corner, the best line gets crammed several inches into the earth, and it makes a fantastic berm—especially on flat or off-camber corners. When the ruts get deeper than 6 inches (15 cm) or they develop big holes, they become a hazard. Find a different line.

Ruts can be your enemies or your friends. This one is definitely a friend. Todd Bosch pulls some major g's. Note his complete lack of braking.

Riding the Skinnies

Bridges sprouted up in the North Vancouver woods as a way for riders to ride over heavy foliage and deep sogginess. As riders got better at clinging to the log-and-lumber structures, the bridges ceased being practical ways to traverse unrideable terrain and became a focal point for a whole new style of riding: part cross-country and part downhill, but mostly trials. Nowadays, freeriders roll 15 feet (4.6 m) above the forest floor on 4-inch-wide (10 cm) logs. No wonder these "bridges" are now called skinnies.

Skinnies range from burly lumber ladders to spindly soggy branches, and heights range from less than a foot (30 cm) to over 20 feet (6 m). Technically, skinnies are no harder to ride than any other narrow line, such as a thin rut or a tiny rock takeoff. Skinnies just look scarier and carry a higher price for error. If you learn to ride skinnies, you'll be able to flow nicely on modern freeride trails, and you'll become a master of balance and pinpoint line control. Just remember:

It's all mental.   You can easily ride the white stripe at 20 miles per hour (32 km/h), but put a two-by-six a few feet off the ground, and you forget how to ride. Remember that your tires need only a few inches of surface; the rest is just decoration.

Stay neutral.   A centered, balanced position is key. Keep your hands neutral—no clenching!—and make sure your bars are free to make small corrections. Keep your cranks level and your weight pressing evenly into both pedals.

Keep your arms bent.   At least a little bit. This is key to adjusting your line and balance.

Sitting can make balance easier.   Standing helps you power onto bridges and make wheelie-hop saves. Do whichever feels best. Try running your seat somewhere between your full-XC and your full-DH positions.

Look as far forward as possible.   Scan ahead, from where you are to the awesome exit, for all the typical reasons. This is easier said than done, but you must not stare exclusively at your front tire. Doing so leads to the dreaded low-speed wobble, which leads to sudden vertical acceleration—and sudden deceleration.

Maintain a soft focus.   You need all of your peripheral vision and spatial awareness to manage your speed, fine-tune your line, and keep your balance. Here's a yoga trick:

In Whistler, British Columbia, Brian's attention is way ahead on that tricky left turn.

Let your eyes sink into your head. Try to see the entire scene from the back of your skull, with your eyes as the window. This can help you take in the entire scene—and keep you from staring at the wrong thing.

Momentum is your friend.   Ride the white stripe at 20 miles per hour (32 km/h); then try it at 2 miles per hour (3.2 km/h). Harder, eh?

Run a taller gear than normal.   Spinning a low gear makes you feel all lumpy and out of control. Turn a harder gear for a more controlled burst up that slimy ladder. You'll maintain better balance, and you're less likely to burn out on that green moss.

Be careful in the turns.   As you round a bend to transfer to an even skinnier bridge, turn your front tire out wide so your rear can track inside without falling into oblivion. Top-notch skinnies have little platforms for just this purpose. To keep max rubber on the tree, keep your bike upright and lean with your body.

Run big, sticky tires.   Lower your pressure for dedicated skinny sessions, but beware pinch flats when you drop onto rocks.

Don't give up right away.   If your tires start to slip off a rounded log, lean the bike (carefully) toward the middle. This generates camber thrust, and it might get your tires to claw back onto the good line.

Choose your exit.   Like we said, riding a skinny bridge is just like riding any other skinny line—until you get off line. If you start veering to the side and you're close to clean ground, just ride off and drop to safety. If you experience a balance blowout close to a smooth surface, ditch the bike and land on your feet. When you're suspended way above gnarl, jettison your steed and hug the bridge.

Thanks to Brandon Sloan for sharing his tips. Sloan is director of Specialized's High-End Mountain Bike Group, and he schools most locals when he goes out to test his new weapons.

THE SKINNY EVOLUTION

Although skinnies are no longer mountain biking's poster children, they're still a fixture in bike parks, and options are popping up on trails everywhere. What's changed over the past few years:

More flow. Skinnies are being integrated ever more cleverly into the movement and flow of trails. Huge hucks to flat are going extinct. Sinuous lines with multiple options are flourishing in the undergrowth.

Better riders. As a species, we mountain bikers are getting better at riding high, big lines, and doing so with grace.

Smaller bikes. Thanks to the flowier terrain and better riders, the hugely overbuilt freeride bike is a thing of the past. Today's freeriders are rocking DH race bikes and nimble, mid-travel all-mountain/slopestyle bikes.

Brian and Richie Schley enjoy some new-school elevated flow in Whistler.

Start wide and low.   Lay a piece of lumber on the ground and ride it. When you get a two-by-eight dialed, step up (down?) to a two-by-four. When you can stay on that as long as you want, try elevating it a bit at a time. Like we said, most of skinny riding is mental. Build your confidence gradually. Never put yourself into a situation where you freak out a dozen feet above pointy rocks. Not cool.

SHOOT YOUR TROUBLES

Problem: You feel like you're getting beaten to death on rough terrain.

Solutions: Make sure your bike is set up correctly. Shift your weight to your feet, loosen your grip, and relax your upper body. Look ahead. Load the bike in smooth sections and unload the bike in rough sections.

Problem: On rough terrain, you feel like you're balling up and getting stuck.

Solutions: Go faster. Unweight your bike, especially your front end, when you encounter obstacles.

Problem: When the going gets slick and loose, you feel like a sick goose.

Solution: This is pretty philosophical. When the ground sticks as well as a nonstick pan coated in cooking spray, you have to be willing to be out of control and go with it. That sounds pretty nutty, but that's the way it is. Wear pads if that helps your confidence. Like Steve Peat says: Expect your bike to slip. There, no more stress.

Problem: On loose ground, your front wheel digs in and pushes the dirt. Sometimes it catches and pitches you forward.

Solution: First, do not steer in loose dirt. Lean. Second, make sure your weight isn't too far forward. Start in your perfect attack position; then shift your weight a bit farther back.

Problem: On loose ground, your front wheel skims over the surface and refuses to steer.

Solution: Your weight is too far back. Move forward until your hands are neutral. To stick turns in loose ground, *carefully* press down on your bars.

Problem: You have trouble holding a line, whether it's between two ghastly ruts or atop an elevated two-by-four.

Solution: Stay loose and look where you want to go (as always). Remember that a little momentum will carry you through a situation in less time than it takes to worry about that situation.

Problem: As you go down rough terrain, your bike feels like it won't move around. You feel like you're getting pitched forward. It's hard to lean into turns.

Solution: Your thighs might be interfering with the movement of your saddle. Spread your knees apart to let your bike bounce around and pitch into corners. Lower your seat!

Problem: You get beaten up while trying to pedal over rough terrain.

Solution: Get off the saddle, even if only a fraction of an inch. Put all your weight on your pedals and let your bike react to impacts. For lots of rough pedaling, lower your seat a quarter-inch (0.6 cm) or so to give yourself more room to work. For more powerful pedaling on relatively smooth sections, slide back on your saddle. This will approximate your normal height. Seriously consider a remotely adjustable seatpost.

Crazy conditions have a way of freaking out riders who aren't used to them. Bury a southern Californian in deep mud, and he'll wig out. Slide an East Coaster on a hardpacked fire road, and she'll feel sketched. Although these conditions might seem strange and different, their solutions are the same: You should stay loose, look where you're going, and have fun!

CHAPTER 12

Avoid Injuries

Many riders (and their wives and mothers) believe injuries are an integral part of mountain biking. We disagree. If you ride correctly, injuries are not inevitable. Mountain bikers are susceptible to two basic kinds of injuries: chronic and acute.

Chronic Injuries

The Man Himself: Ned Overend is in his mid-fifties and fast. Not fast for an old guy. Just plain fast. One reason: He trains smart and takes great care of himself.

Although they're not as glamorous as the big breaks, chronic injuries cause plenty of pain, time off the bike, and even disability. These long-term issues are caused by all manner of overuse, misuse, and abuse of your bike and body, including:

- Knee damage from too much or improper pedaling
- Nerve damage from heavy hands and tense riding
- Excess fatigue from too much riding (Among serious riders, overtraining is more common than undertraining.)
- Previous injuries that never healed (see above)
- Poor posture and general weakness

Chronic injuries can be avoided with some awareness and common sense.

- Make sure your bike is set up for you, especially for extended pedaling.
- Maintain overall mobility and strength. The more you push your body, and the older you are, the more crucial this is to injury prevention. See Top Five Mountain Bike Training Exercises, page 202.
- If something hurts, stop. Make a smart adjustment on the bike or in your technique before you continue.
- If you're tired, rest. You won't get slow and fat if you take today off.

TAKE CARE OF YOUR BIKE!

Equipment failures are often gruesome and almost always avoidable.

- Ride the right bike for the conditions and your skills. (Unless you're Brian, don't rip your hardtail at Whistler.)
- Keep your bolts tight and everything properly adjusted.
- Keep your wheels tensioned.
- Make sure your suspension is working properly.
- Watch for cracks and weak spots in your frame and components.
- When in doubt, take your bike to your local shop.

- If you get hurt, let yourself heal. The more you hammer on an injury, the worse it will get and the more it will impair your riding.
- Always ride with proper form. If you're too weak, tired, or unskilled to ride a section properly, go get strong, get some sleep, and learn to ride (we've heard of a great book).
- When in doubt, seek professional help. Orthopedists and physical therapists make great friends.

If you end up with a chronic injury, we're sorry, it's your fault. Pay attention and take care of yourself.

Acute Injures

Acute injuries are a different story. They happen suddenly, typically because of crashes. Many riders think they're victims of circumstance, but pay attention here:

- All crashes can be avoided.
- Most would-be crashes can be saved.
- Many actual crashes can be survived without injury.

Of course, the best way to survive a crash is to avoid it in the first place. Let's start there.

Stay Out of Trouble

As a rider who very seldom crashes, Brian has a very holistic approach to crash avoidance. Here are his four tips:

Know the Trail

When you know the trail or race track, you know when you can speed up, when you have to slow down, where the tight turns loom, and where that rock is hiding. The better you learn your local trails, the faster you can go.

But what about new trails?

It's all about creating cushion between the moment you perceive an obstacle and the moment you have to react.

1. Slow down.
2. Look ahead as far as possible. Even farther than normal.
3. Follow someone. When you follow someone who knows the trail, you can see when he slows down; it's like following on the freeway—see brake lights, time to brake. Even if the other rider doesn't know the trail, it's still a good idea to follow. Let him be surprised; treat yourself to that cushion. But don't entrust your life to him completely; try to look around and through him, as far ahead as possible.

INSURE YOURSELF

Good health insurance is a must, especially in the United States.

- Ride with more confidence knowing you can get—and pay for—quality medical care.
- Take responsibility for yourself. Unless you are insured well enough to cover any conceivable injury, you cannot guarantee you won't have to sue someone to help pay your medical bills. If you want to be ultra-responsible, look into long-term disability insurance, which takes over after your health insurance lapses.

LEE'S TOO-LATE LESSON

I had left shoulder surgery in 2002 and broke my right clavicle in 2003. These injuries were 100 percent my fault; my technique was terrible.

Since then I've raced, ridden, and coached harder than ever, and I've kept up a consistent strength and mobility program. My shoulders were always sore, and they made funny noises, but I figured that was penance for my lifestyle, and I sucked it up.

In 2008, I got some bad news:

○ The right clavicle had never healed, and the inside of the joint was badly damaged. The only thing holding my arm on was muscle.

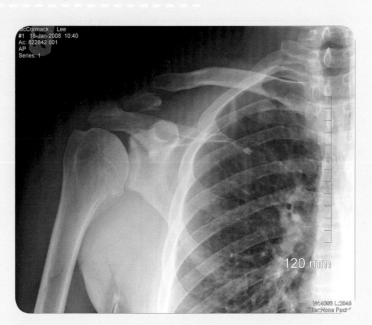

Lee's right clavicle, four years *after* it supposedly healed. Apparently Lee doesn't take great care of himself!

○ The left shoulder was filled with bone fragments, and it was basically destroying itself. The doc said I'll eventually need a replacement.

As of this writing, the left shoulder has been worked on but hurts more than ever, and the right shoulder needs a major rebuild. Being tough all those years was not a good idea. I did more damage, and I'll be paying for it for the rest of my life.

Lessons

1. Learn proper technique so you can avoid getting hurt in the first place.
2. Listen to your body. If you feel joint pain, don't try to tough it out.
3. Take care of yourself. There are no extra points for ripping while injured.

Ride Within Your Limits

Your "limit" is completely relative. It depends on your skills, fitness, confidence, mood, equipment, the conditions, and the terrain. If you want a long career in mountain biking, you should spend very little time on the edge.

"Me at 90 percent may be way faster than most people want to ride," Brian says. "But that's 100 percent within my comfort level. There's no fear, no chances or risks. But when I get to 99 to 100 percent, then every little teeny thing puts me on the edge of crashing. That's when I get scared."

Gravity racers make a living riding the ragged edge, shaving milliseconds without crossing the line. Cross-country racers don't need to push so hard—they're not going to win a two-hour race by 0.01 second. The same goes for recreational riders.

"Some guys, maybe some you know, are constantly riding over their limit," Brian says. "They have flashes of greatness, but they end up on the ground and hurt a lot. Guys like Steve Peat or Sam Hill are consistently at the top of the downhill race results. They're pushing their limits, but not to the point where they're out of control or s----ing themselves down the hill. Most of us can't do that consistently, or we'll end up on the ground."

The more time you spend pushing your limits, the more likely you'll crash. That's why, statistically, downhill racing is so much more dangerous than cross-country racing—and racing of any kind is far more dangerous than just riding.

Stay within your limits—below the point of stress. Finding flow is more fun, and is easier on your body, than seeking thrills.

Ride With Confidence

This ties to the previous items, but it bears mentioning. The smoother and more relaxed you are, the better your bike, body, and mind can flow through any situation. Once you get nervous, you get tense, and a crash is imminent.

Whatever you're doing, wherever you are, whomever you're with: Ride with confidence. If you need to slow down, follow someone, walk a section, or even ride a different trail, that's fine. Do whatever it takes to ride with an open, happy mind.

Wear Your Safety Gear

This is such a "Duh" that it pains us to mention, but please wear proper safety gear.

Mandatory for all rides:

- Helmet
- Gloves
- Eye glasses

In order of importance as your riding gets riskier:

- Knee/shin guards
- Elbow guards
- Full-face helmet
- Goggles
- Upper-body armor
- Hip pads/lower-body armor
- Protective shoes
- Neck brace

Wear whatever you need to feel confident. There's no such thing as too much protection.

Limits are relative. This turn is gnarly/ rocky/tricky, but Abby Hippely is relaxing within her comfort zone (and she's balanced right over her pedals— always advisable).

At the downhill in Crested Butte, Colorado, this rider is rocking a moto-style neck brace. The brace prevents his head from rotating too far backward or forward, thus reducing the risk of neck injury. Gloves would be a good idea, but some downhillers prefer the feel of bare hands. (Awesome position BTW!)

Common Mistakes and Their Fixes

As a more "normal" rider than Brian, and as a coach who works with all sorts of riders, Lee is intimately familiar with the specifics of crashing.

Here are the main ways people lose control of their bikes, and the main ways to avoid them. Ninety-nine percent of crashes are caused by one of the following issues. They are all avoidable.

Over the Bars

THE PROBLEM

Flying over the bars is the leading cause of injuries that require hospitalization. How do you fly over the bars? Put simply, your center of mass has gone forward of your forward-most base of support, aka the contact patch of your front wheel.

Causes include hitting obstacles, improper braking, and—our favorite—hitting obstacles while braking improperly. Another classic cause is leaning back because you're afraid of going over the bars, but hitting rear-wheel heavy and getting bucked forward.

AVOIDING THE PROBLEM

Keep your feet heavy and your hands light. As long as you drive your weight into your pedals, you cannot flop over the bars. It's impossible. So:

- Always practice effective braking technique.
- Maintain a neutral attack position.
- When you encounter a rollable obstacle (say, a water bar), stay centered.
- Repeat the mantra: Heavy feet, light hands. Heavy feet. Light hands!

So you're going over the bars. If you stay loose and roll it out, you'll finish your race. If you stiffen up and try to stop yourself . . . well . . . let's not talk about that.

CORRECTING THE PROBLEM

If you feel the rear wheel coming up and your body rotating forward over the bars, push your bike down in front of you. The idea is to keep your body as stationary as possible and push the front of the bike down to meet the ground. The sooner your front wheel makes contact, the sooner it can support you.

But don't linger. Over-the-bars crashes can be ghastly. If you feel a major buck, or if you feel yourself flying over your bars, there's no way to prevent calamity. Get away from that bike!

Hitting Things

THE PROBLEM

You're going too fast, and you hit a rock, log, or whatever. The speed and size aren't absolute; it's the combination of speed and size that causes trouble, and, more important, it's your reaction that can create or prevent problems.

- You're careening out of control. Your front wheel hits a rock and bounces off to the side. You tense up. You crash.
- You hit a log, bounce into the air, and freak out. You crash.
- You're hauling mail at a square-edged water bar. You're afraid to get bucked forward, so you lean back. Bad idea. Your rear wheel hits extra hard; then Earth pushes back extra hard. Newton's third law. You get bucked forward. You crash.

Believe it or not, the best way to stay safe in rough sections is to actively absorb them. In this case, that means pulling up before the rock pushes you up.

AVOIDING THE PROBLEM

Great riders ride over big things all the time, and they do it with style. All it takes is the proper technique, and the confidence to pull it off.

- ○ Control your speed. *Do not* drag your brakes. Brake hard to slow way down. Coast and pump through the rough sections.
- ○ Maintain a low attack position. This gives you the arm range to let your bike bounce without trouble.
- ○ Never run into anything. If it's big enough to be afraid of, you should (1) ride around it or (2) pump it. Rather than freezing, push down extra hard right before the obstacle; then pull up just as hard as you encounter it. You might not clear the Log of Death, but you'll hit it much lighter—and it'll hit you much lighter in return.
- ○ Keep your hands and feet moving. The rougher it gets, the more you must mirror the terrain. As soon as you brace for impact, it's over.

CORRECTING THE PROBLEM

First, recognize that not every impact is a problem. If a surprise impact sends your bike on a new line into the netherworld, first try to keep riding. You'll be amazed at what you and your bike can handle, especially if you're in the right position.

Blowing Turns

Corners are the most complex skill in mountain biking, and many crashes happen when the trail changes direction.

Look where you *want* to go. Put them in a gnarly enough situation, and even pros get balled up. Alexander McGuinnis gets target fixation at the Snowmass, Colorado, downhill.

THE PROBLEM

- You enter a turn with your weight too far back, and the front end slides out. You crash.

- You're too involved with your upper body, and you're stiff to boot. You enter a turn with your weight too far forward. Your wheel catches and you get sent forward. You crash.

- You're not leaning the bike enough, and it just doesn't want to make the turn. You see the cliff/cactus/boulder (take your pick) on the outside of the turn, and you desperately turn your bars in the direction you want to go. You wash out or flop forward. Either way, you crash.

AVOIDING THE PROBLEM

- Corner correctly. Duh. Low attack position. Lean your bike. Look toward the next turn. Keep your hands light and neutral. Load the turn if needed. See chapter 5, Carve Any Corner.

- Be diligent with your attack position. When you get nervous, you will stiffen up and raise your head and shoulders. Don't! Keep your shoulders low; it's the only way to maintain the arm range you need to control a wayward turn. And keep reading . . .

- Let it go. Yep, that's right. If your shoulders are low and close to the bars, your front wheel can wander at least 2 feet (60 cm) in any direction before you run out of arm range and the drift becomes an issue.

CORRECTING THE PROBLEM

- Lean the bike even more. This increases cornering force.

- Put out your inside foot. But don't hang it to the inside like an outrigger. Push it forward, up near your front wheel. If something catastrophic happens, save yourself with that foot.

- Lean forward onto the front wheel. As long as it's tracking, it doesn't much matter what your rear wheel is doing. This is for experts only; it's easier to screw this up than to save yourself. See chapter 5 on cornering, page 81.

Freaking Out

THE PROBLEM

- Basically, once you feel a certain amount of stress, you lose your mind, your skills, and your control of the bike. You are nervous the whole ride. The trail is hard, the group is fast, maybe you've crashed here before, or maybe you're just weak willed. Every move you make is tainted by tension. This makes your bike feel uncontrollable, which makes more tension, which makes your bike feel even more uncontrollable, and so on until the ride ceases to be fun or you make any one of the common mistakes. You crash. And now you're *really* tense!

- You freak out in a specific section. The drop is too tall, the jump too far, the hill too steep, the roots too wet, your speed too high. You tense up. You lose your mind. You lose control of your bike. You crash. And now you're *really* freaked out!

No matter what happens, if you keep smiling, you'll stay loose, and you'll probably be fine. A little XC action at the 2009 SolVista Nationals.

○ That "Oh s---!" moment. You know what we're talking about. That feeling you get when your front wheel bounces wildly or washes out. Your heart jumps, your hair stands up, your muscles tense. You lose your mind. You lose control. You crash. That feeling happens when your head gets displaced. The balance centers in your inner ear get a sudden, unplanned shake—and that creates instant stress.

AVOIDING THE PROBLEM

○ Don't put yourself into scary situations. Although it's good to push yourself to a certain extent, you learn little and have even less fun when you're scared. Ride easier trails. Ride with slower people. Or at least give yourself permission to slow down to the point where you feel safe. Pushing yourself has its place, but not if you're too stressed to ride to the best of your ability. Anytime you ride stressed out, you're that much closer to melting down—and that much closer to a nasty crash.

○ Always ride with confidence. If that means riding easier trails, riding with slower people, or wearing full body armor, then do it. You'll have fun—and improve— only if you feel good about what you're doing.

○ Find another way. This is supposed to be fun. If a section wigs you out, slow down, take another line, walk your bike, or just find another ride.

○ Always, always, always rock your low attack position. This gives you the range of motion to let your bike bounce around without moving your head. As long as your head is going straight and level, it truly doesn't matter what your bike is doing.

CORRECTING THE PROBLEM

○ In that instant of panic, you are helpless. Do your best to avoid fear. If you do freak out and survive the aftermath, take some time to reboot your brain.

○ Know exactly why you crashed. That's the only way to be confident about avoiding that same crash.

○ Refocus on fun. Release all other expectations. Get back to that sweet feeling of flow.

○ Focus on the basics. If your attack position and other techniques are dialed, it becomes really hard to screw up.

○ Change the situation if needed. Slow down. Change lines. Wear pads. Ride with nicer people. Whatever it takes.

BRIAN KNOWS BIKE JUMPS

I've been jumping bikes all my life. I have a lot of confidence that in that split second when something happens, I'll react correctly. As soon as I take off on a jump, I have a pretty good idea of whether I'm gonna make it. How much will I miss the landing by? Can I case it and pull it off? How bad will it be? Should I abort? I know in an instant. Not that I always make the perfect decisions, but more times than not I do.

I consider myself just OK at riding motocross [Brian

Been there, done that. Brian samples the air at Oakley's test track.

actually races at a local pro level, but he's friends with top riders like Jeremy McGrath and Bubba Stewart, so he knows what fast really is. —Lee].

If I'm riding a supercross track, I might be eyeing a jump I want to do. Sometimes I'm like, "Dang, if I come up short, what will I do?" I know in that split second that I might not have the knowledge I need. If something did go wrong, it might be bad. So I don't try it.

What that means for you: Don't go for something unless you are confident you can handle the worst-case scenario.

Listen to Your Friends (Sometimes)

If your riding partner knows the terrain (say, a big jump), and he knows your skills, and he assures you that you can do it, it can be a great confidence boost. But only if you trust the person. "I'm not gonna listen to some yahoo on the side of some DH course telling me I have enough speed for the jump," Brian says, "but if it's Peaty, sure, I'll probably go for it."

So You're in Trouble . . .

Once you lose control, things can devolve very quickly. Some crashes take a moment to unfold; others are instantaneous. Here's where great instincts and deeply honed bailing skills come in.

If you decide to bail, there's one fact—you're hitting the ground.

Try to ride it out.   If it's minor—a slight buck or tweak—you might be able to pull it off. Nothing gets your heart pumping like a great save. It's happened to all of us. You hit a jump wrong, get bucked into an endo, and dead sailor through the air, just holding on, and somehow you pull it off. It's like, "Oh my God, thank you," then "Yeah! That was so rad!" You don't always make the right decision, but that's life.

Bail sooner than later.   If your bat sense tells you this is gonna be catastrophic, don't wait around to see what happens next. Get out of there. The slow-motion crashes usually happen when you've gotten in over your head. You enter a rock garden way too fast and get out of shape. Uh oh . . . oh oh . . . uh oh . . . it takes a while before you finally flop over the bars or hit that tree. Try to ride it out, but definitely bail before you panic and turn stupid.

If you get bucked forward, get off that bike!   Start running in the air. Keep your head up and hope you land feet first and tumble out. If you hold on to a buck too long, it's a ride to the ER.

Try to come off the low side of your bike, rather than flopping over the top. When a turn or a steep, loose section goes awry, grab your rear brake and lean into the hill. This gets your bike sliding so you can let yourself down easy. Let go of the bike and start rolling.

Don't try to stop yourself.   Falling isn't the problem. It's the sudden stop. If you put your arms out and try to stop yourself dead, something will give (frequently your collarbone; there must be a better design!).

It's all in the tongue. Michael Lobojko surfs out a potential crash at the SolVista Nationals. Note how his rear tire is skidding, but his heavily weighted front tire is tracking. Awesome.

Time to go. No sense hanging on in this situation. Jeremiah Bishop shows us a very pro dismount.

'Tis better to slide under than to flop over. Alex Vidal chalks this one up to experience.

Run it out.   This is ideal. Jump off your bike and stay on your feet. Keep running as long as you must—until all that wayward kinetic energy has been expressed. BTW: This is a great reason to be a competent trail runner.

Roll with it.   This is where good instincts make the difference between a nonevent and a helicopter ride. The elements of a good, safe roll-out:

- Land on your feet.
- Bend your knees to absorb the main impact.
- Cover your face and hold your arms in.
- Roll onto your shoulder.
- Let your body roll over. Don't fight this. Let yourself roll as many times as it takes.
- Finish on your feet. Find your bike. Rip it!

THE ULTIMATE NONCRASH

Lee was chasing pro XC/super D racer Mike West down a technical trail in Colorado. They were going super fast, and the traction was iffy. Mike lost his front wheel in a turn, jumped off his bike, ran alongside the trail dragging his bike by the handlebar, jumped back on, and resumed his speed in less time than it took to read this sentence. Very impressive. If you "crashed" like that, imagine how confident you'd be.

Crashing is a skill like any other. The more you do it, the better you'll get—but who wants to practice crashing? Some hard-core dirt jumpers intentionally practice pitching their bikes in the air. For the rest of us, it's probably better to take a gymnastics or martial arts class and practice tumbling there. Or just practice tumbling on the carpet in front of your TV. Every time Tyra says the word *fierce* . . . tumble!

A crash is only a crash if you get hurt. If you run or roll it out, it's just an . . . unplanned dismount!

Top Five Training Exercises—or— James Says, "Do These Exercises"

James Wilson is a strength coach and serious mountain biker in Grand Junction, Colorado. He specializes in mobility and strength training for mountain bikers. As James teaches, the stronger and more mobile you are, the faster you ride and the healthier you stay. Not only are you less susceptible to chronic injuries, but you're also more durable in case of a crash.

Here are his top five exercises:

Deadlift. The deadlift is most important exercise a mountain biker can do. It helps you maintain a good attack position, and it gives you the mobility and power for awesome pedaling and pumping.

Core activation sequence. The glute bridge, plank, side plank, and bird dog build backward, forward, side-to-side, and rotational core stability for hard pedaling and high g's.

James Wilson is ridiculously strong in the gym and very good on the bike. Training near home in Grand Junction, Colorado.

Quad and hip flexor stretch. Tight quads and hip flexors—common among cyclists—inhibit hip function; cause lower back pain; and rob you of strength, power, and endurance. Stretch those puppies!

Push-up. The classic. Push with your upper body while keeping your core strong and your shoulders packed down on your back, rather than hunched forward.

Single-leg deadlift. This tricky variation makes the deadlift even more functional. (We do pedal one leg at a time.)

To learn more about Wilson's training approach, and to check out his mountain bike–specific training programs, check out www.leelikesbikes.com.

BRIAN KNOWS 360s

With tricks, you know really quickly if it's gone bad. Say you're going for a 360 off a double jump. Your front wheel leaves the lip, and your head is turning for the rotation. In my mind I'm doing a 360, but maybe the back tire is hung up on the lip. The front of the bike and my mind and everything are starting the rotation, but the back of my bike is saying "Not now, buddy." In that case, even before the bike is in the air, I know I'm not going to make it. I let go of the bike and I'm in the air spinning. But at least I'm not tangled with the bike.

Rip It for a Lifetime

Bumps, bruises, and broken bones are not badges of honor. They're signs that you're doing something wrong. If you continue to ride in ways that hurt you, you won't be riding for much longer.

The fact is, you can enjoy a lifetime of fun and improvement if you follow some basic principles:

- Set your bike up properly for your body.
- Listen to your body. If something hurts, stop and make a change.
- Keep yourself as mobile and strong as possible.
- Learn proper riding technique.
- Ride within your limits.

And tell your loved ones: Injuries are not an integral part of mountain biking.

CHAPTER 13

Race Like a Champ

Racing is just like riding, only it's for keeps. On race day you need all your play-day skills, plus a few special tricks to give you an extra edge.

Strengthen Your Mind

In any competitive class, a handful of people have the physical strength and skills to win. To win, you need the emotional and mental skills to hold it together throughout the race. Here are some tips to make you as stony as a statue.

Race for the Right Reasons

Racing is just like riding, only a result sheet tells you exactly where you rank. Competition can stoke you out and inspire you to new greatness, or it can bum you out and spoil you on riding. The determining factor isn't whether you win or lose the race; it's how you perform in relation to your expectations and goals.

We enter races for myriad reasons: to wield our powers against others; to see how we stand against the best; to make a living; to challenge ourselves; to ride as fast as we want on fun courses; to travel to cool places; to bash elbows with our buddies; to commune with the racing tribe; to validate the time, money, and energy we put into our sport; and, for some of us, to validate ourselves as riders and as people.

Before you reach the starting line, take the time to figure out what, exactly, you expect to get from the experience. By setting clear expectations, you'll know what to strive for, and you'll know how to measure your success. Here are some things to keep in mind:

Why is more powerful than what. Think about the reasons you race. Whether you race for self-improvement (good reason) or to destroy other people (not such a good reason), your fundamental goal will drive you through the inevitable difficulties—and successes.

Enjoy the process. Riding (and living) is a never-ending process of increasing your strength and skills. When you become serious about racing, you dedicate yourself to the process of finishing higher and higher in more challenging events and, eventually, in higher classes. Just as learning to jump a 10-foot double is a step on the way to jumping a 12-footer, then a 15-footer, and on and on until the requirements outweigh the rewards, earning 87th place is a step toward 10th place, then 3rd, then 1st, and then up to a harder class. Write down your racing goals and keep track of your progress. When you feel defeated or question your motives, your racing log will keep you motivated. Remember: Keep striving to improve, but enjoy where you are and take the time to appreciate what you've already accomplished.

Racing is 90 percent physical. The other 90 percent is mental. Put Billy Owczarski on a race course, and he's all business.

Remember: It's only bike racing. What? Blasphemy! After you strip away your ego, winning a race means only this: You were the fastest or first rider on that day, in those conditions, among that group of racers. Anything—different terrain, weather, racers, or luck—could have dropped you to number two. Shoot, if you were in a higher class, you might have been 87th! In racing (and in life) you can control only yourself—and then sometimes only barely. Try not to worry about things that are outside your control. If someone flats and you move up a spot, don't be too proud of yourself. In the same way, if a competitor makes a clever move and you fall a spot, don't be too bummed.

If you believe the old No Fear T-shirt that said, "Second place is the first loser," you are in for a world of pain.

Have reasonable expectations. The most reasonable expectation is, "I will do my best," whatever that means to you. For most people (except Brian), the most unreasonable expectation is, "I will win." If you expect to win all the time, expect to be disappointed much of the time. In a time-trial event, you have no influence on other people's runs. If they are fitter, better skilled, more clever, or ride in faster conditions, they might beat you. Do everything you can to ensure a good time, but in the end realize that times are what they are: just times. Racing head-to-head is even more complicated. You can get beaten because of a crash, a clever pass, superior fitness, or mental toughness. Win or no win, either way, do your best.

Set personal performance goals. As we've been saying, "winning" is arbitrary and, in large part, out of your control. Set goals for yourself: In a downhill, lay off your brakes through the tricky rock section; in a cross-country, maintain 176 beats per minute on the climbs; in a bikercross, don't let anyone low–high you. Whether you win or not, judge yourself by how well you met your goals. But keep in mind that this is racing. Keep striving to do better. Otherwise, go for a fun ride and save the entry fee.

Pick the right class. Racing is a great opportunity to compare yourself with other riders of the same caliber. The best racing class for you depends on your reasons for racing. If you want a challenge, race in a class that lets you ride fun courses with riders who will push you. For the most intense competition, race in a class that you have a chance, but no guarantee, of winning. There's nothing as exciting as battling it out with close competitors. Losing makes you hungry, and winning is definitely something to be proud of. If you must destroy other

DON'T LET A BAD RESULT RUIN A GOOD TIME

I (Lee) have been completely stoked on a race run and then been devastated when the results ranked me lower than I wanted to be. What a shame, to let my placing ruin a good time. On the other end, I've completely blown race runs and then been jazzed when the results showed everyone else blew it worse. How shallow, to take pleasure in other people's catastrophes. Both extremes—letting a bad result ruin a great race and letting a good result erase a bad race—show a lack of internal goals. Not only will this not help you improve, it's also no fun.

Have fun! Bobbi Watt, post-crash, filthy and stoked to be out there.

people to feel good about yourself, go ahead and stay in an easy class. Enjoy your five overall titles in Beginner 30-34; then move on to destroy Beginner 35-39. But be warned: There is a special hell for sandbaggers, and your competitors will try to send you there.

Use your losses.   You can always go faster. Learn from your mistakes. In a way, second place is more exciting than first place. When you win, you feel good and there are no excuses, but you start wondering about where to go from there. When you take a close 2nd (or 3rd or 87th or whatever), you get really hungry and hypermotivated to do better next time. The drive toward improvement is much more powerful than the satisfaction of accomplishment.

Get Into the Racing Zone

You've heard all types of competitors talk about getting into "the zone." The zone is like the state of flow (chapter 10), only it's more intense. You've blocked out everything but what you need to win the race. There are good riders—people who flow smoothly while they're out playing with their buddies, but who crumble under pressure—and there are good racers—those who can reach the zone and drop the hammer on command. Brian is one of the best. Here are some tips to help you reach the racing zone.

Visualize.   This is the key to a great performance. Imagine yourself having a great race. Fill in as much detail as you can—sights, sounds, sensations. Run your race in real time. Imagine what you'll do if you get off line or get passed. If you imagine something in enough detail, it's as if your brain is practicing in real life.

Before their race, some riders get excited and talkative. Others get quite and reflective. Current world bikercross champion Jared Graves does the latter.

LISTEN TO JUDY

In her six years as a pro cross-country racer, currently with Tough Girl Cycling, Judy Freeman has learned some important lessons about integrating life and racing.

You Need Discipline

"One of the hardest things about being a serious racer is giving up fun rides with your friends to do solo intervals and honor your rest days. When I think about being in form for April, it's easier to say no to a sweet ride this weekend.

"I saw a quote once that helps: You can only say 'no' and smile when you have a bigger 'yes' burning inside you."

But Not Too Much Discipline

"I have gotten to where I'm wound up so tight on stuff, nothing is fun. Training too hard, trying to eat just the right foods . . . I've deprived myself and been miserable. There were a couple years when I was going to quit. I wasn't liking biking, or anything. It was a big struggle financially and emotionally.

"The more I focus on what I love about racing, the more fun I have—and the better my results are."

Judy gets it done in Crested Butte, Colorado.

Balance Your Life

"Every aspect of your life affects your racing. If one part of your life isn't working right, you can usually rein yourself in and still have a good performance. But if you let things get too out of balance, you get to the point where you can't rein stuff in. You show up unrested, with your mind in a bad spot.

"Racing has a certain priority. Relationships have a certain priority. Work has a certain priority. You have to make it all fit together in a way that works and makes you happy.

"For me right now, racing is the big thing. I'm not in a relationship, and I'm not working. Racing is my priority. To wake up every day and know what the day is about helps me feel good.

"You have to find that balance that fits you, not your concept of *should*. Be true to yourself. You might think that you should be training more, adopting someone else's program, trying to maintain the social life you had before racing, doing this or that, being 'a better person.' Be honest with yourself on all levels. Make sacrifices for the meaningful things in your life. Focus on what's most important to you."

Naps

"I'm unemployed right now so I can do two-a-day workouts, lifting and riding. That really helps. And I try to nap as much as possible."

continued ⇒

Savor the Grays

"Being a racer is hard psychologically.

"Racing has clear rules. There's a winner. It's black and white. But we are humans with desires, hopes, fears, maybe even feelings of inadequacy. It's important that you not process a bad result in a black and white way. But unless someone teaches you how to look at this, how do you know how you should feel about yourself when you don't win? If I'm not number one, I'm no good? You need a healthy way to look at racing and competition.

"Ask yourself, what can you work on specifically? Externalize the result, instead of internalizing it. I think women have more of a tendency to internalize a bad result than men."

Be a Good Sport

"We all can have our jerky moments.

"How many times have you been told 'Congratulations' for a good race only to have it followed by a list of why that person wasn't as fast that day? That's not cool.

"When people complain about their equipment, make excuses, explain why they didn't have a good race, when they came up to congratulate you in the first place, I think they're totally coming from a bad emotional space—and they don't even know it. They're usually just be trying to make themselves feel better, but they're using the wrong opportunity.

"We all have the capacity to be that person. It can be really hard to pull yourself out of a disappointment to be a good sport. Even if you feel bad, just say congratulations; then walk away. Don't take away from someone else's high so you can feel better about your low."

Before the start of the 1993 Mammoth Kamikaze, Missy Giove sat by herself on a rock outcropping, pedaling with her hands and leaning into each corner, imagining every detail of the race course. The phrase "If you can see it, you can be it" is usually true. The phrase "If you can't see it, you can't be it" is always true.

Focus, But in a Relaxed Way.   When your Stanford MBA left brain starts to chatter about race pressure, the huge jump, or whatever, it's time to wake up your Berkeley hippie right brain and chill out. To quiet the inner Republican, try focusing on your breathing. Bring air deeply and easily into your belly, and focus on your center, right behind your belly button. This sounds all new-age hippie-dippy, but it really works. You will feel the nervous energy leave your noggin and settle comfortably in your core. Use this to focus before your event, and try it when you're pedaling so hard the entire universe consists of pain. Here are some other things to keep in mind—well, not really *in* mind 'cause that would be a distraction:

○ Keep your mind quiet, with no extraneous thoughts whatsoever.

○ Think positively and don't let negative thoughts distract you.

○ Relax and let your body and mind do what they know how to do.

○ If you're having a great race, don't let the catastrophic "Hey, I'm gonna win" thought enter your mind. It's hard to keep those thoughts out, but you must. Concentrate all your energy on finishing the race.

WHY DO YOU RACE? HOW HAVE YOUR REASONS CHANGED OVER THE YEARS?

Lee

In the beginning I raced to prove myself as a good bike rider. I'd never been competitive in any sport, and the podium seemed like such a glorious place, a place for studly people (I saw myself as an overweight wimp). After a few years, the need to win started taking over. I focused on downhill, finally won a Sport race, and jumped to Expert. I really thought I'd win races and go pro. At a very deep level, I needed to win to feel good about myself. Second place made me angry. Around this time, I stopped having fun.

After I suffered a concussion in a downhill, I took a break from racing. Once I relaxed, my skills grew like crazy and I started having fun again. I tried a race in late 2001, just for kicks, and won it. Then I goofed off at another race and won that one, too. In late 2001 and 2002, I raced 20 times and won eight times in Expert. I wasn't really training; I just showed up and relied on the skills and fitness I'd gained from playing. I was enjoying the scene, the competition, and my ever-increasing skills. In 2003, I set the goal of winning a national. I quit my day job to focus on riding and writing, and I rode just about every day with fast pros. We trained extremely hard—distance, intervals, the whole thing. My skills and strength jumped dramatically, but I was so intense I couldn't find my flow, and I wound up blowing all the nationals. I went into 2004 hoping to have faith in my abilities and to let the results take care of themselves—and it seems to have worked. I won the Expert downhills at the Sea Otter Classic and the Durango national, and I ended the year as the top-ranked American Expert downhiller in my age group.

The following year, the first edition of *Mastering Mountain Bike Skills* came out, and I shifted my focus to coaching. I still went to the races, but in a supportive role, which was actually more satisfying than my own wins. My junior team won some championships, and I did the occasional race, to stay sharp.

These days, I'm happy to pay the bills, take care of my family, help people through my site, write great how-to books and coach all sorts of riders—and to kick some occasional ass.

Judy Freeman

When I first got into it, it was all a new adventure. I was meeting new people, riding new things, doing things I never thought I could do, seeing new places. Then I started winning.

Once I focused on winning, it was no more fun. The highs are so fleeting, and the lows are so low. I ended up on a treadmill of always trying to be faster, trying to win. I felt like I was losing myself. I'm a generally nice person; I like hanging out and having fun. But I'd show up to the races, and I looked at the people there as competition, and I didn't like that. Sometimes when I'd have a bad race, I'd be negative, feel jealous, or make excuses to myself. It just wasn't fun anymore, and I didn't like who I was as a person.

Spiritually, it was also a big contradiction for me. Wanting to beat someone flies in the face of taming the ego. It's like, why do you need to win? I didn't know what attitude to adopt, how to be competitive, motivated, and effective, yet still be myself.

Now I don't want to beat anyone. In the past year I've changed how I see the other racers. Instead of seeing them as my competition, I try to see them as people who are helping me get stronger.

continued ➡

It's an ongoing process—a practice. I went from wanting to *be* the best to wanting to *find* my best.

Now when I get passed, instead of being upset, I'm like "Right on! Thanks for bringing it!"

I'm a lot happier. You never know when you're gonna stop racing. Instead of being riddled with fear—Am I ever gonna be fast? Will I lose everything I've gained?—I'm enjoying the process. All people—doctors, artists—have ways of expressing themselves. Racing is my expression. It's the path I'm walking now.

Brian

Well, I have a house to pay for . . .

No, actually, I love winning and I love riding my bike. I'm lucky enough to get paid to do it. If I didn't race, I'd still ride. It's all I know how to do; I've been doing it since I was four and a half. That's my life—bikes.

For the past eight years I've specialized in bikercross, dual, and dual slalom. That's what I did, and that's what people expected from me. But there's not much else I can achieve in that area. (Brian has won 16 national, World Cup, and world titles in dual slalom, dual, and bikercross.) It's like riding the same trail two to four days per week for eight years. You get a bit burnt. You still love riding, but you need a new trail.

That's where I am in my racing career. I still love riding and racing. I just want to do a new kind of racing, set some new goals. Now I'm more focused on endurance downhills, and I had fun racing cyclocross last winter.

I'm only getting older. There are so many fun disciplines in cycling—MTB, road, BMX, cyclo-cross, freestyle, trials—I might as well start chipping away a bit. It's all fun.

Follow Your Prerace Routine. Do you remember the way you felt the last time you had a great race? Do whatever it takes to get into that same place. Eat your special dinner, get your sleep, practice in the morning, check every bolt on your bike, take a nap, wear mismatched socks, warm up with your Ab Lounge, or whatever. Your prerace routine is a ladder you climb to your peak performance. Your racing gear—jersey, armor, shoes, or whatever—can help you get that extra eye of the tiger.

Your routine should be flexible enough to withstand sharing a condo with 19 guys, but your warm-up and the last few minutes before your race should be sacred. Do whatever you need to feel warm, relaxed, and centered.

Right before the race, some riders vent nervous energy by goofing around, while others prefer to separate themselves from the frenzy. A lot of riders joke around and stuff, but I (Brian) keep to myself and concentrate on what I have to do. Steve Blick, my Oakley rep, is one of my best friends, but I don't even talk to him up on the start line. I just hand him my dirty glasses and he hands me clean ones. We hang out and party after the race.

Don't Spaz Out. Many beginning racers get too excited and they lose their minds on race day. After five perfect practice runs, they'll fall in the first corner, pedal too hard to make up time, blow up, fall again, and then forget where they left their car keys.

Don't put too much pressure on yourself. If 1 is sleep and 10 is panic, shoot for an 8 or 9. Remember: This is just a bike ride. With results. And series points. And sponsorship on the line . . . Oops, sorry. Just chill out and have fun.

Don't Let Mistakes Freak You Out.   Some tennis players symbolically wipe their mistakes off their rackets before they continue their game. Maybe you could wipe your mistakes off your handlebar. No matter where you wipe them, you have to get over your mistakes and get back onto your race plan. Don't go nuts trying to make up for lost time, either. Stay within your abilities, and everything will go as well as it's supposed to.

Remind Yourself With Keywords.   Pick a word that encapsulates what you're trying to do and say it to yourself to keep you focused. "Spin" might help you climb efficiently. "Float" might carry you over a rock garden. "Bam!" might help you holeshot a World Cup 4X . . . but probably not.

Listen to Tunes.   Music has a powerful ability to shape our thoughts. If you need to relax, go for some Kenny G. If you need to get amped up, crank up Metallica's *Frantic.*

Bikercross

In bikercross (aka mountain cross, four cross, and 4X), four racers blast out of a steel gate and race down a course with humps, jumps, berms, and flat turns. The runs last about 30 seconds. To qualify, each rider runs an individual time trial. Depending on the size of the race, the fastest 4, 8, 16, 32, or 64 riders advance to the finals. The fastest two are pitted against the slowest two, the next fastest two are matched with the next slowest two, and so on until all the brackets are filled. Following each heat, the two fastest riders advance to the next round, while the other two become spectators. This continues until only four are left and the winners cross the line.

To excel in bikercross, racers need good all-around bike skills—explosive pedaling, confident jumping, clean cornering—plus fast starts, decisive passing, and clever tactics. In bikercross, sometimes the winner isn't the fastest rider—it's the smartest rider.

Start Like a Bullet

Many bikercross races are won on the starting line. If you get the holeshot, there's a strong chance you'll hold the pack at bay and win the race. If you come out last, you have to work your way through some ferocious traffic. So work on those starts!

There are few excitements like ripping down a turny/jumpy course with three other people—especially if you're in front. Ross Milan wins a heat in Nathrop, Colorado.

Choose the Right Lane. Lane choice can make or break a race. The fastest qualifiers get the first lane choice. Since you're reading this book, we know you'll be qualifying fast, and you'll have to deal with this situation.

The shortest route to the first corner usually wins. On most courses, this is lane 1. Of course, there are exceptions.

Sometimes lane 1 is so far inside that you have to swing into lane 2 to enter the first turn. If the lane 2 rider is right there, you have to slow down—"shut down"—and let him in first. Not cool. Next time pick lane 2.

Know your competitors' strengths. Just because you qualified first doesn't make you the fastest starter. If you think you'll get beaten to the first turn, line up on the outside rather than the inside. If you get shut down in lane 1, you have to slow down and let everyone go by. If you get beaten in lane 4, you can follow with speed and stay in the game.

Be sure to look at the course. Maybe the first jump is faster on the outside lane, or maybe there's a mud puddle on the inside lane. And this one seems obvious, but it's important: Make sure your gate is clear of rocks, sand, mud, or anything else that can slow you down.

Choose the Right Gear. As always, you want a gear that's not so hard that you bog down and not so easy that you spin out and have to shift right away. Gear choice depends on the grade and the length of the run-out. When in doubt, choose a low gear that gets you out front right away. The faster you can spin, the more speed you'll achieve before you have to shift. For example, a racer who turns a 34×19 gear to 80 rpm has to back off the pressure and shift at 11 miles per hour (18 km/h). A competitor who can whip up to 120 rpm will reach almost 17 miles per hour (27 km/h) in the same gear. In an event that's won by fractions of seconds, that's a huge difference.

You should be able to achieve your optimum cadence in just a few strokes. If you're struggling to tach up, you're wasting time.

DEALING WITH LANE 4

If you get the last gate choice, you're likely to get the outside lane. If you enter the first turn to the outside of the leaders, they're likely to trap you high on the berm.

Options

1. Get a great start, get out front, and corral everyone to the inside. Sweet.
2. Hang outside and just behind the other riders. When everyone dives into the first turn, try a high–low pass, or at least get a great drive into the second straight.

Keep your eyes open and never give up. You never know what's gonna happen.

Position Your Pedals for Power.   Start with your strongest foot forward, with your pedal around 2 o'clock. In a flat gate, run the pedal closer to 3 o'clock for ultimate impulse power. On a steep gate, run the pedal closer to 1:30 to carry you farther down the slope.

The All-Important Gate Start.   For those of you who came to bikercross from cross-country and downhill, BMX-style gates seem like crazy contraptions. You press your front wheel against a metal gate, put both feet on the pedals, and balance while you wait for the cadence.

4X start cadences have seen some changes over the years. They started with a standard, predictable BMX cadence, but the BMXer were killing everyone. Then they went to a special mountain-bike-only random cadence (and BMXers still killed everyone). These days, most 4X and dual slalom races use the new UCI/NBL cadence.

This new random cadence was implemented in 2007 to prevent riders from slingshotting—pushing back from the gate and pedaling before the gate drops. The hope is to make racing more fair. This cadence is the same as the old UCI/NBL cadence; the only difference is the random pause between "Watch the gate" and the first beep:

OK, riders, random start.
Pause.
Riders ready.
Short pause.
Watch the gate.
Random delay of 0.1 to 2.7 seconds.
Beep beep beep beeeeeep!

The lights go with the beeps: red-yellow-yellow-green. The gate starts dropping on the fourth beep/green light.

If you're a slingshotter, it's time to learn a new trick. You can no longer anticipate the gate. The keys to a great start are now a good starting position, a quick response, and awesome power.

Three-Step Sequence

Go on red. That's pretty simple. When you see red (or hear the first beep), go! The time from the red light to the start of the gate drop is about 0.35 seconds. The average human reaction time is about 0.25 seconds. So you're not likely to hit the gate. (If you do hit the gate, keep doing the same thing; just move your start position back a bit.)

1. When the command starts, stand up. You should be balanced over your pedals, with your arms straight and your hands lightly weighted. Set your pedals level or one click down.

2. As soon as you hear the beep or see red, thrust your hips forward. Your bike will roll back a bit, but only because it's lighter than your body, which is now moving forward.

3. Extend fully into the first stroke. Align your ankle, knee, hip, and shoulder into one plane of power. By now the gate is starting to drop. Sprint like your entire race depends on the first few strokes—which it does.

Wheelying off the line looks cool, but you want to go forward, not up. When you pull the bars and accelerate, make sure your weight is forward and the front end stays low.

The First Straight

When four competitors leave the gate and there's only one good line into the first turn, they politely get in line according to their qualifying times. Not! Racers blast off the line and roar forward with the intensity of a freight train. It's one of the most exciting moments in bike racing.

Focus all your energy forward. Look forward, hold your line, and stay straight. Don't go veering this way or that, and don't look at the racers next to you. If you do, you'll unconsciously slow down for a better look. Remember, you are a hurtling juggernaut of the forward type.

Follow up that snap. Your second and third pedals are almost as important as your first. When you snap downward, pull the other foot forward for that second stroke.

Pointy elbows. When I (Brian) raced pro BMX, I was one of the smallest guys out there—but I had the sharpest elbows. If a competitor creeps up on you, work your elbow into the crook of his arm and pull him backward. Physical contact like this isn't exactly legal, but it isn't exactly illegal either. At national races, many a high-level mountain biker has been juked by this old BMXer trick.

Assert yourself. If you're even slightly ahead, move toward the good line. A lot of riders are intimidated by the closeness. Hold your course, and maybe they'll back down. If not, too bad. Wear your pads just in case.

Be patient. If you get beaten into the first corner, back off. Instead of risking a nasty tangle, start planning your pass.

QUALIFYING VERSUS RACING

In qualifying, do whatever it takes to get down the course as fast as possible. Take the fastest lines without worrying about passing. If you can, on rough courses run a dual suspension bike for maximum overall speed and a fast qualifying time, and then race a hardtail so you can start fast and control the race from the front.

Passing

The back-and-forth of changing leads makes bikercross exciting to watch and even more exciting to race. You take all the physical and emotional skills needed to haul ass down a tricky course and add three other racers, each scheming for the lead. In bikercross, the action is fast and places change in an instant.

Here are some general passing tips, along with the two main types of passes:

Do your recon. Each track has a few good passing spots. Look for places where you carry lots of speed into corners, places where you carry lots of speed out of corners, and places where you ride faster than everyone else.

Plan ahead. Watch the other racers to see their lines and where they're fast and slow. Plan what might happen—"If I'm behind here, I'll rail the outside of this turn, carry speed out, and then pass on the rhythm" or whatever. The more thinking you do ahead of time, the more quickly you can act in the heat of battle.

Stay ready.   Don't be a sheep. Be spontaneous, creative, and devious.

Don't follow.   You can't get by someone when you're right behind him. You can't see or react, and you certainly can't ride straight through him. Hang back a bit or take a different line. Accelerate before you reach your passing point, then shoot on past.

If you can outpedal, outpump, or outjump someone on a straight section, that's fantastic. But for the most part, passing happens in corners. There are two basic approaches:

○ **High–low pass.** If the leaders dive into the inside of a berm, stay high. As they drift upward and slow down on the exit, drop down and accelerate for a pass. This works best in a berm, but the same idea applies for flat turns. In general, the faster you dive into the inside, the more speed you end up scrubbing on the exit. By being patient, you can set up wider and later and drive out of the turn while the other goofballs struggle for traction.

○ **Low–high pass.** When the leaders sweep outside to rail a berm, dive inside. But don't blow by and drift high on the exit, or they'll high–low you. Instead, get next to them, squeeze them toward the top of the berm, and gain speed on the exit.

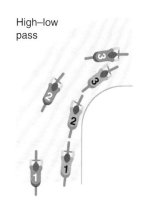

High–low pass

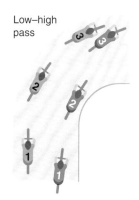

Low–high pass

A classic low-high pass. If the kid in front is extra-smart, he'll stay high and corral the other riders to prevent them from diving down and trying a high-low pass.

This works really well on flat corners. While you're squeezing a racer to the outside, you're in control. When you decide to sprint for the next corner, you usually have a slight head start. When you bust out a low–high pass, watch out for someone trying to high–low you from behind.

Keep it clean. A little contact is OK, but don't ram into someone on purpose. In general, if you're in front, you can push a rider behind you to the side. If you're in back, you have to find a way past. T-boning someone is not cool. There's a fine line between a clean pass and dirty racing. If you do pull a dirty pass, it'll come back to you eventually.

Preventing Passes

Sometimes you don't know someone's right behind you until he flies past, but most of the time you can feel him. If you're still in front, cut him off. If he's already caught up with you or is ahead of you, let him go and start planning your counterattack. If a guy low–highs you, hit him with the ol' high–low.

Know the good passing spots and think through the possibilities so you're ready for anything. Learn two lines for any bikercross race: your qualifying line, which is the fastest way down the course, and your race-leading line, which will pinch all the corners and prevent racers from barging in on you. If the qualifying and racing are done on different days, practice your qualifying line on qualifying day and practice your various race lines on race day. If you have a really clever idea, don't reveal it until your final run.

Pay attention to where the other racers are, and plan your lines accordingly. They might react to you and change their plans, but if you know where they are, at least you have a chance to counterreact. In time, you'll develop a sense for these things. Until then, you might want to run a helmet mirror and maybe even some handlebar mirrors. These really help you keep tabs on your competition.

Practice These Skills

If you want to improve your bikercross performance, here are some specific things to work on:

Starts. This is huge. Go to the BMX track, buy a year's membership for $40 or so, and then show up for practice sessions. For about a buck, you can sprint your brains out for an hour and a half, which is plenty of time. Remember that quality is more important than quantity. Try to do 10 good starts per session. Blast the first straight; then pull off to recover for the next gate. If you feel strong after your start practice, try some full-lap intervals.

Jumps. Carry maximum speed over jumps. Stay low. Work on bigger jumps and a variety of lips so you don't get caught off guard at the races.

Rhythms. Dirt-jumper doubles are good for learning to pump transitions, but you need a long set of rolling humps like you find at most BMX tracks. Practice them every which way—doubling them up, manualing, any combination you can think of. Go as fast as you can.

Berms.   Get the hang of going very fast with your tires above your face. Get on the gas as early as possible. Practice low–high and high–low lines. Even better: Dice with your friends.

Flat turns.   You can get great practice on any old fire road. For a real challenge, throw some cones out on a dirt lot and race your buddies. Carry max speed through a variety of lines; then sprint back up to speed as quickly as you can.

You can practice all of these skills in your car on public roads. Hard acceleration, late braking, forced passing, cutting people off . . .

Intensity.   Go as hard as you possibly can for 30 seconds at a time, followed by rest and a few repeats. Intervals on a trainer or the road are brutal. Intervals on actual terrain are brutal too, but at least they're fun.

Fuel Up

On the day of the finals, let's hope you'll have an hour of practice followed by round after round of grueling racing action. You might be out there for hours, so make sure you bring food and drinks. Nothing that'll weigh you down; just enough to stay sharp. Maybe some water and Cytomax. Don't bring beer with you—that's just admitting you'll be a spectator soon.

Dual Slalom

Back before bikercross tried to grab TV airtime, dual slalom was the king of gated racing. Take every element of a sweet trail—the flat turns, the berms, the jumps, the flow—boil it down, and pour it onto a grassy hill. In dual slalom, the fastest overall rider—not just the best starter—wins the day.

Dual slalom is fun for the riders and spectators: Joey Schusler and Rudy Unrau go after it in Nathrop, Colorado.

Making a Comeback

Dual slalom is returning to small and large events alike. Thank goodness.

○ For many riders, dual slalom is less intimidating than bikercross. You have your own lane, and there is no (intentional) contact. Cross-country racers, who know how to pedal fast and ride smooth, make excellent slalom racers. Especially if they can jump.

○ Because they don't require four-rider-sized berms and jumps, dual slalom courses require less earth moving than bikercross courses. This saves money for promoters.

How It Works

There are two parallel courses, usually named Red and Blue.

You take a qualifying run down each course. Your times are combined. If the weather is bad or the schedule is tight, you might qualify on one course.

Depending on the size of your class, the top 2, 4, 8, 16, 32, or 64 riders qualify. You are placed in a bracket, fastest qualifying time against slowest qualifying time. Try to qualify fast, or you'll be facing Brian in the first round.

In each round you take two runs, one on each course. Total time doesn't matter. It's all about the differential.

Run 1: When rider A crosses the finish, the timer starts. When rider B finishes, the timer stops. This is the time differential. On most courses there's a maximum differential, usually about 1.5 second.

Run 2: If rider B beats rider A by more than the differential, rider B advances to the next round. If rider A wins, or if rider B wins by less than the differential, rider A advances. This can be a bit confusing; that's why bikercross plays better on TV.

In each round, the field gets cut in half. This goes on until Lee and Brian face off in the final!

BE PATIENT

Number of runs it takes to cut the field from 32 qualifiers to a winner:

✓ Bikercross: 4

✓ Dual slalom: 62

There's a lot of waiting around in dual slalom, but those 30 seconds are so sweet!

Bike Choice

Because most bikercross races are won on the start, hardtails are almost mandatory at the higher level. In dual slalom, the start isn't as important as your total time down the course.

Pick whichever bike lets you carry smooth speed the whole way. Brian rides a hardtail on smooth DS courses; on rougher and rawer ones, he rides with suspension.

No matter what kind of bike you ride, use a short stem, a chain guide, and a low seat.

Strategy

Know the courses. Although the two courses should theoretically be identical, they never are. Learn the lines and jumps. Know where to slow down, and where you can go fast. Also know how to gauge yourself with the rider in the other lane.

You know he's right there, but you don't want to pay too much attention. Mitch Ropelato and Petr Hanak race hub to hub.

Maintain flow.   Good slalom courses have a constant, connected flow. If you blow one turn, you'll blow the next one, and so on. Stay in control, and let each feature build on the previous one. The most important part of the course is the finish line. Conduct your entire run to get you there asap.

Be smart.   Know where the other rider is, but ride your own race, and don't panic and try to make up time—unless the other rider's way ahead. If you're on the slower course, don't worry if you get beaten by a bit. You can make it up on the faster course.

Be very fit.   Compared with 4X, dual slalom requires twice as many runs. As you go through the rounds, the racing gets more intense, and you get less rest. Rock those intervals. Make sure you can recover quickly!

Have fun.   Dual slalom is an awesome form of racing.

A HISTORY OF GATED RACING

Dual slalom: The original mountain bike gated racing. The gated turns and format were patterned after skiing.

Dual: The UCI's attempt to make slalom more spectator friendly (and make the races run twice as fast). Two riders started on individual courses and then funneled onto one line. Dual ran from 1998 to 2001.

Bikercross: Straight-up head-to-head racing, four at a time. Bikercross races are easy to run and easy to watch. Bikercross was supposed to get major TV exposure and tons of outside sponsorship money, and it did (for a while).

Downhill

30 seconds

You lean on the start ramp.

20 seconds

You click into your pedals.

10 seconds

You adjust your goggles.

Five . . .

You stand.

Four . . .

You lean back.

Three . . .

Deep breath.

Two . . .

OK.

One . . .

Your mind goes silent.

Go!

Your body erupts. Pedal, pedal, pedal, turn, turn, turn. Over the rocks, down the chute, off the drop. Heart pounding, lungs gasping, legs churning, you fly down the course you have etched in your memory. Here's that rock; take the inside line here. You ride the fine edge between control and catastrophe, victory and violence.

There are as many different kinds of downhill as there are mountains. Most races are two to five minutes long, but a few, like the Downieville Downhill, run up to an hour or longer. Terrain varies from easy and fast to gnarly and slow to gnarly and fast. Top downhillers possess quick reflexes, otherworldly bike-handling skills, total-body strength, and a mix of anaerobic and aerobic fitness. A certain amount of confidence doesn't hurt either.

Here are some tips to help you dominate your next downhill race.

The faster, steeper, looser and rockier it gets, the more aggressive (yet flowy) you need to be. Australian tough guy (and nice guy) Jared Graves strikes the balance in Snowmass, Colorado.

Learn the Course

Downhill racing is just like normal trail riding, except you get to memorize the course and go as fast as you want. The better you know the course, the faster you can go. At most races you have limited time (and energy) to learn the course, so getting effective practice is important. Following is some advice from World Cup champion downhiller Steve Peat.

Walk the course before you ride it. Don't try to memorize every rock, but definitely get the overall layout. Figure out how you'll handle the tricky sections, and imagine yourself riding the course. Don't waste a short, crowded practice session checking out the course for the first time. If you formulate a plan while you walk the course, you'll be able to ride faster sooner.

Get lots of practice runs. Peat usually gets six to seven runs on day 1 of practice, four to five on day 2, and two runs on race day. Be sure to learn something every run. Blindly doing runs only tires you out.

Do full runs. Many racers ride short sections, rest a bit, scope out the course, and then continue. Not Peaty. He rides top to bottom every time, and he emphasizes different sections on every run. When race time comes, he knows exactly how long he has to withstand the pummeling.

Practice fast. Some racers start slow and get faster as they do more runs. This is a safe way to go, but things always change when you go faster in your race run. Peaty hauls the mail on every run. "People say my first practice run could be my qualifying run," he says. Peaty hits some sections faster in practice than he does in his race run. In a full-out race run, he might be too tired to pedal as much or hold on as well. But by hitting everything at full speed plus, he knows he and his bike are ready and nothing will catch him by surprise. "Some people say I should be more methodical," he says, "but this works for me."

Stay flexible. Courses change. Roots and rocks break out and kick loose. Lines grow out of nowhere. Keep your eyes open and adjust your plan. Sometimes you have to adjust during your race run, so when you make your final race plan, leave room for interpretation.

Keep thinking. Between runs, go over the course, your lines, and your speed. Which lines should I try this time? Where can I go faster? Compare notes with people you trust. Watch fast riders, but keep in mind that pros easily do things that would maim you.

"Sometimes it hurts to watch other people," says Peat. "It looks like they're hauling ass, and you get all worried, but if you watch yourself ride the section, you're hauling ass too. It's a big mind trip. You have to concentrate on your own thing."

Pay attention to people you respect. If Peat is at a 4X and he is watching or maybe gets eliminated early (youch!), when he tells me (Brian), "You got it," that assures me that I definitely have it. I kind of know already, but when I hear that, it really clicks.

Don't freak out on the tough sections. Don't spend too much time working on any one section, be it a humongous jump, slippery rock garden, or whatever. Do what you can to get through the section; then move on. If you have time later, come back and get it dialed.

Imagine a race down the A-Line trail at the Whistler Mountain Bike Park. You haul the mail down this grooving trail, with berm after berm and dozens of perfect tabletop jumps. Then, all of a sudden, there's a big rock drop, with a wimp line that goes around it. A lot of guys would stand at that split all day watching other people and considering what to do, but if they just decide to skip the drop and lose two seconds, they can easily make up that time by learning the rest of the course.

Avoid the big hits. In a race when your eyes pop out of your skull and your hands pump into useless claws, even a moderate hit can knock you out of whack. Besides, downhill bikes take enough of a beating without you bashing stuff willy-nilly. Says Peaty, "I run my bottom bracket low for better cornering, but I land on my bash guard two or three times every run. If I hit things really hard in practice, I might break it in my race run, so I go smarter instead."

Do runs in your head. From your last practice to your race time, keep running through the course. Some racers even draw the course on paper. Relax and visualize yourself flowing down the course. Know you can do it; then go do it.

Prepare to pin it. "A downhill run isn't always fun," says Peaty, believe it or not. "There's a certain speed that's fun and flowy. You go beyond that."

At the Mountain States Cup in Crested Butte, Colorado, Blair Reed takes the high line while Cody Wilderman stays low. Which line is better? That depends on your skills, fitness, and riding style. Smart riders time both options.

Don't Go Too Hard

A two- to five-minute downhill run is smack dab in the "mystery zone" between your aerobic and anaerobic energy systems. You basically want to go as hard as you can without becoming stupid. When each of us gets over a certain heart rate, we lose focus and make mistakes. It's better to ride a bit too easy and clean than to ride too hard and sloppy. In a perfect run, lactic acid should build up in your muscles the whole way, so when you finally cross the line, you can barely hold on or pedal. There's a nice satisfaction in knowing you left nothing behind on the course. Practice at different intensities to learn where your line lies.

A downhill run is a series of short sprints and recoveries. Drop the hammer on flat sections, and try to recover before you reach the technical sections. Decide where to pedal, where to pump, and where to rest. On steep descents, pedal up to speed and then coast. You waste a lot of energy pedaling against wind resistance.

Qualify Smart

At some races, you do a qualifying run before the final run. The faster you qualify, the later you race. If the course is likely to get rained on as the day progresses, try qualifying with a slow time so you can race earlier on a nice track. This is a bit risky, but every once in a while a nobody wins a big race because the honchos raced on a bad course.

The opposite applies as well: If it's going to get drier as the day goes, you'd better pin it in qualifying.

Ultimately, the point of this steep, rocky section is to set you up for the flat turn afterward. Ask yourself: Which line will let me carry the most speed through that turn?

Avoid Arm Pump

You know the feeling: You barrel down a rough course and your forearms start to ache. Pretty soon the aching becomes unbearable and you can barely hold on to your bars, much less control your bike.

Your forearm muscles are surrounded by a thin, inflexible sheath called a *fascia*. When you work those muscles hard, they swell up with blood and a painful pressure builds within the sheath. The higher the pressure gets, the more your veins get squished and the less blood can flow away from the muscles. Meanwhile, your arteries are squirting blood like a high-pressure fire hose, and even more blood gets trapped in the muscles. This further increases the pressure and pain and makes it even harder to ride your bike.

Some motocross racers, including Shawn Palmer (also a mountain bike downhill racer), have gotten their fascias cut open or removed to relieve this pressure. Don't worry: You can control the pump with less-invasive remedies. In order of importance:

Relax. Your forearm muscles work best when you use them for a short time and then let them rest. Be sure to loosen your grip in the smooth sections, even if just for a second. In hectic situations it feels like a little demon is pulling on your forearm tendons, but you must concentrate on relaxing those muscles. You'll get less arm pump, plus you'll ride more smoothly.

Be in great shape. The better your aerobic condition, the better your circulation. To prepare your hands for the stress of downhill racing, ride rough terrain a lot or ride motocross. If you can hang on to a moto, your DH bike will feel like a basket of flowers.

These exercises will give you Popeye forearms:

- **Wrist curls and extensions.** With a barbell or light dumbbells, bust out three sets of 20 or more reps.
- **Dowel of death.** Take a 5-pound (2.3 kg) weight, tie it to a 4-foot (120 cm) rope, and hang it from a wooden rod. Use both hands to turn the rod and wind the weight upward. Lower the weight slowly; then wind it back up in the opposite direction.

Practice These Skills

Downhill racing rewards exceptional strength and bike-handling skills. Here are some things to focus on.

Go fast. If you want to race fast, you have to practice fast. "I ride fast all the time," says Peat. "It keeps your body and reflexes in tune. Anything to stay faster than the next guy." Of course, you should haul ass only in designated areas and never on public trails.

Get used to gnarl. If you go to a race and encounter something—a huge jump, sticky mud, pointy rocks—and ask yourself, "Uh-oh, how am I going to do this?" you're going to end up slow, struggling, or crashed. The terrain on race courses should never shock you; it should challenge you to go as fast as possible. Be sure to practice on the most extreme terrain you can handle, and pay special attention to the things that give you fits: off-camber turns, slippery roots, or whatever. When you get to your next race, you should be saying to yourself, "Aw, this is easy. Now, what's the fastest line?"

Pedal everywhere. Practice cranking out of every turn and between every rough section. If you're not pedaling, you should be pumping.

Intensity. Get used to spending two to five minutes going as hard as you can without losing control. You can do intervals on the road, but there's no substitute for fast runs on real terrain. Pedaling until your eyes bleed is step 1; maintaining control while you're seeing red is step 2. Downhillers need good aerobic fitness, but they don't need the mileage the XC guys need. A few hard, one-hour rides per week will do the trick.

Fuel Up

You don't need much fuel to get through a three-minute race. Just make sure you're hydrated and sharp. A Clif Shot 15 to 20 minutes before your run should give you the snap you crave.

GET OUT OF THE WAY!

"I would have let you by, but it would have cost me 5 or 10 seconds"—this from a racer who had been caught after a 60-second interval.

If you're in a downhill or other time-trial event and someone makes up 20, 30, or even 60 seconds and appears on your tail, don't try to speed up or block him. Get out of the way! Don't ruin someone else's winning run just to elevate yourself from 27th to 26th place.

If you're the one doing the catching, call out from way back so your fellow racer can find a good spot to let you by. When you do pass, do it all at once. There is a special hell for people who refuse to let faster racers pass. It's right down the hall from sandbagger hell.

Cross-Country

Cross-country racing, whether for 20 minutes, two hours, or an entire day, is just like normal cross-country riding, only it's faster, harder, and more painful. That, and you ride in a tangle of type-A go-getters. And let's not forget the pain. Oh, the pain.

Colorado State Championships at Snowmass: Regional tough guy Mike West leads out an all-star cast including soon-to-be state champ Lance Armstrong.

Hecka Tips

Cross-country racing demands a mix of strength, tactics, and toughness. If you're into cross-country, you probably enjoy doing things the hard way. That's all well and good, but you might as well race smart.

Pace yourself.   Know your threshold and stay there. Push to the redline on the climbs and recover on the descents.

Respect your physical condition.   Do you feel well? Where are you in your training program? Don't shoot your wad if it's going to harm your future results or, worse, your health.

Know your competition.   Know which guys to go with in case they attack. If you're a better technical rider than a competitor, make sure you get to the singletrack before him. If you're a great climber, don't take chances on the descents. Just get down safe and hammer on the way up.

Preride the course.   Know where to push and where to recover, when to hold 'em and when to fold 'em.

Use the feed zones.   Don't carry any more food or water than you need to. For short laps, pick up half-filled water bottles and maybe a shot of energy gel.

Pick the right bike.   Hardtails rule smooth courses. Dual suspension treats you right on rough courses. The longer and more brutal the course, the more likely you should run suspension.

Deal With Traffic

Unless you start like a nitro-burning funny car, you'll eventually have some characters in your way. And that means choking dust, annoying slowdowns, and possibly a poor result. To dominate the world of mass-start racing, you'd best learn to pass.

Warm up to start fast.   If the starting straight leads to a singletrack, you need to get there ahead of the sheep. Warm up thoroughly, line up near the front, and pin it to the singletrack. Once you're safely ahead of the flock, use your superior handling skills to recover—while still hauling.

Don't follow.   Think of other racers as obstacles, like trees. You wouldn't ride up to a tree, hit the brakes, and wait for the tree to move out of the way, would you? Most cross-country races end up being parades, with each racer sheepishly following a rear wheel. As long as you follow, you can't keep an eye out for passing spots, and you end up part of the flock. Baaa.

Pass smoothly.   Don't waste energy catching someone, slowing to the same speed, and then accelerating past. As you overtake another racer, plan your pass so you can whiz by without braking or accelerating. Try to pass in corners. Sorry to say this, but most recreational cross-country racers can't turn worth a damn; they slow down too much, take early apexes, and stall on the exit. Bust out a high–low or low–high pass, or blitz through a far-inside line. Remember: If it's within the course markings, it's legal. That narrow strip of tracked dirt is fine for slow sheep, but not for a speedy wolf like you. (Check out the passing section in this chapter, page 216.)

Roll like a freight train.   If you must pass on a pedaling section, start accelerating from behind and zoom right by. If possible, slow your breathing, smile, and say something like, "Nice day!" or "When does the race start?" When your competitor is already on the brink of emotional collapse, this can be enough to make him trade his bike for a bass boat.

Embrace the Pain

Bike riding is hard. Bike riding at race pace is very hard. Sometimes it feels like the universe is made of pain and a funnel is pouring all of it onto your head.

Know your pain.   Most of us think all pain is unpleasant, uncool, and worth avoiding. But there's a bad kind of pain—the kind you feel when you void your clavicle warranty—and a good kind of pain—the kind you feel when you push hard. Realize that the pain of effort is a good sign. It means you're pushing hard, getting stronger, and, hopefully, putting the hurt on someone.

If you feel terrible, take a moment to figure out why. Are you tense? Relax. Are you pedaling poorly? Smooth it out. Are you yanking on the bars? Let 'em be. Are you panting like a dying dog? Breathe slowly and deeply. Are you going as hard as you can? Sorry, that straight-up hurts. But at least you're getting stronger. Pain is a doorway between the rider you are and the rider you want to be.

XC racing hurts, especially at the national championships. Judy Freeman knows a sweet descent is coming right up—and that everyone else is hurting just as bad.

Breathe.   When you panic, your breathing gets fast and shallow. And when your breathing gets fast and shallow, you tend to panic. It's a two-way feedback situation. So when you're panting and apprehensive like a Chihuahua, take it slow and deep like Jacques Cousteau. That should mellow you right out. Focus on slow, deep breaths down in your diaphragm.

Relax.   If a muscle isn't directly carrying you up the hill, it should be slack. Make your hands, arms, and shoulders as limp as possible. When we get uncomfortable, we unconsciously contort our faces like gargoyles. Relax your jaw, your cheeks, and your eyes, and the rest of your body will follow.

Consult your HRM.   A heart rate monitor is a tachometer for your body. If you feel like you're going to die but your heart is in the green zone, then something else is going wrong. You might be tired, sick, dehydrated, or mired in terrible form. If you think you might be able to go harder and your HRM shows a safe reading, then go for it. If you're at redline, then it's a matter of maintaining the pace and dealing with the pain.

Think about something else.   The more you focus on your pain, the more it fills your entire consciousness. If you focus on something else—anything—your pain will fade to the background. Perfect your stroke. Sing a song. Remember that everyone else is hurting just as much. If you can put your discomfort on the back shelf and get your competitors to concentrate on their agony, you can break them.

You can get through this.   One of the biggest milestones as a new rider is when you realize you can bust a gut to clear a rise, and then recover and feel fine afterward. If you're in good shape, the pain is temporary.

Pace yourself.   When you reach a long climb, start relatively easy, find a rhythm, and push harder as you reach the top. Upshift and keep pushing until you start to coast downhill. Recover on the way down. The buffoons who blasted from the bottom will hit their walls partway up, and there won't be any rest for them.

Remember, this is supposed to be fun. Right? Ha!

Fuel for Cross-Country Racing

Know your body. Know how long you can hammer without food. Try different drinks, gels, and solid foods on your training rides, especially those that mimic your race distance. We've seen guys consume pork chops and sardines on group rides. Gnarly. But, hey, do what works for you.

Super D

Super D races have become very popular, and for great reasons. You get to ride your normal trail bike. You get to ride normal trails. And you get to ride as fast as you can with a bunch of like-minded people.

If there was ever a real test of the total mountain bike rider, super D might be it. A typical super D race consists of:

- ◦ A hairy-scary running start and sprint to the first turn
- ◦ Riding trails very fast, in heavy traffic
- ◦ Making and blocking passes
- ◦ Carrying flowy speed through a wide variety of terrain

Super D LeMans starts are usually mayhem. And they are always fun. Open Men mount up in Crested Butte, Colorado.

○ Pedaling harder than you think you can
○ Basically pinning it and having a great time

In the age of specialized fitness and equipment, super D might be the last bastion of the all-around, all-mountain rider.

What Is Super D?

Super D is the fun half of your typical trail ride. Super Ds start at the top of a mountain and barrel down a mix of dirt roads and singletracks to the bottom. Courses usually employ XC trails—often parts of XC courses—but some include a bit of DH flavor.

Races range from as short as seven minutes to as long as an hour. Fifteen to thirty minutes is about average.

Terrain is mostly downhill, with some climbs thrown in along the way. Officially, if there is such a thing in mountain biking, up to 30 percent of the course can be uphill.

The original super Ds were time trails, just like downhill races. One year at Snow Summit, the race promoters were running behind schedule, so they ran everyone at once. That was exciting for the racers (and easy for the promoters), and since then most super Ds have had mass starts. The most common style is Le Mans.

In a Le Mans start, you lay your bike in a designated area and then walk to a start line, where you line up on foot. When the gun goes off, you run to your bike, jump on, and pin it. This theoretically spreads the riders out to reduce contact—but a competitive Le Mans start can get pretty hectic. Elbows fly, bikes get stepped on, inner beasts become unleased. Braaap!

Equip Yourself

Most super D racers compete on their trail bikes. Smoother courses favor more XC race–oriented bikes. Rougher courses favor burlier all-mountain bikes. You can make yourself crazy trying to optimize for the huge variety of super D courses. Ride what you're used to.

A remotely adjustable seatpost is a great idea. If lets you climb and descend with full kung fu.

XC gear and open-face helmets feel good on mellower courses. The gnarlier the terrain, the more you want to dress like a downhiller. On an XC-ish course, Lee wears an open-face helmet and full Lycra with neoprene knee guards. On a gnarlier course, he still rocks the Lycra, but with burlier knee guards and a full-face helmet.

Get a Great Start

A successful Le Mans start is massively important, and it's the single most shocking thing about super D. Some tips (to be used when you're not racing against Lee):

○ Set your bike away from the rest. You're less likely to trip over other bikes, and your bike is less likely to get stepped on. And: You'd be amazed how frequently harried riders grab the wrong bikes.

PRACTICE THESE SKILLS

✓ Running (especially sprinting uphill on a rough surface)

✓ Jumping onto your bike at speed (see Mounting and Dismounting section on page 59)

✓ Passing and preventing passes (see the bikercross section)

✓ Pedaling super hard

✓ Descending super fast

- ○ Put your bike in the gear you want. For a downhill start, that usually means big ring and middle cog.
- ○ Most riders mount from the left side (on horses and motos too). Lay your bike on its left side, with your right pedal at around 2 o'clock.
- ○ Line up early so you have a short, straight run to your bike. Check your line to make sure you don't step into a hole or roll your ankle on a rock. Details, baby!
- ○ When they say "Go," run as fast as you can. You've been practicing your off-bike sprints, right? If you're a serious super D racer, you *must* work on your running and sprinting form.
- ○ Run up to your bike, and don't stop. Grab the right handlebar as you go by. Drag the bike behind you, flip it upright, and jump on.
- ○ Catch your right pedal and start pedaling. Who cares whether you're clipped in? PEDAL!!!

Pacing and Tactics

Ariel Lindsley is a pro downhill and cross-country racer who, with his Maverick team-mate Mike West, dominated the Mountain States Cup Super D series for several seasons. Ariel's thoughts on the fine art of super D:

First, do your intervals. You should be able to pin two- to four-minute intervals, full bore, with only 30 to 60 seconds of rest, for the duration of your super D race.

Do whatever it takes to get a great start. "The mass start can be pretty scary," Ariel says. "I'm a pretty big, aggressive person, and I feel like a bully. You gotta run to your bike, elbows out, and fight for your position. It's super important that you start close to the front. It's really hard to battle your way up from the back."

Spend it all at the start; then settle into your own pace. "Go full agro on the start—as hard as you can without maliciously hurting people," Ariel says. "When things sort out, ride smooth and smart, and make good decisions. Count on the people behind you to do stupid stuff." If you're in front, you'll eventually reach some clear trail where you can relax (sort of). If you're stuck in the pack, you'll never find your flow.

Be the slow traffic. "If you're in the back, you get stuck behind people. It's better to be taxed out and in front. That way you're the one who's slowing traffic."

Learn to ride without vision. Cross-country racers are used to racing in heavy traffic and blinding dust. "Coming from cross-country racing, I'm able to just blank out and ride without seeing."

Plan your passes. During practice, identify spots where you can get by people without endangering any lives. That grassy area after that one turn . . . If you get stuck behind someone, just relax and save energy until you reach that spot—then go!

But measure your risk. When you're fully pinned, elbow to elbow, you'll be tempted to do things you normally wouldn't. Ask yourself, How important is this win? "If you're a pro, maybe a crash and getting hurt is worth the risk," Ariel says. "But if you're racing for fun, and you have to take your kids to school on Monday, just relax and enjoy the ride."

THERE GOES ARIEL

Angel Fire, New Mexico: The super D course starts on a wide-open, lava-strewn ski run; then funnels into a tight, rocky singletrack.

I (Lee) lined up early and followed my normal pre-start routine The dirt road swung wide around the ski run before it hooked onto the singletrack. I knew the sheep would follow the road; I planned to dive straight down the run, through all the lava rocks, straight into that turn.

I reached my bike in midpack, jumped on, and sprinted full-bore toward the turn. I was 20 feet (6 m) off the main line, pinging off rocks, my eyes rattling, pinning it at the edge of what I thought was reasonable.

And there was a noise.

A violent noise.

And it was Ariel, 10 feet (3 m) farther off the main line, bouncing sideways through the air as he passed me. I fought him for a second, but it was just too spicy, and I backed off.

"Go Ariel!"

Ariel rocks some local rocks.

24-Hour Races

24-hour races have grown from hyper-hard-core fringe events to fun festivals where you can race with your buddies or push your own limits (or both).

Pick Your Pain

Solo races are exactly what they sound like. You race all 24 hours by yourself.

Team races are much more popular because you share the fun with one to four buddies (depending on the event and your racing category). Most teams have four people. Six hours of riding in a day—fully pinned, of course—is enough for most of us.

Ariel's Advice

Pro racer Ariel Lindsley has ridden 24-hour races solo and with teams. Here's his team routine:

Before the Race

Bring warm clothes—warmer than you think you'll need. Even if it's 60 degrees Fahrenheit (15.5 °C), you'll get cold just sitting around. Rock your biggest, warmest jacket.

If you wanna ride at night, you gotta rock the lights. Kevin Goodman rides bleary at the 24-hour solo championships.

Bring a team mom. She (or he) is in charge of rider care: fire, food, drink, clothes, batteries, rest. "It helps to have someone tell you what to do: 'Dude, eat this; put your clothes on.'"

Bring a riding manager. This person walks back and forth from camp to the start area, takes your jacket when you're riding, greets you when you're done, tracks the other teams, relays messages, makes sure you're on schedule, and—when needed—lies to you. "I've been lied to many times. Saying I was a minute behind when I was 10 minutes ahead, whatever it takes. You need someone who knows you, so they now how to motivate you. 'Tinker is right behind you!'"

Set up a trainer in the handoff area. Use a seatpost quick-release, so all of your team members can hop on and spin. This gets you warm and ready to hammer, and it gives you an outlet for your nervous energy. Ride the trainer right after your lap, too; this helps you cool down and reduces soreness and tightness that would make your next warm-up harder.

Designate a team jacket for everyone to wear on the trainer. The riding manager is in charge of this, as well as snacks for right before and after laps.

This is important: Make sure you have designated drivers. None of the racers should be driving home—especially after those postrace beers.

During the Race

Ride exactly how you always ride. You're not going to win a 24-hour race with one bold move.

You'll get to know the course well. Take the same lines every time. Try to shift in the same places, and try to pull the same gears up the hills.

As soon as you finish your lap, change into dry clothes. Change before you eat—and definitely before you tell your 30-minute story.

Rocking It Solo. Keep moving. Don't stop. Don't take breaks. "The more you keep your mind off the comfort that exists in the pits, the better. Pretend that place doesn't exit, which is hard because you smell hot dogs every time you come into the pits. Hot dogs . . ."

Food can be a problem. Some people can gut cold pizza. If you're not one of the lucky, experiment with drinks, gels, and protein shakes. Try electrolyte pills and even Pedialyte, which is designed to rehydrate sick children. Chances are you'll be a sick kid.

Your pit crew has to be even more on it. They can't let you sit around. "No, dude, you can't sit there. Go. Please. No, get the hell out of here." Lying can help— "Here comes Tinker . . ."

Weir's Advice

Pro racer Mark Weir has won numerous team races and turned many a fastest lap—once on a single speed. His 24-hour tips:

Strategy. Prepare everything in advance. All of your food, your lights, all your gear, everything. That leaves less for you to worry about at the race.

"I don't do any special training. I just try to drop some pounds." But this is Weir. For him, riding one quarter of a 24-hour period is a rest day. To prepare for a 24-hour race, he leans down by riding lots of road and less pump track.

Decide who will do the Le Mans start and first lap, and who will ride second to get the fastest lap. Practice your handoffs.

In a 24-hour race, someone has to be in charge of bike maintenance—and that someone cannot be you. Lars Thompsen of Trail Head Cyclery in San Jose, California, keeps Kevin Goodman rolling.

Plan how long each person will ride. After midafternoon, have each rider do two laps so everyone else gets more rest—four to six hours rather than two to three hours.

"A four-man team is the hardest thing I've ever done. I can ride for 19 or 20 hours nonstop, no problem; but when you ride with a team, you pin it as hard as you can every lap. After 10 of those, your legs are dead."

Bring a power strip for your battery chargers. And write your name on all your batteries.

Food. "I drink a lot of shakes, and sometimes I'll buy a bunch of burritos and eat them cold right out of the cooler."

Whatever you eat, you'll get sick of. "Bring food you usually wouldn't throw down your neck, because you'd feel guilty—like Pop Tarts, Lucky Charms, or Golden Grahams. If I brought PB&J, I'd get sick of it, and I don't know what I'd eat after the race."

Keep eating all night, and be sure to stay hydrated.

Rest. Lie on your back with your feet up on a chair. Elevating your legs helps drain out all that evil blood.

"I believe in the no-sleep program. The time is so short, it's not worth it."

"I like to cruise the pits and heckle people—especially if my team is leading. I once got kicked out of the LUNA Chix pit 'cause I woke 'em up."

BRIAN'S APPROACH TO TRAINING

Keep it fun. I don't follow a specific plan. I listen to my body. If I feel tired, I back off. If I feel strong, I ramp it up.

Adapt with your body. As I've been getting older, I feel like my body needs more rest between hard workouts. It's all about getting adequate rest. (Cross-country legend Ned Overend, now in his mid-50s, says the same thing.)

Change with your events. When I was focused on 4X and DS, I did a lot more weightlifting and gate starts. Now that I'm more focused on endurance downhill type events, I'm working more on

If it has wheels, Brian will race it. He braaaps a mini-moto at the 2005 Crossover Challenge at the San Francisco AMA Supercross.

my endurance—not to the XC extreme, but I do need some endurance. I do a lot of longer rides, some downhill runs, and some dirt jumping, because it's fun.

Match your gym workouts to your needs. Nowadays I go to the gym maybe twice a week (down from four when I was focused on power for 4X). I do a lot of stretching and circuit workouts, to build strength and endurance. I do push-ups, pull-ups, and sit-ups, plus power-lifting moves like squats and power cleans. Those I do with light weight, but I try to move the weight as fast as possible; then I go right to the next exercise.

Try cyclocross. This winter I did some cyclocross races, which I've never done before. It was a perfect training tool for endurance downhills—45 to 60 minutes pinned, lots of pedaling, some short climbs. It's a really good winter sport on the bike. (BTW: YouTube has videos of Brian hopping over barriers that the rest of the field is running over.)

Simulate your race. When I was racing 4X, I rode a lot of BMX track. When I'm racing cyclocross, I do simulated races during the week. I go max effort, recover a bit, repeat.

And then there's moto. I love riding motocross. You can do everything on a moto that you can do on a bike, only twice as fast, twice as far, and twice as high. It gives you a full-body workout, and it gets you used to going really fast over crazy terrain. I used to have a motocross track in my backyard. Heck, if I could make a living as a motocross racer, I'd do it in a second.

Special Olympics. We'll be hanging out at someone's house and I'll say, "Let's see who can jump up the most steps" or whatever. Competition is a way of life for me, and I'm always ready to go. [Note from Lee: The last time Brian visited my house, we had an epic Special Olympics in my basement. If you see him, ask him how many dips he did. (One fewer than me!)]

SHOOT YOUR TROUBLES

Problem: Fellow racers accuse you of sandbagging.

Solution: Thank this book for making you faster—and then upgrade to a higher class!

Competition adds challenge, excitement, and validation to an already-cool sport. If you've never raced before, we suggest you pick an event that appeals to you. Race locally against your buddies, or travel to a new place. Go in with an open attitude and reasonable expectations, and you'll have a great time. If you're already a serious racer, keep training, baby! We'll bet this book helps make you even faster.

GLOSSARY

20—A bike with 20-inch wheels. Almost always a BMX bike.

24-hour race, solo—A 24-hour race in which one rider races the entire time.

24-hour race, team—A 24-hour race in which two to five riders take turns racing on the course.

24-hour race—A cross-country race that takes place over 24 hours.

29er—Any mountain bike with 29-inch wheels. Standard mountain bikes have 26-inch wheels.

air spring—A device used in some forks and shocks that uses air pressure, rather than a metal spring, to support the rider. Widely used on cross-country bikes. Lighter than a coil spring.

all-mountain—A form of riding characterized by a mix of cross-country, downhill and freeride terrain and styles. Riders seek to ride all sorts of trails with cross-country endurance, downhill speed and freeride expressiveness. All-mountain bikes are a rapidly growing segment because they can be ridden almost anywhere.

attack position—A neutral position on the bike that gives you ideal balance and maximum range of motion to negotiate terrain.

baby head rocks—Loose, round rocks about the size of a baby's head. These are a tricky riding surface.

backside—Any surface that faces away from the rider, in the direction the rider is traveling. Landing on the backside of a jump is smooth. Pumping the backside of a roller is fast. Opposite of frontside.

bash guard—A round plate that protects the largest chain ring from impacts. Often an integral part of a chain guide.

berm—A banked turn.

bikercross—A racing form in which four riders race head to head down a course featuring a start gate, berms, jumps and other obstacles. Races last 30-40 seconds. Also known as mountain cross, four-cross or 4X.

BMX—Acronym for bicycle motocross. A form of racing conducted on a track consisting of a start gate, start ramp, several berms and a mix of jumps and rollers. Most popular among younger riders, but a great stepping stone into and training ground for mountain biking. Now an Olympic sport.

BMX bike—A small, responsive, extremely agile bike designed for sprinting, jumping and pumping around a BMX track. Available with 20-inch or 24-inch wheels. Awesome way for a mountain biker to improve core skills.

bottom bracket—The part of the bike frame, located at the bottom between the wheels, where the crank arms are attached. Also the axle and bearings that attach the crank arms to the bottom bracket of the frame.

bottom out—To use all of a bike's suspension. The components hit their stopping point, often with a metallic clank.

braaap!—A statement of intent derived from the sound of an off-road motorcycle—and the aggressive flow possible on such a machine. Braaap can be used as a noun, verb or, most often, an interjection. Braaap!

brake dive—The tendency for the front suspension to compress under braking forces, which causes the front of the bike to drop and the head angle to get steeper.

bump jump—To catch air by bouncing the rear wheel off of an object, typically a rock, log or other trail obstacle. In bikercross or dual slalom, racers might bump jump off a small roller.

bunny hop—To bound over an obstacle by lifting the front then rear wheel, preferably without pulling up on the pedals.

carve—To aggressively ride a tight line through a turn. This line would be tighter than the main line, which would be railed.

cassette—The cluster of rear gears attached to the rear hub. Each of those gears is a cog.

chain guide—A device that uses channels, rollers and often a bash guard to keep the chain on the chain ring. Used in more aggressive styles of riding.

chain ring—One of the front gears attached to the crank arms.

clips, clip-in pedals—Pedals that attach to the rider's shoes via metal cleats. This aids pedaling power. Also called clipless pedals.

cockpit—The area in which a rider can move on the bike.

cog—One of the gears in the cassette, which is attached to the rear hub.

coil spring—A traditional metal spring used in some forks and shocks, especially for downhill. Typically yields a smoother ride than an air spring.

compression damping—Hydraulic circuit inside a suspension fork or shock that controls the speed and amount of suspension compression. More compression damping resists movement and creates a firmer ride.

countersteering—A high-speed turning technique in which the rider momentarily steers counter to the desired direction of travel. For a left turn, the rider first steers slightly right. Gyroscopic forces lean the bike to the left. The rider then steers to the left and finishes the turn.

cranks, crank arms—The metal or carbon fiber levers that the pedals are attached to. They convert leg motion into rotation.

crank set—Crank arms, axle, bearings and chain rings sold as a matched set and ready to attach to the frame's bottom bracket.

cross-country—A form of riding and racing conducted on traditional trails for long distances. Race durations range from 45 minutes to multiple days. The vast majority of mountain bikers ride cross-country trails.

cruiser—A BMX bike with 24-inch wheels.

cyclocross—A form of racing conducted on a mix of paved roads, dirt roads, mellow trails and manmade obstacles. Because of the high speeds and relatively smooth terrain, cyclocross bikes are like road bikes, but with wider tires. Many cyclocross obstacles are designed to force riders to dismount and run with their bikes. The dismount, run and remount are key cyclocross skills. Race durations range from 30 to 60 minutes.

differential—In dual slalom, the difference between two racer's times on their respective courses. If Rider A wins the first run by a 0.5 second differential, Rider B must win the second run by a larger differential to win that round and progress in the race.

dirt-jump bike—A bike designed with agile handling and durable construction for dirt jumping. Also called DJ bike.

dirt jumping—A style of riding performed on manmade jumps, usually constructed of dirt. Riders strive for air and style. Also called DJ.

double jump—A jump with a gap between the takeoff and landing. This gap cannot be rolled through; it must be jumped over.

doubletrack—A trail, typically on an overgrown dirt road, with two paths created by ATV or automobile wheels.

downhill—A form of racing conducted on steep, rough terrain that requires a purpose-specific long-travel bike, full-face helmet and body armor. Race duration is typically three to five minutes.

drift—When cornering forces exceed available traction, and the tires get pushed sideways through the turn. Unlike in a skid, the tires are still turning, and the rider can maintain control.

drop-in—A drop-off where the rider must land on a near-vertical surface. Examples: half pipes, very steep cliffs.

drop-off, drop—A trail feature that is so steep the rider must fly through the air from the top to the bottom. Examples include cliffs and steep rock faces.

flats, flat pedals—Pedals used with regular rubber-soled shoes. They typically use metal teeth and/or pins to help grip the shoe soles.

flatten (your bike)—To lay your bike on its side, usually in the air while performing a tabletop trick.

flow—1. The psychological and physiological state of optimal performance. 2. The act of riding smoothly and gracefully. 3. The way trail features connect to encourage graceful riding. 4. What we are all looking for.

fore–aft position—The rider's position front to rear in relation to the bottom bracket. In most cases the rider's center of gravity should be directly above the bottom bracket.

fork—The part of the bike that attaches the front wheel to the frame. May feature suspension.

freeriding—A style of riding in which riders ride creative lines and perform expressive tricks on natural and manmade terrain. Much less linear and results-driven than racing.

frontside—Any surface that faces toward the rider, opposite the direction the rider is traveling. Landing on the front side of a jump is rough. Loading the front side of a roller is slow. Opposite of backside.

front suspension—A front fork with telescoping legs that allow the front wheel to move independently of the bike frame and rider.

full-face helmet—A helmet that covers the rider's face. Most often used in downhill, bikercross, dual slalom, BMX and freeriding.

full suspension—A bike with both front and rear suspension. In contrast with a hardtail, which has only front suspension, or a rigid bike , which has no suspension.

gated racing—Any form of racing that uses a starting gate to hold racers back until the moment the race starts. Examples: BMX, bikercross and dual slalom.

hardpack—A trail surface made of tightly compacted dirt. It offers fast rolling and high traction.

hardtail—A mountain bike with a rigid frame and a front suspension fork. Because of their affordability, lightness and sturdiness, hardtails are favored by beginners, cross country racers and freestyle riders.

hauling the mail—Going fast. An expression Lee snagged from Mark Weir, derived perhaps from Lance Armstrong's racing performance while sponsored by the United States Postal Service, but more likely it comes from the Pony Express.

high–low pass—To pass another racer by entering a berm on a higher line, then dropping behind the racer then accelerating past on the lower line.

hip jump—A jump with the landing pointing in a different direction than the takeoff. The rider turns in the air.

holeshot—In head-to-head racing, to reach the first turn in the lead. Applies to bikercross, BMX and, to a lesser extent, Super D and cross country racing.

huck—To ride off a large drop with abandon, often with a stiff, bike-breaking style. As freeriding has become more technical and flowy, hucking has fallen out of fashion.

kickout—To swing the rear tire sideways while keeping the front tire on the ground.

le mans start—A start in which racers must run to their waiting bikes, which are lined up on the starting line, then jump on and start riding. Named for the original starting procedure at the 24 Hours of Le Mans auto race, in which cars were lined up according to qualifying time and drivers ran across the track to their cars.

line—A specific path through a section of trail. Most sections have multiple lines. The line you choose can make any trail harder or easier, slower or faster, less exciting or more fun.

load—To apply extra down force to your tires. Loading is synonymous with weighting.

loose over hardpack—Sand, dust or fine gravel on top of hardpack dirt. Like riding on ball bearings: slippery!

low–high pass—To pass another racer by entering a berm on a lower line, blocking the racer's path then exiting on the high line.

manual—To raise the front tire off the ground while coasting.

open-face helmet—Helmet that covers the top of the head but leaves the rider's face open. Used for cross-country riding.

overbake, overcook—To enter a turn or obstacle too fast (too hot) to ride it easily.

pedal hop—To bound forward by pedaling powerfully as you bunny hop off the rear wheel.

pedal strike—When a fully extended pedal hits a rock or other trail feature. Best avoided.

pin it—To ride as fast as you can. Derived from motocross, to hold the throttle wide open.

predictable start—A BMX, bikercross or dual slalom start cadence that drops the gate at a consistent time. Throughout the gated racing world, these are being replaced by random starts.

preload—In coil spring suspension, the amount the spring is compressed with the suspension fully extended. Increasing preload, usually via a threaded collar, makes the suspension stiffer.

prerace routine—The sequence of tasks and habits you perform to prepare your bike, body and mind for peak performance. Different color socks are the key!

pump—Actively working terrain—unloading frontsides and loading backsides—to gain speed and control.

pump-manual—To lift the front wheel between a pair of rollers by pumping the rear wheel through the trough.

pump track—A continuous loop of rollers and berms that can be ridden without pedaling. Riders Actively work the track—unloading frontsides and loading backsides—to gain speed.

quick-release—A lever-and-cam device used to fasten and adjust hubs and seat posts without the use of tools. Allows quick wheel changes and easy adjustment of seat height.

rail—To follow a steady, consistent line through a turn.

random start—A BMX, bikercross or dual slalom start cadence that uses a random-length pause before the gate drops. Random starts are becoming the norm because, some say, they encourage fairer racing than predictable starts.

ratchet—To repeatedly turn the pedals forward and backward about one-quarter of a turn. Useful while climbing in very rough terrain, where a fully extended pedal might strike a rock.

rear suspension—A system of lever arms on the rear of the bike frame that allows the rear wheel to move independently of the bike frame and rider.

rear-wheel drift—To drift the rear tire while the front tire stays planted.

rebound damping—Hydraulic circuit inside a fork or shock that controls the speed of the spring's rebound. More rebound damping means slower rebound and a less bouncy ride.

rhythm section—In dirt jumping, typically a sequence of double jumps. In bikercross, dual slalom and BMX, typically a sequence of rollers, double jumps, tabletops, step-ups and step-downs.

rings—Chain rings.

roller—A smoothly shaped mound of dirt. Often used in bikercross and dual slalom courses, as well as pump tracks and dirt jump areas.

run-out—In bikercross, the slope that extends from the start gate to the first obstacle.

semi-slick—A tire tread that's slick or slightly textured in the middle and has knobs on the sides. Used for racing on hardpack surfaces.

shock—The part of the frame that controls the movement of the rear suspension.

singletrack—A narrow trail that fits only one rider in its width. Singletracks tend to be more curvy and fun to ride than doubletracks and dirt roads.

six-pack—A set of three consecutive double jumps. An eight-pack is four doubles, and so on.

skid—To lock a wheel so it longer turns, then let it drag across the trail surface. Usually to be avoided.

skinny—A narrow bridge, log or plank. Originally created to allow trails to flow through densely wooded, rugged terrain. Now a trademark feature of freeriding.

slalom/dual slalom—A style of racing in which two riders race head-to-head down a series of turns, jumps and bumps. Slalom bikes are quick and agile. Races last 30-40 seconds. Also known as DS.

slingshotting—A starting technique used with predictable start cadences, in which the rider rocks backward and begins the start before the gate drops. This creates a significant advantage over racers who wait for the gate to start dropping. The adoption of random starts is an attempt to eliminate slingshotting.

start cadence—The recorded message (and often the sequence of flashing lights) that precedes the drop of a BMX, bikercross or dual slalom starting gate. Racers use this message to time their movements and get fast starts. Some start cadences drop the gate predictably. Others drop the gate randomly.

step-down jump—A jump with the landing lower than the takeoff.

step-up jump—A jump with the landing higher than the takeoff.

style—A rider's expressiveness on the bike.

super D—A form of racing in which the entire field (up to about 50 riders) races head-to-head on a course that is mostly downhill but has enough climbing to reward pedaling fitness. Many Super D races are kicked off by a Le Mans start. Races usually last 10 to 30 minutes.

suspension—A system of springs, shock absorbers and levers that allows the bike's wheels to move in relation to the frame. Suspension insulates the rider from bumps, increasing comfort and control.

switchback—A very tight turn built into a steep hillside. After entering the turn, the rider must immediately switch back to the opposite direction. The same turn on flat ground would be called a hairpin.

tabletop, jump—A jump with a flat top between the takeoff and landing. Can be safely rolled over.

tabletop, trick—To lay the bike flat in the air.

T-bone—To collide with another rider at a right angle, thus forming a T.

track stand—To balance on your bike in one spot. Derived from a starting and tactical move used in track racing.

transfer jump—A jump with the landing off to the side of the takeoff. The rider changes lines sideways in the air.

travel—The distance suspension allows the wheels are allowed to move in relation to the bicycle frame. On a bike with four inches of suspension travel, the wheels can move four inches before they "bottom out" or hit the suspension's stopping point.

turn-down—A jumping technique that uses gyroscopic forces to lay the bike flat and keep it low to allow greater speed. The front wheel is turned down toward the ground. Also known as a whip or moto whip.

two-wheel drift—To drift with both tires. A sure sign of high speed and great skill.

unload—To reduce the down force on your tires. Unloading is synonymous with unweighting.

unweight—To reduce the down force on your tires. Unweighting is synonymous with unloading.

weight—To apply extra down force to your tires. Weighting is synonymous with loading.

wheelie—To raise the front tire off the ground while pedaling. (You can also "pop a wheelie" without pedaling.)

zone, the—The mental state of optimal performance. Like flow, but more intense and competition oriented.

PHOTO CREDITS

INDEX

ABOUT THE AUTHORS

The name **Brian Lopes** is synonymous with American mountain bike racing. Since his professional debut in 1993, Brian has been a constant presence on race podiums worldwide. Brian is recognized as the winningest American pro mountain biker: He holds the most World Cup titles (25) of any male racer to date and has four World Championship titles and nine National Championship titles in both downhill and dual slalom.

In 2008 his winning ways were recognized when Brian was inducted into both the Mountain Bike and BMX Halls of Fame.

Having raced BMX for most of his childhood, Brian learned how to ride a bike at the age of 4, turning pro at the age of 17 and competing in the BMX circuit for 7 years before channeling all his efforts to mountain biking. He has appeared on EuroSport, Universal Sports, CBS Sports, and Outdoor Life Network and has graced the covers of every major national and international mountain biking magazine: *Mountain Bike Action, MBUK, Dirt, Bicycling, VeloNews,* and *Mountain Biking.* Brian also has received coverage in such mainstream media as *Men's Health, Rolling Stone,* and *USA Today.*

Brian currently has various signature mountain bike products: TLD knee guards, Bell helmet, Kenda tires, WTB bike seat, and a signature Sportsmobile design. Other career highlights include being nominated as the ESPY Extreme Athlete of the Year and starring as himself in Playstation's video game Downhill Domination.

Lopes resides in Laguna Beach, California, with his wife, Paula.

Lee McCormack is the world's leading technique instructor and uses his own sequential teaching curriculum to coach riders of all types and levels—from homemakers to pro downhillers—to ride better, safer, and faster. He is a journalist who has written for *Bike, Mountain Bike Action, Twentysix, Flow,* and *Mountain Biking.* He is also the author of the book *Pro BMX Skills,* which is available at www.leelikesbikes. com, a mountain biking Web site maintained by Lee and visited by thousands of readers worldwide.

McCormack has won numerous writing and informational graphics awards at the state and regional levels and was part of the team that won the 1998 Pulitzer Prize for public service. Lee has been a bike nut for over 20 years and enjoys all riding disciplines, including single-track, road, dirt jumps, pump tracks. McCormack lives in Boulder, Colorado, with his wife, Arlette, and four children: Kate, Ian, and twins Finley and Fiona.